Shanghai Forum 2013 Conference Papers Edition
Fudan Development Institute Series

This book is funded by Asia Research Center, Fudan University

复旦发展研究院
FUDAN DEVELOPMENT INSTITUTE

Asia's Wisdom

Explorations on Regional Integration and Economic Growth

Yuan Tangjun   Zhang Yi   Editors-in-Chief

復旦大學 出版社

Preface

2013 is a challenging year not only for the world economy but also for the Asian and the Chinese economy. After 2008, the trend of the global economy has been changed. The America-led TPP negotiation and the new reforms in China have just started, whereas the recovery of the Europe has been slow or remained doubtful. The U. S. economy has started to recover after several rounds of QEs, while the emerging economies such as the BRICs are not doing well in the wake of the change of the global economic division. Reviewing the changes of economy and politics in Asia this year, we find that although the geopolitical friction has almost reached the most intense level after the World War II, the pace of the economic integration in this area has been continuing, which has influenced and enhanced the change of the global economic division. Especially in the recent years, while WTO negotiations seemed to have stalled, bilateral free trade negotiations became the main stream. Now, there are more than 350 FTAs that have been implemented around the world. Although China has signed more than 10 FTA agreements with various countries, its main trading partners such as the U. S., Japan and Korea have not yet entered any agreements with China. Japan's recent announcement of joining TPP has indeed made China feel to be marginalized.

While there are both economic and political reasons to explain the fast development of FTA, the most important two factors are the stagnation of WTO negotiation and the rapid evolving of the global value chain due to the deepening global economic division. For the first reason, with the fast growth of international trade and direct investment, thanks for the participation of the large emerging economies such as the BRICs, the way to reaching free trade has been changing. Now, the key issue is how to reduce the non-tariff obstacles barriers rather than tariff barriers. Obviously, with the active role of developing countries such as China, it becomes difficult for the Doha Development Agenda to satisfy the interests of all parties, which inevitably stalled the trade negotiation. As for the second reason, with the development of the global value chain which is multinational company centric, apart from trade policy, issues like investment laws, intellectual property protection law, fair competition, subsidies, labor policy and infrastructure supply, all have become more important. In order to bypass the difficulties or break the stagnation, WTO members are exploring ways to reach their goals without the Doha Development Agenda. After entering the new century, especially after the global financial crisis in 2008, FTA has become a hot choice, more and more countries want to boost their domestic economy by establishing FTA and hence promoting economic integration under that umbrella.

The area integration has two types. One is production network-centric which is called de facto economic integration, and the other is government agreement-centric which is called de Jure economic integration. In the former situation, the trade of intermediate goods such as components and raw materials increase a lot. Both inter-industry and intra-industry trade have increased through the further divisions in manufacturing process between China, Japan and Korea. The formation of the manufacturing network between the three countries was initially based on China's opening up and then benefited from economic globalization in the 1990s. Through the development of the network China has gradually integrated with the global value and manufacturing chains. The reduction of transportation and telecommunication costs, and the increase in modular production have lowered the transaction cost and boosted the international integration of manufacturing. In such a process, large companies, especially multinational corporations have made a significant contribution to the development of the global network. Driven by profit maximization, they have played an indispensable role in allocating resources between countries and building up logistic systems through trade and FDI. The global financial crisis in 2008 has shown that countries have closely integrated in the global value chain. Therefore, cooperation is the only way to benefit all parties. It is therefore reasonable for us to expect the implementation of FTA to further enhance the economic integration. It is fundamental for a sustainable growth in Asia, especially for China.

However, because of some non-economic reasons in Asia, FTA and EPA have been crippled because economic integration has been going ahead of institutional integration. This situation is however both challenging and opportunistic for Asia and China. In general, in the areas where economic integration has been achieved, the agreement of free trade is subject to the existing net work of production. In other words, the development of Asian FTA has to be in line with the interests of multinational companies operating in the area. From the economic point of view, this facilitates the development of FTA and hences an opportunity for China to open wider and deeper. But one thing we need to know is that self-interests-maximizing multinational companies do not always satisfy the interests of local countries. To overcome institutional obstacles, higher level cooperation of each party is necessary.

Until now, the objective of China's FTA is to expand economic scale and secure resources. Both political and economic strategies have been used in diplomacy. However, China has not clearly set up its objectives from the view point of the global production and value chains. It is sure that the countries, such as the US, Japan, Korea, ASEAN, who have involved in GVCs, will not give up the chance to corporate with China in FTA. So China should precisely evaluate its current status and future trend in the global value chains, and based on different factor endowments, economic division and the stage of development of the countries involved develop various types of FTA. In doing so, not only can China further develop foreign trade and direct investment, but it will also be able to gain more time for institutional reform which is an important condition for China to join TPP. When implementing FTA, the interaction between China's FTA and the global production and value chains should always be considered.

Asian countries are different in culture, institution and the model of economic development. Therefore, an integration of such multi-cultural and multi-institutional region requires a good collaboration of all countries involved. In 2013 Shanghai Forum, under the general theme of "Asia's Wisdom: Seeking Harmonious Development in Diversity", more than 500 leaders and experts from government, business and academia discuss and debate on issues in politics, finance, law, urban development, social development, environment and energy, and provide insights and suggestions for the development of Asia. The consensus that "the 21st century is the Asian Century" is not just a slogan, but a trend. Integration and corporation are the two keys to achieving healthy and sustainable development in this region. As the most dynamic area in today's world, Asia should use its unique wisdom to resist shocks and reduce risks, hence contributing more to the global development in economy, finance and trade. The key to a harmonious world with a great diversity in many aspects is the peaceful share of economic development.

The forum selects the papers focusing on the following topics: "After the Asian Miracle: Problems, Challenges and Choices"; "Global Economic Recovery without Asset Security"; "The Integration of Regional Economy in Asia: Target, Path and Policy"; "Asia's Wisdom: Approaches to Disputes"; "Asian Legal Wisdom: Diversity and Unification"; "Global Governance and Asia's Wisdom"; "Innovation-driven Urban Development in Asia"; "How to Assure Health for 4 Billion People in Asia?"; "Emerging Asian Renewable Energy: from New Technology and New Industry to a New Market"; "Climate Change and Environmental Protection: the Focus of Human Attention". These papers are the results of the intellectual efforts of the authors. They provide valuable views and suggestions from historical and international perspectives as well as interesting case studies. Due to limited space, we are only able to select some of them in both Chinese and English proceedings. We hope that the proceedings will encourage more debate in searching for a better development of Asia.

Tangjun Yuan

March 2014

Contents

1

CHAPTER 1 "Asia-Pacific Security in the Age of Interdependent Survival: Need for a New Paradigm"

Kirill Barsky

1.1 THE GLOBAL CONTEXT

The world is living through rough times. The international system which emerged in the wake of World War II has been seriously undermined by deliberate breaching or bypassing of the international law, by growing reliance on military power, including in the settlement of conflicts, by hubris of national ambitions at the expense of other players, as well as by the unfolding trend of exacerbation of regional tensions and bilateral controversies. Elements of instability, uncertainty and unpredictability are gaining dominance.

The ongoing recession of the world economy as a repercussion of the financial crisis of 2008-2009 has further complicated the international situation. It has demonstrated gravity of the crisis of the global governance.

Against this gloomy background members of the international community are trying to find solutions to the problems of security and economic development on a regional level. They resent to strengthening regional organizations and boosting regional economic integration.

Meanwhile the regional landscape remains very unusual. Strong drive for economic cooperation in the Asia-Pacific and Eurasia and the unequivocal shift of balance in the international affairs towards this part of the world do not correspond with potentially unstable security situation in many corners of Asia. So far the speedy economic growth has not been influenced by security concerns or strained bilateral relations between countries of the region. The largest trade turnover in the region is between the US and China — USD 3. 87 trillion in 2012 — while their political interests often clash.

But we also witnessed a different picture when a crisis between China and Japan over the Diaoyudao islands broke out last October. It resulted in a dramatic 30 percent drop of the Japanese investments in China. The 3. 3 percent downfall of the Sino-Japanese trade volume delivered a painful blow to most vibrant sectors of bilateral cooperation, in particular to automobile sales which plunged by 41 percent. Total Japanese export to China fell by 10. 4 percent.

History teaches us that close economic relations do not ensure lasting peace and security. Before World War II the best economic ties and diversified cooperation existed between those countries who later became the worst rivals during the War. A conflict between the thriving economy and poor security may play a dangerous trick on the Asia-Pacific region which is full of all kinds of problems, conflicts and disputes.

Lack of security guarantees in Asia is a big issue. Therefore, something needs to be done to ensure a better security environment for all the countries of the region. But in doing so regional countries will have to face a host of various challenges.

Conclusion. Regional economic cooperation has become a mainstream of the modern day in Asia. However fast economic development cannot be taken for granted. In the absence of a reliable political framework it seems very fragile. Sustainable economic growth and integration require firm security guarantees.

1. 2 SECURITY LEGACY IN THE ASIA-PACIFIC REGION

The complexity of building reliable security in the Asia-Pacific region and

Eurasia lies in their immense diversity and the messy legacy of the past.

Problems inherited from World War II and its implications:

(1) Peace accord with Japan; the Treaty of San-Francisco was not signed by the Soviet Union and DPRK.

(2) US military presence in Asia.

(3) Break-up of India; India-Pakistan relationship has been bumpy since then.

(4) Taiwan issue

Legacy of the Cold War:

(1) Korean Peninsula

(2) Afghanistan

(3) Remnants of ideological confrontation

(4) "Cold War mentality"

(5) Lack of transparency, and mutual suspicion

Historic problems:

(1) Territorial claims and disputes

(2) Border delimitation problems

(3) Internal ethnic and religious conflicts

(4) Cultural and confessional prejudice

(5) Negative popular stereotypes of neighboring countries

(6) Influence of former colonial powers

Conclusion. Given cultural, ethnic and religious diversity of Asia and complicated historic legacy it is not an easy task to bring security interests of the countries of the region together. However at the time of globalization and in the face of challenges of interdependent survival most Asia-Pacific countries recognize the need to join hands to overcome problems of the past and to build a better future.

1.3 "ARCHITECTURE OF DANGER" IN ASIA

There is no coherent and comprehensive security system either in the Asia-Pacific or in Eurasia. Evident deficit of security arrangements is one of the key flaws of the regional mosaic.

First, currently regional security is based on military power of individual countries and their coalitions. The most powerful nation — the US — believes that its military presence in the region, its strategic alliances with Japan, the Republic of Korea, Australia, Turkey and military cooperation agreements with a number of other Asian countries and quasi-state entities are sufficient to ensure regional security and stability.

However the recent developments show that national security of the US is not equal to regional security. Multilateral security architecture should be based on a balance of interests instead of deterrence and imbalances of military might. Legitimate security interests and military capacity of other regional players should be taken into consideration.

Secondly, throughout the post-War history the American military power has failed to win most of the wars where the US was involved (Korean War, Vietnam War, military operations in Iraq and Afghanistan). The American defense umbrella turned out futile in preventing international conflicts in the Asia-Pacific region and Eurasia (wars between India and Pakistan, Pakistan and Bangladesh, Iran and Iraq, China and Vietnam, conflict in Cambodia and crisis between Indonesia and East Timor, border clashes between China and India, Malaysia and Thailand, Indonesia and Malaysia, Thailand and Cambodia), dangerous aggravation of tension in regional flashpoints (Korean Peninsula, Taiwan Strait, territorial disputes in South China Sea and between China and Japan) and civil wars and internal disturbances in some countries (Sri Lanka, Indonesia, Thailand, Myanmar, the Philippines, Iraq, Afghanistan). This is a clear evidence of the fact that the military power of the US and its regional allies is unable to serve a guarantor of regional security. Neither can the US be an honest broker.

Thirdly, American defense policy arouses anxiety of quite a number of Asian nations, among them China, Russia, India, Indonesia, Vietnam, DPRK etc. They believe that they have good reason to feel threatened by the existing "hub and spokes" security system and American unilateralism which ignore their own interests or even infringe them.

Fourthly, the existing security arrangements in the Asia-Pacific and military actions by the US and its allies (arms build-up, development and deployment of regional ABM systems, weapon sales, expansion of military bases, growing naval activity, regular military exercises, frequent relocations of troops etc.) are playing a provocative role leading to further mistrust between countries of the region. The Mutual suspicion is rooted in the lack of transparency of the military alliances led by the US, its arrogant and selfish policy towards many countries of the region. It triggers counter-measures and instigates arms race across Asia. The architecture that Americans have constructed in the Asia-Pacific is the "architecture of danger", not the architecture of security.

Last, but not least. Under the enormous pressure of domestic financial and economic problems as well as the systemic slow-down of the US economy, Washington has difficulty in sustaining the burden of military spending. In January 2012 the White House decided to cut its defense budget by USD 487 billion over five years, to reduce troops by 80,000 (up to 15 percent) over the next ten years and to "rebalance" American military forces worldwide.

When introducing a new US Defense Strategy President Obama stressed that the US "will be strengthening its presence in the Asia-Pacific, and budget reductions will not come at the expense of this critical region". At the same time he mentioned that "the US should abstain from flexing its muscles as this won't help solve regional disputes". Although the US officials reassured their allies in Asia that America will continue to be committed to its security obligations, in reality deep defense cuts put a big question mark over the reliability of the US military might in the region which looks clearly overstretched for smaller expenditures. Even the Pentagon had to admit that "with reduced resources, thoughtful choices will need to be made regarding the location and frequency of presence abroad related operations".

Conclusion. The security system based on the US-led military alliances has proved to be unable to replace a genuine multilateral security system. Its focus on the US strategic domination and non-transparent character of existing military blocs are not conducive to regional stability and mutual confidence. Moreover, the posture and actions of these defense alliances provoke a sensitive reaction on part of some regional players, pushing them to take symmetric and asymmetric measures and to expedite steps to enhance their military capacity. This leads to growing mistrust, arms races and conflicts.

However due to historic and political reasons, establishment of a multilateral non-bloc regional security system is a challenge that the regional community so far fails to meet.

1.4   MAJOR REGIONAL FLASHPOINT AND EFFORTS TO EASE

1.4.1   Korean Peninsula

A system of maintenance of peace and stability on the Korean Peninsula where two Korean states have been technically in a state of war for six decades is in high demand. The Armistice Agreement of 1953 did not bridge the political gap between Pyongyang and Seoul. Since the Korean War no bilateral, regional or international mechanism has been set up to mitigate tension. Ideological enmity of DPRK towards the Republic of Korea and economic hardships in the North have been aggravated by the unfavorable external environment. The US military bases in South Korea and Japan alongside with the anti-Korean rhetoric in the West are viewed in Pyongyang as a proof that the US and its allies are nourishing plans to attack DPRK or to overthrow the North Korean government. By the same token the policy of self-reliance and inculcation of an army-style values in social life exercised in North Korea make the US and other Western countries believe that DPRK is a hostile regime which needs to be changed. In addition persistent efforts of Pyongyang to obtain nuclear weapons and means of delivery forced the UN Security Council to impose sanctions on DPRK.

The recent crisis on the Korean Peninsula was another dangerous signal showing the fragility of peace in the Northeast Asia. Regretfully, DPRK refuses to abandon and dismantle its nuclear program and to return to the NPT regime. Its audacious declarations threatening to unleash a war against the Republic of Korea and to destroy targets in the US and Japan add fuel to the hostilities. It is equally regretful that the US and the Republic of Korea have chosen the path of exerting growing pressure on Pyongyang instead of making efforts to start mutually respectful negotiations with it. One should admit that by enhancing their military infrastructure in the Southern part of the Peninsula, in Japan and Guam, by deploying Patriot systems and by conducting US-South Korea joint military exercises in the vicinity of DPRK, they are provoking Pyongyang to tough response thus creating a vicious circle of instability in the sub-region.

1.4.2 Taiwan

The Taiwan issue clearly falls under Chinese internal affairs, and it is up to the people on both coasts of the Taiwan Strait to solve it. However it is impossible to deny that situation around this issue has both bilateral and international dimensions. Since 1950 Taiwan has become a 'hot potato' in Sino-American relations. Throughout the 60-year-long history military confrontation at times prevailed and even led to dangerous crises, later giving way to peaceful initiatives and agreements between Beijing and Taipei. But the "explosive potential" of this issue has not been diminished — the Taiwan issue remains a factor casting a dark shade on the prospects of lasting stability in Asia. The PRC Government announced that it reserves the right to use force against Taiwan in certain circumstances. Therefore the regional community is interested in an early and sound solution of this issue for the benefit of regional security.

1.4.3 South China Sea

Five Asian countries — China, Vietnam, the Philippines, Malaysia and Brunei as well as China's Taiwan — claim their sovereignty over archipelagoes and waters of South China Sea. Over the years this territorial dispute has become a permanent factor of instability in the sub-region, a cause of mutual accusations and a source of political and at some instances military confrontation.

The complexity of the issue is determined by the following:

(1) Overlapping nature of the claims;

(2) Effective control over different islands is exercised by different claimants (for example, regarding Spratly Islands Vietnam takes hold of 21 islands, China — 9 islands, the Philippines — 8 islands, Malaysia — 3 islands, China's Taiwan — 1 island);

(3) Variable composition of claimants with regard to different islands and waters (China and Vietnam assert that they have sovereignty over all Paracel islands and Spratly islands, the Philippines claim sovereignty only over the Kalayan islands, etc.);

(4) Solidarity within groups of claimants (ASEAN Member-States vs. China, China vs. others, etc.);

(5) Oil and gas reserves discovered in South China Sea;

(6) Growing importance of safety of navigation and security of sea lanes crossing South China Sea;

(7) Temptation of ASEAN Member States who are parties to the territorial dispute to use a "China threat theory" in order to form "a united front" vis-à-vis China, as well as to involve third parties, namely the US, to exert additional pressure on Beijing.

Another serious difficulty is that all the claims are poorly documented. As a result claimants have to appeal to myths and legends, ancient literature and other unreliable sources, to allude to national pride and habits of local people or to resort to harsh emotional statements, thus making rapprochement of the positions even more problematic.

Given a considerable number of countries involved in this territorial dispute and the fact that the issue has already caused serious international implications (incidents endangering sub-regional stability, need to ensure safety of navigation, need to guarantee necessary security conditions for exploration and exploitation of energy resources discovered under the seabed, etc.) the situation in South China Sea is attracting growing attention of the regional community.

In 2002 China and ASEAN adopted a *Declaration on the Conduct of Parties in the South China Sea (DOC)*. Now the parties concerned are working on elaboration of a *Code of Conduct in the South China Sea (COC)*, but so far this work remains unfinished.

Conclusion. Both regional community and countries involved have failed to find a lasting solution to regional and sub-regional conflicts and disputes. They also appear unprepared to establish necessary security mechanisms to prevent escalation of tension in major flashpoints in Asia. Urgent and consistent efforts should be taken to put those flashpoints under effective control until they break up again.

1.5   NEW CHALLENGES TO REGIONAL SECURITY

Meanwhile the world was shocked by the emergence of new challenges and threats. They have been multiplying and proliferating for the last two decades. Since the end of the Cold War the vacuum left by the confrontation between the Western and Eastern blocs has been filled by various destructive forces which capitalized on the loopholes in the international law and security cooperation mechanisms.

The evolution of these new threats was accompanied by the outbreak of a series of various calamities. The intensity of natural and man-made disasters is a result of the rapid development of industrial and post-industrial societies and damages caused by this development to the environment.

The list of new challenges and threats includes:

(1) Terrorism

(2) Separatism

(3) Extremism

(4) WMD proliferation

(5) Threats to cyber security

(6) Drugs trafficking

(7) Money laundering

(8) Trafficking in small arms and light weapons

(9) Human trafficking

(10) Natural disasters

(11) Infectious diseases

The dynamic growth of the world and Asian economy in the 1990s ended up with an Asian financial crisis of 1997-1998. The economic recovery in early 2000s was achieved mainly thanks to the resilience and responsible economic policies of China, Japan, Republic of Korea, India and Southeast Asian nations. However this recovery was again interrupted by the global financial crisis of 2008-2009 and ensuing economic recession. This added new challenges to the problems Asia is facing with. Their implications are not limited to just volatility of the financial markets. The crisis reflected qualitatively new intensity of international competition for shrinking mineral, energy, food and water resources, for financial reserves, investment and technology, for an access to transportation routes and for political influence. As a consequence of this new reality the Asian countries feel more motivated to cooperate with each other in coping with security, political and economic challenges.

"**The newest generation of challenges and threats**" Against the backdrop of the ongoing reshuffle of global and regional power balance struggle between states, coalitions, organizations, companies, cultures, ideas, development models and civilizations is intensifying. Political and economic interests are now more frequently advanced through circumvention of international law, use of military power, elaboration of new weapons and destructive application of new information and communication technologies.

Recently we have seen the emergence of a completely new set of threats to security and stability. They are:

(1) Arbitrary interpretation of norms and principles of international law, unilateral actions breaching the international law, attempts to justify unlawful actions by UN Security Council resolutions, abusing of international sanctions, introduction of unilateral sanctions, imposition of national legislation on sovereign states;

(2) Attempts to break up global strategic stability and regional strategic balance, including through weaponization of outer space and deployment of ABM systems, implementation of strategies of controlled tension in latent regional conflicts and

territorial disputes;

(3) Attempts to threaten the information security of states, government agencies and private corporations, development of information weapons by governments, growing links between computer hackers and extremists;

(4) Galloping drug-trafficking intertwined with terrorism and extremism, strengthening of links between drug-trafficking and terrorism, use of drug revenues to finance terrorist and extremist groups, separatist movements, illicit trafficking in small arms and light weapons;

(5) Rise of piracy as a new type of organized crime connected with terrorism, extremism, illicit arms and human trafficking;

(6) Incitement to a regime change in sovereign states, attempts of military intervention or external interference into home affairs of sovereign states under a pretext of providing assistance to insurgents against authoritarian or corrupt regimes;

(7) Attempts to resolve internal conflicts or to calm down social unrest through a violent regime change, supplying of arms to opposition forces;

(8) Use of modern information and communication technologies for the purpose of a violent regime change;

(9) Attempts of external forces to change the direction of social unrest through mobilization of the Internet, electronic and printed mass-media, use of biased coverage, deliberate distortions, negative image-making etc. ;

(10) Use of foreign-funded NGOs by external forces to influence direction and intensity of public protests;

(11) With ethnicity replacing ideology as the prime factor of conflicts the risk of ethnic clashes has increased;

(12) Radicalization of public sentiments on the grounds of inter-confessional differences, especially provoked by the escalation of confrontation between the West and the Islamic world;

(13) A sharp rise of xenophobia and intolerance in the societies, growing disrespect of religious feelings of believers;

(14) Attempts of terrorists and extremists to use social unrest and radical groups

to provoke ethnic, inter-confessional and intra-confessional confrontation to achieve their goals.

Conclusion. "The newest generation of challenges" poses a serious threat not only to international or regional security and to external security of states but to sovereignty, territorial integrity, stability and social order within states. They emerged at the time when what we knew as "new challenges" — terrorism, narcotics, etc. — have not been successfully countered, old conflicts have not been settled and traditional security threats continued to exist. Such a "mix" makes it even more urgent to change a paradigm of regional security cooperation.

1.6 ARMS RACE IN ASIA

Two recent studies accomplished by the International Institute of Security Studies (IISS) in London and the Stockholm-based International Peace Research Institute (SIPRI) have shown that an arms race is in full swing in Asia. According to these reports, now Asia accounts for 19.9 percent of worldwide military spending and has become No. 2 among regions (North America accounts for 42 percent). In 2012 military expenditures in Asia for the first time ever exceeded those of the European Union (17.6 percent of global military expenditures).

Over the last five years the world's biggest arms importers were Asian countries. As of today they are India, China, Pakistan, Republic of Korea and Singapore.

In their purchases of advanced military systems Asian countries are making emphasis on Navy and Air Force. The major fleets are now concentrated in Northeast Asia. Ignoring its constitutional limits, Japan has become a nation with the second largest Navy in the world. A powerful ocean Navy including a strong submarine fleet is being developed by South Korea.

Japan, the Republic of Korea and China's Taiwan remain the biggest importers of most sophisticated American weapons, including elements of ABM systems.

Arms export market has also been changing resulting from the ongoing shift of global strategic balance towards Asia. China has risen to the world's fifth largest weapons exporter. Other Asian countries are actively engaged in a defense build-up. Some of them have started to develop their own defense industries. The share of weapon deals between Asian countries is growing. This helps Asian buyers to weaken their dependence on the US which is often reluctant to transfer its military technology to partners in Asia.

Conclusion. Intensifying arms race in Asia raises risks of inadvertent conflicts and escalation of tensions. This phenomenon deserves attention as an important factor undermining regional security. A possibility of establishing regional arms control mechanisms, promoting transparency and military CBMs should be considered.

1.7 THE INTERDEPENDENT WORLD AND THE NEED FOR A NEW PARADIGM OF REGIONAL SECURITY

The analysis of the global and regional situation leaves no doubts that the world has become multipolar, diverse, unstable, insecure and dangerous. The evolution of the human society is characterized by both unbelievable progress of the civilization and an all-out decline and self-destruction. The world has clearly entered a new age of its history. I call it the Age of Interdependent Survival. Everything has become so closely linked that it is only through cooperation not competition that can the humankind survive. This new age demands from all the participants of the international relations to bear in mind the following rules as guiding principles for policy making.

General rules of the Age of Interdependent Survival:

(1) The world is interconnected and interdependent.

(2) Problems and conflicts are trespassing boundaries faster than capitals, goods, services and people.

(3) Even if you are geographically far from me, I am your closest neighbor.

(4) What happens miles away may become your problem too.

(5) Rapid development with shrinking resources leads to tougher competitions.

(6) Politics are interdependent; your political decisions may become my

problems, social unrest in my country may spread to your country.

(7) External interference, regardless of its goals, may lead to violence and chaos in the country which became a target of the intervention.

(8) A violent regime change, regardless of its goals, may lead to disruption of institutions, renewed conflicts and economic decline.

(9) Economics are interdependent; economic and financial problems are "contagious", no open market economy has immunity against this "contagion".

(10) Even if today you are rich and stable, tomorrow you may have economic and social troubles.

(11) Security is interdependent; you cannot ensure or strengthen your security at the expense of weakening mine.

(12) Whatever your military or economic power, in the interdependent world you are not invulnerable.

(13) My and your survival depends on many things beyond my and your control.

(14) You have many ways to influence my ability to survive.

(15) I have many ways to escape collapse and to retaliate.

(16) If I am weakened by your policy, indirectly you may be also affected in this or that way.

(17) If you infringe my vital interests to your benefits, new dangers to your vital interests may emerge from elsewhere.

(18) If you and I are engaged in mutual struggle, others will have a chance to use it to their benefit thus affecting your and my ability to survive.

(19) No international threat or problem can be tackled by you or me alone.

(20) International problems in the interdependent world have no simple military solutions.

(21) Survival, security and prosperity have become global problems; to resolve them you and me must cooperate.

(22) In the light of mounting problems and conflicts in the interdependent world mutual survival must become a top priority issue.

Conclusion. To ensure survival and sustainable development in the Asia-Pacific region and Eurasia today and tomorrow countries of this region should immediately start to learn lessons of living together in peace and cooperation. The alternative option can be only internal collapse and international chaos. Therefore regional nations should agree on proper regional security arrangement and cooperation mode.

1.8 NEW SECURITY ARCHITECTURE IN ASIA

No one is interested in a negative scenario in the Asia-Pacific region since in the age of interdependence it would boomerang affecting the rest of the world. But such a scenario is possible if economic growth is not underpinned by equal, just, transparent and effective security institutions.

Many experts are concerned about a probability of a simmering conflict between the US and China. By 2030 China may catch up with the US on many fronts. That will make them not only two most economically and militarily powerful nations in the region (and in the world) but also the two nations of comparable power and clashing interests. In the light of this possibility it is crucial, they believe, to have China and the US as well as other major countries of the region firmly committed to legally binding multilateral instruments containing fair and clear security obligations.

At the same time multiplying threats and challenges facing the Asia-Pacific region require further efforts of all the countries of the region to maintain regional security and stability. Even a strong country cannot protect oneself from trans-boundary threats, emanating from the non-governmental level, without international cooperation. Unilateral actions have become obsolete and useless.

A multipolar nature of the modern world presupposes a new distribution of power and a new balance of interests. No country in Asia wishes to be anybody's satellite. No country would like to be in a position when decisions on its security, domestic, economic or cultural policy are made in other capitals. Multifaceted strategies, diversified bilateral relations, overlapping participation in various regional organizations and coalitions, intensive diplomatic maneuvering allow players of the game of international politics to enjoy a certain degree of freedom and stay relatively independent. For this purpose they need multilateral diplomacy.

Conclusion. The evolving architecture of security in the Asia-Pacific region is a reaction to the wide range of security problems, threats and challenges burdening Asia. It also shows that the regional community is mature enough to build a comprehensive, indivisible, equal and fair security system Asia deserves. Many people view this new architecture as the best way to avoid bilateral and regional conflicts in the future.

1.9 THE OSCE EXPERIENCE

To build new architecture of security and cooperation, experience of other regional projects should be studied. In this "league", Europe is the absolute champion.

The Organization of Security and Cooperation in Europe (OSCE) with 56 Member States and an impressive history of collective efforting in political and military dimensions of security is the most authoritative regional organization in terms of security building expertise and CBMs implementation. The OSCE takes a comprehensive approach to security, which includes a number of commitments by participating states and mechanisms for conflict prevention and resolution.

In 1994 the participants of the OSCE Summit in Budapest adopted the *Code of Conduct on Politico-military Aspects of Security*, which reaffirmed and reiterated their determination to act in solidarity in case of violation of the CSCE norms and commitments and to facilitate the concerted response to security challenges. The Code also broke new ground by formulating norms regarding the role of armed forces in democratic societies. It was followed by the *Vienna Document on Measures to Strengthen Confidence and Security.*

The OSCE Member States are strongly committed to the full implementation and indefinite and unconditional extension of the NPT. They reaffirmed their commitment to prevent proliferation of nuclear weapons; to prevent the acquisition, development, production, stockpiling, and use of chemical and biological weapons; to control the transfer of missiles capable of delivering weapons of mass destruction and their components and technology. Important documents on small arms and light weapons and on stockpiles of conventional ammunition have been adopted.

Among the greatest achievements of the OSCE one should register an arms control regime. The end of the Cold War resulted in a huge amount of surplus weapons becoming available in the international grey market for weapons. The OSCE set before itself a challenging goal — to make a new step towards the enhancement of security in Europe by striking a balance of conventional weapons between the NATO and the Warsaw Pact at lower levels, to limit their capacity to deploy conventional weapons along the line of contact between the two blocs, to prevent illegal spread of conventional weapons and to provide assistance with regard to their destruction.

In 1990 a *Treaty on Conventional Forces in Europe (CFE Treaty)* was signed in Paris. However after the break-up of the Soviet Union and the dissolution of the Eastern bloc it became clear that the Treaty could not be effectively implemented because the provisions of CFE Treaty no more represented the real balance of power on the ground. Upon the initiative of the Russian Federation an *Adapted CFE Treaty* was drafted and signed in 1999. But the NATO Member States hindered the document from entering into force.

The OSCE also works on a wide spectrum of issues from conflict prevention to post-conflict management, crisis management and early warning, capacity building and institutional support, border management, combating terrorism, police operations, military reform etc.

The OSCE has established a Forum for Security Cooperation which provides a framework for political dialogue on various aspects of security. The Forum organizes annual OSCE Security Review Conferences, High-Level seminars on military doctrines etc.

Conclusion. The OSCE has achieved substantial results in elaboration of security mechanisms and in codification and implementation of CBMs. These patterns should be thoroughly studied and utilized as appropriate by the Asian countries.

However mechanical application of the OSCE experience will not do. It should be adapted to the Asian reality. At the same time Asian multilateral organizations and fora need to have a somber view of its achievements and advantages, on the one hand, of its flaws and limitations including agenda imbalances, political motivation, double standards etc., which weaken the OSCE and tie up its further work in the field of security, on the other.

1.10　THE ASIAN EXPERIENCE: ASEAN, ARF, ADMM PLUS AND CICA

ASEAN has been working on security issues since its inception. But initially the Association set before itself very modest goals — to promote regional peace and stability as stated in the Bangkok Declaration of 1967.

The ASEAN Charter adopted in 2007 devoted much more attention to security. Now "The Ten" are aiming at establishing Political Security Community. Among the tasks of ASEAN we find shaping and sharing norms of good conduct and solidarity; promotion of maritime cooperation, including establishment of the ASEAN Maritime Forum; building of a cohesive, peaceful and resilient Political Security Community; conflict prevention and confidence building measures, preventive diplomacy and post-conflict peace building.

To strengthen confidence building measures ASEAN is promoting greater transparency and understanding of defense policies and security perceptions, organizing regional meetings of ASEAN defense officials at all levels, exchanging observers invited to military exercises, publishing an annual ASEAN Security Outlook etc.

ASEAN is trying to play a role in conflict resolution and pacific settlement of disputes relying on "rational, effective and sufficiently flexible procedures, avoiding negative attitudes". Under the ASEAN Charter, it may establish appropriate dispute settlement mechanisms. However "The Ten" have not been very successful in this regard failing to stop numerous disputes and clashes between ASEAN Member States.

ASEAN can be proud of elaborating in 1974 a *Treaty of Amity and Cooperation in South East Asia* which prescribes that Member States refrain from threat or use of force and settle disputes peacefully through friendly negotiations, and a 1995 *Southeast Asia Nuclear Free Weapons Zone (SEANFWZ) Treaty*.

ASEAN initiated a Regional Forum — ARF — which provided a platform for cooperation between regional and non-regional countries on security issues. ARF is an important forum for discussing a broad agenda from confidence building measures and preventive diplomacy to conflict resolution. The CBMs are promoted on the basis of principles enshrined in the *Chair's Statement of the 1995 ARF Second Ministerial Session* as well as in the 2009 *ARF Vision Statement*. The agreed CBMs include organization of multilateral seminars and meetings on sensitive aspects of security in Asia, arrangement of joint exercises and training, exchange of information, best practices and contact data, elaboration of documents etc. Implementation of CBMs is supposed to pave way to next stages — preventive diplomacy and conflict settlement mechanisms.

ASEAN defense officials have been involved in the security dialogue since 1996. At the ARF sessions ASEAN holds voluntary briefings on political and security developments in the region and regularized meetings of high-level defense officials under the framework of ARF Defense Officials' Dialogue (DOD) and ARF Security Policy Conference (ASPC). ASEAN has also established an annual ASEAN Defense Ministers Meeting (ADMM) later supplemented by the ADMM plus Dialogue Partners mechanism (ADMM Plus).

Another forum dealing with Asian security problems is Conference on Interaction and Confidence-Building Measures in Asia (CICA). Since its inauguration in 1999 it has made a good progress in adjusting the CBMs designed by the OSCE and other political entities and research centers to the realities of Asia. In 1999 the Ministerial Conference adopted a *Declaration on the Principles of Guiding Relations between the CICA Member States* which was in 2004 followed by the adoption of *CICA Catalogue of Confidence-Building Measures*. These two documents contain valuable ideas on how security situation in the Eurasian continent can be ameliorated.

The essential problem of CICA is implementation. As a loose forum of extremely diverse nations it has proved too slow and too inefficient to translate the agreed principles and measures into practice.

Conclusion. Being a key regional organization in the Asia Pacific ASEAN is still in the process of building a security community. It plays an important role in maintaining stability in the Asia-Pacific region. However there is a gap between the ASEAN's claim for centrality in the regional affairs and its inability to ensure effective functioning of security mechanisms both within ASEAN and in Asia in general.

At the same time there is no doubt that the legal and institutional frameworks established by ASEAN, ASEAN Regional Forum and CICA as well as their experience in the field of security building are valuable assets that should be used in the process of building of multilateral security architecture in the Asia-Pacific region. Their achievements constitute important investments to "the Bank of Asian Wisdom".

1.11   THE RUSSIAN-CHINESE EXPERIENCE

Russia and China boast good-neighborly relations, mutual trust and strategic cooperation which are rear in the contemporary international politics. To achieve this they had come a long way.

Following the normalization of Sino-Soviet relations in 1989 the two countries faced the need to clear up the border issue and to ensure stability in the border area. In order to understand the value of Russia-China experience of elaboration and implementation of CBMs we should look back into the year 1990.

In 1990 Moscow and Beijing sealed an *Agreement on Guidelines for Mutual Reductions of Military Forces and Strengthening Confidence in the Area of the Soviet-Chinese Border*. It is very concise but truly innovative. The fundamental element of the agreement was embodied in a simple but a far-reaching formula: the principle of mutual equal security enshrined in Article 1 of the Agreement. Bearing in mind ups and downs in the relationship between the Soviet Union and China this was a real breakthrough.

The two sides agreed to cut their military forces along the border to a minimal level and to set limits for those troops which will remain deployed in the border zone. The document further stipulated that military forces of the two sides stationed in the border area shall have structure allowing them to perform only defensive duties and shall not have capacity to launch a sudden assault against the opposite side or to undertake offensive operations.

Article 2 introduced another crucial notion: a principle of asymmetrical reductions. It means that either side should combine unilateral and bilateral cuts. The side possessing superiority must make deeper cuts.

Reductions shall start with offensive components (Article 3) and be implemented within agreed geographical zones (Article 4). The USSR and China agreed to establish a bilateral control and verification mechanism (Article 5) and engaged in elaboration of military CBMs in the border area (Article 6).

Lastly, the Agreement contains an important provision that while executing reductions of arms and armed forces in the border area and implementing the CBMs outlined in the document, with regard to the border line both sides will maintain a *status quo*.

The Agreement was ratified by the USSR and China, entered into force and became a cornerstone of security cooperation of the two countries. Twenty three years later it is still effective. The Joint Control Commission established by the Soviet Union and China in accordance with Article 5 holds meetings on a regular basis supervising the implementation of the Agreement and solving questions which arise in the course of its implementation.

Conclusion. The 1990 *Agreement on Guidelines for Mutual Reductions of Military Forces and Strengthening Confidence in the Area of the Soviet-Chinese Border* should be appraised as a good example of how two countries with a controversial historic background exercised political will and sorted out their security problems peacefully through diplomatic means. This example may be followed by other Asia-Pacific countries.

1.12　THE "SHANGHAI FIVE" EXPERIENCE

The provisions of the Sino-Soviet agreement of 1990 were further developed by a group of neighboring countries which in 1996 shaped the so called "Shanghai Five". Later the club was transformed into the Shanghai Cooperation Organization. Alongside with Russia and China the group included Kazakhstan, Kyrgyzstan and Tajikistan.

This coalition came into being not by accident: all the above mentioned national delegations participated in the marathon-like border negotiations between the USSR and the PRC which lasted for 32 years. When the delimitation issue was by and large resolved[1], the five leaders complemented the border accords with a border security arrangement. They extended the principles entrenched in the 1990 Sino-Soviet Agreement to a broader regional scope. In April 1996 the "Shanghai Five" Summit was marked by a new *Agreement on Strengthening Confidence in the Military Field in the Border Area* signed by the presidents of Russia, China, Kazakhstan, Kyrgyzstan and Tajikistan.

The document was not a replica of the Sino-Soviet treaty. New elements were added. They included the following provisions:

(1) Armed forces of the State-Parties shall not be used for an assault against other sides;

(2) Armed forces of the State-Parties shall not conduct any military activity threatening other sides or undermining calm and stability in the border area;

---

[1]　In April 1991 USSR-China Agreement on the Eastern Sector of the Border was signed. It was followed by Russia-China Agreement on the Western Sector of the Border signed in September 1994. In April 1994 Kazakhstan-China Border Agreement was signed.

As to Kyrgyzstan-China and Tajikistan-China border negotiations they were continued in the second half of the 90's. Both agreements were signed in August 1999.

Russia and China also proceeded to explore possibilities to finalize their border talks. They were faced with a challenge to fix the issue of three islands in the Amur River and the Argun River. Negotiations were a success and climaxed in 2004 with a final border accord between Moscow and Beijing.

(3) The State-Parties shall not conduct military exercises directed against other sides;

(4) The State-Parties shall limit the scope, geographical areas and frequency of military exercises;

(5) The State-Parties shall exchange information on quantity of troops and weapons deployed within a 100-km zone along both sides of the border;

(6) The State-Parties shall inform each other of all large-scale military activities or relocations of troops caused by emergencies;

(7) The State-Parties shall invite each other's observers to their military exercises;

(8) The State-Parties shall take measures to prevent dangerous military activity;

(9) Friendly exchanges ought to be promoted between officers and soldiers of the armed forces of the State-Parties serving in regular armies and border troops.

What is critically important is that in accordance with Article 7 of the Agreement the State-Parties made a commitment to respect the principle of inviolability of frontiers and with regard to the existing border line to maintain a *status quo* until a comprehensive solution of the border issues is finally achieved. This formula is applicable to other territorial disputes in the Asia-Pacific region. Its application may open up a wide window of opportunity to change political climate in bilateral relations between countries involved in those disputes.

Conclusion. The 1996 Agreement among "the Shanghai Five" had a great significance for peace and security in a vast geography from the Pamir Mountains to the Pacific Coast. The five regional countries left the dark shadows of the past behind them. For the first time in the history of the 7520-km-long border a risk of military confrontation was eliminated.

The implementation of the Agreement gave birth to a new atmosphere of mutual trust and good will between the five nations and set an excellent example for other countries. The Agreement played an important role in strengthening military CBMs in the border areas of the related countries as well as in developing between the signatories the so called "Shanghai Spirit" whose essence is mutual trust, mutual benefit, equality, consultations, respect for civilizational diversity and common development.

The signing of the 1996 Agreement helped prepare conditions for the establishment of the SCO which was born in 2001. The Organization followed in the footsteps of the "Shanghai Five" and took the above principles on board. In Article 5 of the *SCO Treaty of Long-Term Good-Neighborliness, Friendship and Cooperation* signed in 2007 the State-Parties declared that they would "take active measures to strengthen confidence in the military field in the border areas aspiring to transform borders between them into frontiers of eternal peace and friendship".

The "Shanghai Five" and the SCO's experience may be helpful as a pattern showing that neighboring countries can enhance regional security through bilateral and multilateral CBMs.

1.13   THE JONT RUSSIA-CHINA SECURITY INITIATIVE

In 2010 Russia and China came up with a new initiative on regional security. They urged all the countries of the Asia-Pacific region to renounce confrontation and mutual cooperation directed against third countries and to promote relations in the spirit of mutual trust, mutual benefit and equality. They expressed their firm belief that it is high time to establish open, transparent and equal architecture of security and cooperation in the Asia-Pacific region based on the principles of international law, non-bloc approaches and due consideration of legitimate interests of all parties.

Moscow and Beijing called upon all countries throughout the region to adhere to the following basic internationally recognized principles:

(1) To respect sovereignty, independence and territorial integrity, not to interfere in internal affairs of each other;

(2) To confirm their commitment to the principle of equal and indivisible security;

(3) To confirm defensive character of their military policies;

(4) Not to use or to threaten to use force;

(5) Not to undertake or support any actions aimed at overthrowing governments or undermining stability of other states;

(6) To resolve mutual disagreements by peaceful political and diplomatic means on the basis of principles of mutual understanding and search for compromise;

(7) To strengthen cooperation on countering non-traditional threats to security;

(8) To develop bilateral and multilateral military cooperation not directed against third countries;

(9) To develop cooperation in the border areas and to strengthen contacts between people.

Russia and China also highlighted that by establishing close relations between multilateral associations in Asia the regional community can also facilitate the advancement of the aforementioned principles and security measures. In the age of network diplomacy it is necessary to develop an extensive network of partnership ties between regional organizations and fora, counterterrorism structures, emergency information and management centers.

Conclusion. Apprehending the urgent need to reconfirm principles of collective security and measures to strengthen transparency and mutual confidence in Asia, Russia and China took the lead and put forward fresh ideas. This is ought to be seen as a new beginning. But words are not enough. Their ideas should be followed by further actions.

1.14 EAST ASIA SUMMITS AND ASIAN SECURITY

The Sino-Russian initiative was positively received across the region. ASEAN Member States echoed by drafting — together with their dialog partners — a new regional document reflecting the same thinking — *East Asia Summit Declaration on the Principles for Mutually Beneficial Relations*. It was adopted at the Sixth East Asia Summit in 2011 in Bali. The document produced very important added value supplementing elements of the Russian-Chinese initiative with the following principles: respect for the diversity of ethnic, religious, cultural traditions and values, as well as diversity of views and positions, including by promoting the voices of moderation; enhancement of regional resilience in the in the face of economic shocks and natural disasters; respect for fundamental freedoms, the promotion and protection of human rights and social justice; promotion of good neighborliness, partnership and community building; enhancement of mutually beneficial cooperation in the EAS and with other regional fora.

It is worth mentioning that a new regional platform — East Asia Summits — turns out to be most suitable for discussions on regional security. Its participants include leaders of all major countries of the region. After the US and Russia joined the EAS in 2010 the forum became ideally equipped to conduct a meaningful dialog on key issues of the regional life including security. The EAS should be strengthened and gradually developed as "a hub" of the evolving Asian architecture of security and cooperation.

One of the tasks of the EAS should be to lay down a legally binding basis for new multilateral regional security arrangements. A time has come to make another step forward in this direction. Russia has suggested that this coming autumn in Brunei the EAS leaders adopt a *Declaration on Framework Guidelines on Strengthening Security and Promoting Cooperation in the Asia-Pacific region*. It could further elaborate and codify principles already listed in the previously approved documents of this kind, as well as formulate some new up-to-date steps to be taken.

Conclusion. With the inclusion of the US and Russia the power and significance of the EAS increased. This forum may become the key regional structure where leaders of the 18 major Asia-Pacific countries could conduct a strategic dialog on vital regional issues ranging from security to economic cooperation to education, health care and humanitarian assistance. In the field of security the EAS should concentrate on elaboration of regional rules of "fair play" as well as on establishment of close coordination and "division of labour" with ASEAN-centric pillars of the security architecture — ARF and ADMM Plus, CICA and the SCO.

1. 15   WELL FORGOTTEN INITIATIVES: VLADIVOSTOK-1986 AND KRASNOYARSK-1988

In 1986 Mikhail Gorbachev, then the top Soviet leader and a reform-minded politician, spoke in the Russian Far Eastern city of Vladivostok where he announced a whole set of bold and far-fetched foreign policy initiatives related to the USSR-US and USSR-China relations and regional issues. Two years later in 1988 he further developed those initiatives in his famous speech in Krasnoyarsk.

There is no need to talk about the ideas which were successfully translated into concrete steps and brought about a warming in the Soviet-American relationship and normalization between the Soviet Union and China. We will focus on security initiatives regarding multilateral diplomacy in Asia.

In fact the crux of what Mr. Gorbachev suggested can be summarized in three words: an Asian security system. It is worth reminding that today, 25 years later, a security system in the Asia-Pacific region still remains a dream.

In particular the Soviet leader proposed:

(1) To hold a regional conference on Asia-Pacific security and cooperation in Hiroshima, similar to the 1975 Helsinki Security and Cooperation Conference in Europe;

(2) To stop proliferation and boosting of arsenals of nuclear weapons in the region;

(3) To downgrade the activity of the Navy of the regional powers, first and foremost of warships carrying nuclear missiles, and to restrict submarines from entering agreed zones of the Pacific Ocean;

(4) To cut military forces and conventional weapons in the Asia-Pacific region to the level of reasonable sufficiency;

(5) To launch a discussion on CBMs and non-use of force in the region starting from elementary measures of securing safety of navigation in the Pacific Ocean;

(6) To hold a multilateral discussion on ways of reducing military confrontation

in the Northeast Asia with a view to a frozen and balanced reduction of Navy and Air Force of the sub-regional countries;

(7) To work out joint measures of preventing incidents in the open sea and air zones above it;

(8) To establish a trilateral USSR, China and the US negotiation mechanism to discuss Asia-Pacific security issues.

A quarter of a century has passed since then but the ideas put forward in mid-80s do not look outdated. Moreover, it seems timely to pick up some of them to promote security in Asia. Combined with commitments proposed in the 2010 Sino-Russian Security Initiative their implementation may fill some of the gaps in the existing regional security architecture.

In particular, the conditions in Asia seem to be ripe for doing the following things:

(1) To convene an Asia-Pacific Ministerial conference to discuss feasible CBMs and best practices and lessons learned in the course of their implementation;

(2) To kick-start a voluntary exchange of information on defense budgets, composition of military forces especially those deployed in the border areas;

(3) To invite observers from regional countries to national and multilateral regional military exercises and maneuvers;

(4) To refrain from conducting military exercises in the vicinity of land and sea borders of other countries;

(5) To inform each other on plans of large-scale movements of military forces;

(6) To elaborate a legal instrument and to establish a mechanism of prevention of dangerous military activity and mutual assistance in case of incidents in the open sea;

(7) To make a commitment to limit the activity of aircraft-carrying fleets and submarines in the Pacific and Indian Oceans;

(8) To make a commitment that Navy forces will refrain from entering the straits and zones adjacent to the coast line of littoral states;

(9) To upgrade exchanges between the military, including mutual visits of top

brass, friendly contacts between rank-and-file officers and soldiers, including those serving in border troops and coast guards.

(10) At a later stage regional countries may engage themselves in the following actions or negotiations on:

(1) Elaboration of guidelines for mutual reductions of military forces and strengthening confidence in the border areas;

(2) Withdrawal of redundant armed forces and weapons from the border areas;

(3) Establishment of a legal framework and an institutional mechanism of control over mutual reductions of conventional weapons.

Countries possessing nuclear and/or missile potentials may unilaterally or upon agreement take the following obligations;

(1) Not to aim their missiles at targets in other countries;

(2) Not to be the first to use nuclear weapons against each other;

(3) Not to deploy strategic or tactical ABM systems in other countries.

1.16 KOREAN PENINSULA AND A POSSIBLE SECURITY MECHA-NISM

In the framework of the Six-Party talks in 2010 Russia proposed to adopt *Guiding Principles of Peace and Security in Northeast Asia* which would include a number of basic principles and means to establish a sub-regional security mechanism. The draft document contained obligations of the State-Parties to respect each other's sovereign equality and individuality, legal equality, territorial integrity, freedom and political independence; to refrain from acts constituting threat or direct or indirect use of force against another party; to refrain from any manifestation of force for the purpose of inducing another party to renounce the full exercise of its sovereign rights; to refrain from any intervention, direct or indirect, individual or collective, in the internal affairs of another party; to refrain from any act of political, economic or another coercion; to refrain from any direct or indirect assistance to activities directed towards overthrowing of the regime of another party; to respect each other's right to belong or not to belong to international organizations, to be or not to be a party to bilateral or multilateral treaties including treaties of alliance; not to permit use of their territory to prepare or launch military intervention or to conduct any other activity which meaningfully infringes security of other parties; to seek settlement of disputes and other problems among them through political, diplomatic and other peaceful means.

The concept of establishment of a sub-regional security mechanism for Korean Peninsula and Northeast Asia also envisaged promoting economic cooperation in the area including constructing Trans-Korean oil and gas pipelines, a Trans-Korean railway and supplying electricity from Russia to the Peninsula. Moscow views economic cooperation as a part and parcel of any sub-regional deal.

Unfortunately the process of negotiations on the draft of Guiding Principles was interrupted by the pause in the Six-Party talks and never resumed. Once conditions are at place the idea of building a multilateral, equal peace and security mechanism in Northeast Asia should be revived.

1.17 SOUTH CHINA SEA ISSUE AND A POSSIBLE SECURITY MECHANISM

In the South China Sea in fact there is a combination of two problems — a series of territorial disputes and an issue of maintenance of peace and stability in this sub-region. Therefore the first step towards a settlement of the South China Sea issue should be to agree on the right approach to the relationship between the two.

Now the countries involved in the dispute either hope to maintain a *status quo* till better times in the future or to achieve a comprehensive solution "once and for all". But both stands are naïve and resemble more a wishful thinking rather than a serious strategy. Due to the complexity of this "multiple territorial dispute" any "package deal" seems absolutely impossible.

I believe that territorial disputes *per se* should be separated from multilateral efforts to ensure maritime security and transparency of military and naval activity in the South China Sea. This would, on the one hand, allow to alleviate the tension in bilateral relationship between the parties concerned and would create favorable environment for the establishment of a security mechanism in the South China Sea, on the other.

The 2002 *China-ASEAN Declaration on the Conduct of Parties in the South China Sea* was an important move in the right direction. However the next goal set by the participants of the negotiations is misleading. A *Code of Conduct in the South China Sea* even if it is going to be a legally binding document would not guarantee peace. The parties concerned should negotiate several security agreements, among them agreements on political principles of multilateral cooperation (such as "mutual equal security", "mutual non-use of force", "renunciation of unilateral military superiority" etc., already tested by the SCO Member States), on decreasing military and naval activity including exercises in the sub-region, guidelines on confidence-building measures, documents on ensuring safety of sea communications, on preventing dangerous military activity and sorting out incidents, on emergency cooperation, on mutual assistance in saving seamen in need, on combating piracy etc. All the arrangements should be based on the premise that the parties to the conflict must strictly observe the border *status quo* until all border issues are finally settled.

Simultaneously a mechanism to oversee the security situation in the South China Sea and to control the implementation of all those agreements should be established. In my view such a mechanism should be participated only by regional countries. The international community having a vested interest in maritime security and safety of sea lanes in the South China Sea may act as guarantors of the agreements, provide technical assistance etc.

* * *

What is Asian wisdom? Different people may have different definitions. I believe that it includes values of tolerance, balance, moderation, mutual respect, non-violence, stability, a habit of resolving conflicts by peaceful means, through negotiations and consultations. At the same time Asian wisdom embraces successful experience and bright ideas accumulated over the years in the course of development of bilateral relations between the Asia-Pacific countries and the evolution of regional organizations. It is my strong belief that this wisdom and experience may and should serve the noble ideals of strengthening security in Asia.

(Kirill Barsky, Special Envoy of the President of the Russian Federation on the Shanghai Cooperation Organization Affairs)

CHAPTER 2   The Western Philosophy of Exploiting the Earth's Limited Resources in Comparison with Asia's Wisdom

Bernd Schünemann

2.1   FOUR CRUCIAL MODES OF THOUGHT THAT HAVE BUILT THE WESTERN LEGAL FRAMEWORK FOR GLOBAL ECONOMY

Parallel to the growth of global economy, the global problems and threats due to over-exploitation of global resources have grown exponentially. On the surface, these problems derive from an unlimited, predator-like capitalism according to economic neo-liberal theory of Chicago. In the deep structure, however, they are the logical consequence of the essence of western religion and philosophy, starting with Judaism and Christianity, followed by the enlightenment, perfected by the democratic form of government and finalized after the decay of socialism. Let me take these four steps that are responsible for the current state of the world into closer consideration.

In the holy book of Christs, the Bible, within the oldest Jewish part at the beginning of the book Genesis, we find God's command to mankind "Subdue the earth". This means a basic perspective which is everything but a matter of course, for example in comparison with the modes of thought of Buddhism or of many Indian tribes in America, and is responsible for a basic attitude of human beings not only as crown of creation but also with permanently prevailing interests so that all parts of nature are obliged to serve men's pursuit of happiness.

However, the real consequences of this normative basis remained insignificant, due to the anti-individualism of early Christianity. With the decay of the Roman empire, the Roman-Greek culture as a whole broke down, the libraries containing the knowledge of a millennium were closed, analphabetism became the common level of education or, frankly spoken, of the complete absence of education. It was not before the era of enlightenment perfected the era of Renaissance, that the individual was re-discovered in philosophy and released from countless boundaries in practice. His old slogan of the Greek sophistic philosopher Protagoras, "a human being is the measure of all things" now took an individualistic turn, tangible in the hypothesized direct dialogue between God and the individual in the religious concept of Protestantism and in its self-legislation in Immanuel Kant's moral philosophy. In Kant's famous words, enlightenment meant the exit of mankind out of her self-inflicted immaturity.

The intellectual liberation of the individual from all constraints caused the rise of the totality of empirical sciences and enabled the establishment of modern techniques and industries. For its unlimited use, however, the democratic form of government was indispensable, and the more thoroughly a formal egality with respect to political and property rights was established, the more efficient were the results of an unleashed economy, fulfilling the old Jewish-Christian command of the book Genesis of the Bible.

Notwithstanding, there were still moral limits to overcome, at least in Europe, less in North America. Out of the principle of "fraternity", which was enshrined in the French but not in the American declaration of human rights, the development of socialism grew which barred a radical capitalism in Europe as well as its legal prerequisite, a rigid concept of property rights. After the Russian revolution of 1917, the socialist countries including the People's Republic of China abolished private property of the means of production, whereas the Federal Republic of Germany invented the so called Social Market Economy on the constitutional base of a concept of property that had to serve not alone the interests of the proprietor but the public and social interests as well. However, with the dissolution of the Soviet Union and the decay of socialist philosophy in the whole Western hemisphere, the Angloamerican concept of predator-capitalism pretended to have won the victory over socialism and, at least in practice, prevailed for the recent two decades. Its crucial legal figures are built by a radically individualistic concept of property rights, a harsh protection of brands and an uncontrolled banking system whose key activity is gambling on a large scale of thousands of billions of US-Dollars.

2.2 THE IMMINENT DISASTROUS CONSEQUENCES FOR THE FUTURE OF THE WORLD

The four steps I have pointed out before lead to four disastrous consequences unless the people of the world will succeed in their extinction: revolving financial crises, increasing inequality of the distribution of income and property and by this of life chances, growing exploitation of workers, especially in underdeveloped countries, and depletion and destruction of the world's natural resources.

In no more than one decade, the global financial system has met three extremely deep crises that have not been solved but could only be overcome by postponing the damages and consequences for the next, even deeper crises with the forthcoming final result of a collapse of the whole system. First the so-called dotcom-bubble, then the American subprime mortgage bubble, and today the European debt crisis. To date, there is no Western state that would be able to pay its debts. This means not only a disability of the debtor but also of the creditor, which is China on the largest scale. Imports from China have been paid with loans that can never be paid back. Thus Western capitalism behaves like a fraudster who has his livelihood paid by a creditor who will never get his money back. His standard of living is not earned by himself unless through false pretense. And what is even worse, only in this way he is enjoying amenities of life that exploit the world's natural resources to a grade several times higher than covered by a calculation of sustainable development, thus leading inevitably to an ecologic catastrophe which we already watch approaching.

The increasing inequality of the distribution of income and property characterizes the social and economic development in all Western countries for the past two decades, even in Germany. As long as the Soviet Union and other socialist countries had challenged the Western Hemisphere with respect to the question of social justice, the situation of the lower classes had improved even and especially in the countries with a capitalist economy, which was the main reason for the collapse of the Soviet Union and the whole Russian-dominated Communist power bloc. However, after the decay of the Soviet Union the so-called turbo-capitalism gained the upper hand with the consequence, that an evermore widening spread between the higher and lower incomes leads to so-called new poverty, even in Germany with its relatively most prosperous economy in the European Union, whereas the number of people with immense fortunes increases.

Nevertheless, even the poorest people in Western countries enjoy a standard of living that goes far beyond the income levels in the rest of the world. In Germany, for example, people without any assets or earned income will be paid by the state about 6000 yuan monthly for housing and living. To assess the high level of purchasing power of this amount adequately, you must take into account that clothing as well as electronic devices including computers, radios, televisions and cameras are either available at a moderate price, or if the consumer prefers an expensive brand, the lion's share is for the owner of the brand, whereas the producer will only be paid a small percentage of the consumer price.

The exploitation of the working classes, especially in the underdeveloped countries of the Third World, has accelerated during and due to globalization. As a matter of fact, de-colonization has ended in neo-colonialism, with all over the Third World stretching kleptocracies that have followed the colonial rule as most feasible instruments to guarantee the exploitation of the population. Indigenous dictators as a substitutes for the international law of colonialism on the one hand, and the separation of brand and product with brands as the core of property rights on the other hand form the spine of Western dominated world economy. As *Naomi Klein* has pointed out, a brand is not created in the factory anymore; it is created in the office. The brand is not a reflection of quality but a reflection of what the marketing department wants it to stand for, no longer producing things, but images of things. The inconvenience of production is contracted out, using third world labour at dumping prices to produce its products. As long as the trade-mark proprietors are companies of the Western hemisphere, there is no recipe to break their domination and their ability to dictate the exchange prices, forcing the production factories to pay scant wages to the workers. Even the huge Chinese economy is subjected to these rules of global market economy, that pervert a sound protection of intellectual property into a dictatorship of brands. To illustrate this point, Klein provided an example of a factory in China called the Liang Shi Handbag Factory which produced Kathie Lee handbags for Wal-Mart.

According to the proponents of liberal market economies, the consumption-fuelled growth, that means driving global growth by consuming more, is the only promising way to overcome these inequalities of the standard of living of the world's population. In recent years, Chinese officials in particular enjoyed what looked like a vindication of their country's model of state-managed economy, albeit helped by a massive stimulus package, kept steaming ahead[1]. And as a matter of fact, the next few decades will see the most extraordinary jumps in the consumption of almost every product and service imaginable as Asia catches up. *Nair* gives the example of poultry and energy. Per year, Americans eat 9 billion birds, whereas the whole of Asian — 30 times as many people as in the United States — eats 16 billion annually. So if the Asian population would become eating the same amount of poultry as each American does now, there would be a need of 120 billion birds per year, a quite incredible number. As for energy, the average American uses 250 kilowatt hours a day, the average Chinese 40 and the average Indian 20[2]. Since development can no longer be allowed that rewards only a few, we have to assume that 4 billion Asians will consume the same amount of energy as the Americans which would be as impossible

---

[1]　See Nair, Consumptionomics, Oxford 2011, p. 23.

[2]　See Nair, p. 43.

as the consumption of 120 billion birds per year. The depletion and destruction of the world's natural resources would become inevitable. Since all natural resources are constrained, economic activity must be subservient to maintaining the vitality of resources[1].

Once again, the advocates of liberal market economy do not deny the necessity of changes and new solutions but still hold that the rationality of the market will be the best way to find them. In their famous book "Varieties of Capitalism: The Institutional Foundations of Comparative Advantage" (2001), *Peter A. Hall* and *David Soskice* argue that technological specialization patterns are largely determined by the prevailing "variety of capitalism". They hypothesize that "liberal market economies" specialize in radical innovation, which would be exactly the remedy to break the deadlock which the world economy to date so urgently needs. However, the experience with the recent financial crises proves the opposite. According to *Joseph Stiglitz*, the global financial "crisis should lay to rest any belief in rational markets. The irrationalities evident in mortgage markets, in securitization, in derivatives and in banking are mind-boggling; our supposed financial wizards have exhibited behaviour which, to use the vernacular, seemed stupid even at the time." [2]

2.3　THE UNDERLYING LEGAL STRUCTURE

My conclusion is that liberal market economy as the final consequence of Western modes of thought will not be able to break the deadlock which has been necessarily created by its own structure, convictions and tendencies. Before I will turn my perspective to the question if Asia's wisdom can help us to find a way out, let us keep in mind that there is a specific legal structure that underlies modern liberal market economy. The two most important features are, in my opinion, the selfishness in the concept of property rights and the weak influence of the liberal state in the field of economy. However, a radical change of these features, which implies public

---

[1]　See Nair, p. 91.

[2]　The Non-existent Hand, London Review of Books, volume 32 number 8, April 22, 2010, p. 17.

utility of property rights and state control over the core of economy, is hardly to accomplish in the Western democracie names, because the decay of the communist power bloc has been interpreted as a proof for the superiority of the market economy and parliamentary democracy to all kinds of socialism. And during every summit from Kyoto to Copenhagen on climate change and how to stop it, the Western countries refused to grant substantial concessions to the developing countries and to wave their usurped claims to take and consume the lion share of the world changes natural resources. Therefore I do not see a chance at the time being to derive an effective solution for the present ecological problems of mankind from Western social philosophy and political theory.

2.4   A SHORT GLANCE ON ASIA'S WISDOM

As a matter of fact, for every European it is a great venture to give comments on Asia's wisdom. Therefore let me quote the Theme Interpretation of our Forum with the following words: "The long history of Asian civilization has given rise to the diverse cultures of this continent. The essence of harmonious advancement is peaceful co-existence, win-win cooperation and joint development. Due to asymmetric growth and complicated histories, Asian countries can only realize peace, cooperation and development through bold, positive efforts. Specifically, Asia should establish shared values based on a cooperative mechanism, and require an agenda for effective action in addition to innovative institutions. We must promote deeper mutual trust and cooperation while appreciating other countries' culture. We cannot accomplish this goal without passion, wisdom and concrete action. While differences are unavoidable, peaceful coexistence comes from proactive hard work. Endowed with a brilliant civilization, when Asian countries are ready to unite, embrace their differences, and seek harmony together, a new Asia will emerge."

Of course, I can fully agree with this statement. However, its criteria are not very specific, therefore I want to try to lay stress on the differences between Asia's wisdom and Western political theory. If I understand well, the Chinese idea of a harmonious society is grounded on a concept of human beings that differs significantly from the concept of "homo economi" whose main goal is to maximize his personal benefits. Such a "homo oeconomicus" will cooperate only when the cooperation brings himself benefits as well, his political philosophy is the philosophy of individualism and selfishness. On the contrary, the members of a harmonious society support the welfare of their co-citizen for its own sake. By the way, there is a strong connection with the moral principles of early Christianity before the era of enlightenment and the discovery of the individual. This connection is not that surprising, because the moral principles of early Christianity seem to have been influenced by Buddhism because the ideas of Buddhism have been brought to the Mediterranean area through the conquests of Alexander the Great. And the modern concept of harmonious society is rooted itself both in Buddhism and Confucianism, notwithstanding that in history there has been a great rivalry between Buddhism and Confucianism. For example, let me quote what Ch'eng Hao, the famous Neo-Confucianist during the Song dynasty. "Simply because of selfishness, man thinks in terms of his own person, and therefore, from the point of view of principle, belittles them. If he lets go with this person of his and views all things in the same way, how much joy would there be! Because the Buddhists do not know with this, they think in terms of the self. If they cannot cope with it, they become disgusted and want to get rid of sense-perception, and because the source of their mind is not calm, they want to be like dry wood and dead ashes. But this is impossible. It is possible only with death. The Buddhists say all that because they in reality love their own persons and cannot let go. They are like those worms that carry things on their backs which are already unable to bear their load and still add more things on their bodies, or like a man who sinks in a river."

Of course, as a European I don't feel qualified enough to decide these quarrels between Buddhism and Confucianism. The common grounds, however, both for Buddhism and Confucianism, is the refusal of radical individualism as I have highlighted with the figure of "Homo oeconomicus". And therefore, the two necessities of change I mentioned before, that is public utility of property rights and state control over the core of economy, are fully compatible with the core of Asia's wisdom.

2.5 NECESSARY CHANGES IN THE LEGAL STRUCTURE OF GLOBAL ECONOMY IN THE 21ST CENTUREY

The first necessity is, that the use of natural resources must be equitable for current and future generations, and therefore collective welfare must take priority over individual rights. As a consequence, resources must be repriced. Whereas market capitalism has downplayed or even ignored negative external factors and external costs, this must be reversed. As a matter of fact, the advocates of liberal market economy have developed a concept of pollution rights some years ago which should be bought by all polluting industries or facilities, thus repricing resources and coercing all activities dangerous for the environment and natural resources to protect and to save them. However, due to lobby activities and as a consequence of the weak position of modern Western democracy with respect to the regulation of economy, pollution rights have remained so cheap that their function is nothing else but an alibi for the state to refrain from any effective measures.

Property rights have to be subordinated to usage responsibilities. Capitalist-style rights have been introduced to facilitate transfers of ownership of land or resources to a company or individual better able to exploit them immediately for short-term gain, as has been the case with so many tracts of rainforest in Indonesia and other countries of South-East Asia[1]. This must be terminated on the spot. Taking the following sentence of the quote the Theme Interpretation of our Forum into consideration: "The essence of harmonious advancement is peaceful co-existence, win-win cooperation and joint development", I want to emphasize that, in my opinion, it would be a misunderstanding to read it as an announcement of a combined exploitation of the rain forests of Indonesia both by the Indonesian and the Chinese timber industry.

---

[1] Nair, p. 107.

The consequence of all of these ideas is, of course, redefining the role of the state. In the Western Hemisphere, the propaganda for liberal market economy was accompanied by the thesis that the state should have lost his sovereignty, remaining only as one player among other players and needing cooperation with the powerful economic players. In the US, in particular, but also in Europe, politicians have largely abandoned the notion of acting for the public good to work instead as agents advancing the narrow interests of business and other constituencies with the financial power necessary to fund elections campaigns, or, even worse, influencing the state agencies by means of corruption. According to media reports, the danger of corruption is imminent all over the world. And in China, India and other countries with a huge population, there is a specific pressure on the government to improve the standard of living of hundreds of millions of people in short terms, disregarding the necessary protection of the environment and of natural resources in long terms. Nevertheless, there is no alternative to the state bringing back in in the Western Hemisphere and to encourage the Asian leaders in those countries in which the state is still in control of the economy to keep this control and to refuse the misguiding temptations of liberal market theory.

Summing up, the classic role of the state is in the current situation of mankind by no means obsolete but more important than ever. It's task is to guarantee public welfare not only for the living generation but also for future generations. It is self-evident that only the state has a chance to achieve this goal. The siren calls of the US American liberal market proponents of the alleged agony of the state are not to be taken seriously. They lead into a dead-end street.

2.6 THE CONTRIBUTION OF ECONOMIC CRIMINAL LAW

To draft the legal framework for reshaping capitalism and saving the planet is such a demanding task that I cannot presume to contribute solutions in this short paper. All areas of the law have to be included. There is a special role for criminal law because of its unique overkill functions. Public Law and Civil Law depend on the effectivity of control, be it by a civil servant of the state, be it by the contractual partner. On the contrary, criminal law has a preventive effect by deterrence, that means by the threat of punishment, even if there is no controlling person present. Therefore economic criminal law is an indispensable part of the new legal framework.

For the time being, there are two different concepts for economic criminal law riveling in the legislation. Within the US and in all countries under the influence of the United States, punishing the legal entity itself has become a standard sanction. The criminal policy of the European Union and of many of the member states goes into the same direction. However, this is the wrong way, because a legal entity cannot act and bears no personal responsibility. On the other hand, sanctions against the legal entity is usually mitigating the sentence against the management people, so it's effect is contra-productive.

Taking everything into account, economic criminal law is an indispensable instrument for the implementation of a legal order that takes the task of saving our planet seriously.

(Prof. Dr. Bernd Schünemann, LMU Muenchen, German)

CHAPTER 3　　Addressing Territorial Disputes — the Asian Way

Maj Gen Dipankar Banerjee (Retd)

3.1　THE BACKDROP

Nation states in the 21st Century are defined by territory, which in turn are sanctified by borders. These borders then go on to delineate boundaries of political entities and thereby define legal jurisdictions of provincial governments or sovereign states. There are various means through which nations manage borders. Some borders are open and completely unguarded, for example in South Asia between India and Nepal and India and Bhutan. Or, in countries and regions that have decided to come together to form a single geo-political entity, such as the European Union or the one that ASEAN proposes to develop in the next few years, trans border movement of peoples and commerce are either free or the procedures have been simplified in a major way.

Before states can open up borders, it is often important to first delineate and then even guard them. Robert Frost's words in his poem, *Mending Fences* explained it well, "good fences make good neighbors" he wrote[1]. Because borders define clear

---

[1]　Robert Frost in, **Mending Wall**, published in 1914. Even though he states this twice, there is also a certain doubt in his mind, an uneasiness. Midway through the poem he also say, "*Something there is that doesn't love a wall,*" as if rebelling against the very idea. Yet, the poem makes a strong case for fixed borders.

jurisdiction over territory within which one is free to enjoy the products of one's labor without hindrance, it was necessary to both mark and then strengthen it.

But, this was not always so, not in history or in Asia. Overlapping territorial jurisdictions were not uncommon in the past. Borders were never entirely barriers to movement. Silk routes emanating from China in all directions traversed through many regions and kingdoms before reaching their markets very far away. Indian kings in the South extended their influences to the east as well as to the west to Arabia across the seas without much difficulty. Afghanistan was always a route for trade as well as invading armies. What in Europe came to be established as the principle of state sovereignty at the Treaty of Westphalia in 1648 with rigid borders, to be defended aggressively were to come about much later in Asia.

Imperial powers in Asia from the 18th Century delineated borders in their own interest to facilitate greater exploitation of resources and to assist political domination. Therefore, they often created borders artificially, separating peoples and cultures in to different nation states. Imposed buffer states for enhanced security where none were perhaps warranted. Even at the time of their departure after World War II they created further divisions by imposing artificial borders and creating new nation states. Much of the conflicts of the later Twentieth century till the present day, can be traced to consequences of colonial rule in Asia. The current state of national and territorial boundaries in Asia must be seen in this backdrop as well as the outcomes of the two World Wars.

In West Asia straight lines were drawn across maps dividing tribes and religions even during the First World War. New states were introduced or created to facilitate exploitation of their mineral wealth. After World War II, the Indian sub-continent was divided arbitrarily, in a few weeks, by Sir Cyril Radcliffe, a British lawyer who had never set foot in the country earlier. The division was based entirely on maps and census data perused alone in closed rooms. In parts of Southeast Asia anti-colonial wars for independence would go on for years before national borders would be rationalized. In East Asia, the Koreas still remain divided.

3. 2   ASIA'S REEMERGENCE AND THE QUESTION OF BORDERS

As Asia re-emerges as the center of global prosperity and generator of wealth, the question of settling borders and territorial disputes assume greater importance and urgency. This short essay will attempt to trace and define the Asian Way of territorial dispute resolution. Can we learn from these even as we move forward in peace and prosperity in Asia in the years ahead? How did Asia address territorial disputes? Is there a distinct Asian way of resolving borders and territorial issues? Addressing these questions will take a more detailed effort. This paper attempts to highlight a few issues.

The first major attempt had to begin with an attempt at re-establishing the Asian identity. This was attempted at the Asian Relations Conference held in Delhi in March 1947. It was not by the Government of India, as India was still not independent; but by the Indian Council of World Affairs an autonomous body created just a couple of years earlier[1]. It brought together many countries and peoples from across Asia. Its purpose was to reframe an Asian view on global affairs, moving away from recent history. From this humble beginning an Asian identity began to emerge, which in turn would impact on Asia's view on geo-politics.

At the inaugural session of this Asian Relations Conference, the future Prime Minister of India, Jawaharlal Nehru said,

> "*For too long we in Asia have been petitioners in Western courts and chancelleries. That story must now belong to the past. We propose to stand on our own feet and to co-operate with all others who are prepared to co-operate with us. We do not intend to be the plaything of other states*". [2]

This was a clear call for a new Asia, even though it was to be a year and a half

---

[1]   For more details, please refer to the ICWA web site at; http://icwadelhi. info/asianrelationsconference/ index. php? option = com_content&view = article&id = 51 &Itemid = 137; accessed on 19 May 2013.

[2]   Speech delivered by Jawaharlal Nehru on 24 Mar 1947 at the Asian Relations Conference, New Delhi, accessed on 20 April at icwadelhi. info/asianrelationsconference/images/stories/jawaharlalnehru. pdf.

before China truly emerged as Mao Zedong proclaimed from Tiananmen Square in Beijing. Though the issues were framed at this Conference and an Asian identity was re-established, more concrete shapes to these ideas were to be given later.

For the purpose of this paper, it is necessary to examine four principal developments in Asia in the last sixty years. First, is *Panchsheel or the Five Principles of Peaceful Coexistence*. Second, is the *Spirit of Bandung and Afro-Asian solidarity*. Third, is the evolution of *Non-alignment* as state policy and the global Non Aligned Movement, in which Asian countries played a major role. Fourth, is the *ASEAN Way* or the *ASEAN Charter* that identifies ways to promote regional peace and stability through abiding respect for justice and the rule of law.

3.3   PANCHSHEEL OR THE FIVE PRINCIPLES OF PEACEFUL CO-EXISTENCE

The first issue that Asia confronted was to define an Asian view of international relations[1]. A view that would differ from the confrontational approach that prevailed in the west, where disagreement over major issues would ultimately and rather early, be resolved through conflict and force of arms. The Five Principles of Panchsheel were to differ from this approach. By adopting a spirit of reconciliation through non-interference in internal affairs of other states and by following a policy of peace and consultation, it was hoped that conflicts would be reduced in Asia.

The five principles of Panchsheel were given shape during dialogue between India and China on trade issues in Tibet. Meetings were held during 1953-54 in both Beijing and Delhi. At the end both premiers issued a Joint Statement on June 28, 1954 laying out the vision of Panchsheel. It was to be the framework, not only for relations between the two countries, but also for their relations with all other countries, so that a solid foundation could be laid for peace and security in the world.

---

[1]   Panchashila is a Sanskrit word, meaning "Panch" (five) "Shila" (virtues). President Sukarno had in 1945 mentioned this, though with some variation, as the five principles on which the Indonesian state would be built.

Later, Premier Zhou Enlai suggested that these guiding principles could be adopted by both countries in their foreign policies[1]. These Five Principles are not unique to India and China, its ideas are shared more broadly in Asia. Particularly in Indonesia and others where these principles have been accorded a high position in state policy. The five principles as found in the preamble, are:

(1) Mutual respect for each other's territorial integrity and sovereignty,

(2) Mutual non-aggression,

(3) Mutual non-interference,

(4) Equality and mutual benefit, and

(5) Peaceful co-existence[2].

Since then the Five Principles have played a great role in developing cooperative international relations and on border and territorial issues. This concept of the Panchsheel was subsequently incorporated in the Bandung Declaration, the Non Aligned Movement Charter as well as in the ASEAN Charter. At the time of signing the document in 1954, Jawaharlal Nehru had stated that,

"Panchsheel can provide the ideological foundation for developing a paradigm of international interaction, allowing all nations to work towards peace and prosperity in cooperation, while maintaining their national identity, spirit and character." He went on to say that, *"those who desire peace for the world must know once for all that there can be no equilibrium or stability for either the East or the West unless all aggression, all imperialist domination, all forced interference in other countries' affairs end completely."*[3]

---

[1] Former President of India KR Narayanan at a seminar in Beijing on 20 July 2004. Accessed on the MEA web site on 4 May 2013.

[2] These principles were first formally enunciated in the Agreement on Trade and Intercourse between the Tibet region of China and India and was signed on April 29, 1954. http://meahindi. nic. in/hindixpsite/celdemo/panchsheel. pdf; accessed on 24 April 2013.

Please also see Dr Swaran Singh on "Three agreements and five principles between India and China", for a balanced Indian perspective on this Agreement, http://ignca. nic. in/ks_41062. htm; accessed on 24 April 2013.

[3] *Panchasheel*, a brochure brought out by the Ministry of External Affairs, Governent of India, on the 50th anniversary of the signing of the Agreement.

The Five Principles of course has had its critics, mainly in the west. Criticism has been based on its lack of practicality, of its lofty idealism and its unenforceable nature. Then this misses the very point of the Asian Way and of the Principles. Just as Panchsheel remains an important tenet of Buddhism, it is but a principle and not a finite directive that can be enforced through force. Yet, these principles continue to have contemporary relevance. President Narayanan of India said some two decades ago, that,

> "*I think a new international order can be built on the basis of the five principles, because these principles recognize dignity and sovereignty of other countries. For any peaceful world order, this is the first requisite that you must recognize the sovereignty of each other and respect others' territories*"[①]

3.4　THE AFRO-ASIAN CONFERENCE AT BANDUNG 1955

The next major step was the Afro-Asian Conference held at Bandung in Indonesia in April 1955. The conference was organized by Indonesia, Ceylon (Sri Lanka), Philippines and Burma (Myanmar) and attended by 29 countries of Asia and Africa, many of these countries had only recently become independent and come out of colonialism. During the meeting, Premier Zhou Enlai advocated the principle of "*seeking common ground while shelving differences*" and suggested setting the Five Principles as a "*base for establishing friendly, cooperative relations between countries of different social systems*".

The meeting was seen in a different light in the west. One western author went on to describe the meeting as representing those who were;

> "*The despised, the insulted, the hurt, the dispossessed — in short, the*

---

① 　KR Narayanan, Five Principles of Peaceful Coexistence at China internet forum at; file:///Users/user/ Desktop/Shanghai% 20paps/People's% 20Daily% 20Online% 20—% 20The% 20Five% 20Principles% 20of% 20Peaceful% 20Co-existence% 20% 3Cp% 20align = right% 3E% 3Cfont% 20size = 2% 3E% 3Cs. webarchive accessed on 13 May 13.

underdogs of the human race were meeting. Here were class and racial and religious consciousness on a global scale. Who have thought of organizing such a meeting? And what had these nations in common? Nothing, it seemed to me, but what their past relationship to the Western world had made them feel, this meeting of the rejected was in itself a kind of judgment upon the Western world!" [1]

Actually this defined the meeting quite well. It was a meeting of the marginalized of Asia-Africa, many of them recently under colonial rule, striving for real freedom and who had come together at Bandung to express their views on the global order. President Soekarno articulated this view very eloquently when he said:

"For long years we Asian and African people have tolerated decisions made in our stead by those countries which placed their own interests above all else. We lived in poverty and humiliation. But tremendous changes have taken place in the past years. Many peoples and countries have awakened from centuries of slumber. Tranquility has given way to struggle and action. This irresistible force is sweeping the two continents." [2][3]

Premier Zhou Enlai played a leadership role at this conference and established his credentials as an outstanding international diplomat and made many important contributions. He also strongly supported Asian-African solidarity[4].

In its final Communique passed on 24 April 1955 under the last section *Declaration on the promotion of world peace and co-operation*, it lists out ten principles. Its essence is, respect for fundamental human rights, sovereignty and territorial integrity of all nations. It calls for the recognition of the equality of all races

---

① The Color of Curtain, *The Mississippi University Press*, Richard Wright.

② Zhang Yan, *The Mississippi Quarterly Report*, 1997.

③ file:///Users/user/Desktop/Shanghai% 20paps/The% 20Spirit% 20Of% 20Bandung. webarchive, accessed on 13 May 13.

④ "Spirit of Bandung Conference will Shine Forever', file:///Users/user/Desktop/Shanghai% 20paps/People's% 20Daily% 20Online% 20-% 20Spirit% 20of% 20Bandung% 20Conference% 20will% 20shine% 20forever. webarchive; accessed on12 May 13.

and abstain from intervention or interference in the internal affairs of another country. It asks sovereign nations to respect the right of each to defend itself singly or collectively and from refraining from acts or threats of aggression or the use of force against the territorial integrity or political independence of any country. It then calls for international disputes to be resolved through peaceful means and to promote mutual interests and co-operation. Finally, the Communique calls for respect by all to respect justice and international obligations[1].

The process resulting from Bandung brought about a number of other changes in Asia. One of which was the formation of the Association of Southeast Asian Nations (ASEAN) a few years later. But, before that a quick look at another movement for developing solidarity amongst the developing world through the Non Aligned Movement.

3.5 THE NON ALIGNED MOVEMENT

Finally, Asian resurgence was taken to its logical conclusion to the global level by involving the newly independent countries of the world through the *Non-Aligned Movement*. The organization was founded in Belgrade in 1961, and was largely conceived by President Tito of Yugoslavia, Indonesia's president, Soekarno, Egypt's second president Nasser, Ghana's first president Kwame Nkrumah and India's first prime-minister, Jawaharlal Nehru. All five leaders were prominent advocates of a middle course for states in the developing world and were for maintaining equidistance between the Western and Eastern bloc countries during the Cold War[2].

Members of the Non-Aligned Movement in reality were often quite closely aligned with one of the super powers. This had more to do with their particular political alignment, security concerns as well as developmental needs. Yet, through the mechanisms of this organization they also maintained an alternate identity, which

---

① http://franke.uchicago.edu/Final_Communique_Bandung_1955.pdf; accessed on 13 May 2013.

② The Non-Aligned Movement: Background Information. Government of Zaire. 21 September 2001. Retrieved 23 April 2011.

helped secure their autonomy and generated a sense of solidarity with other developing countries. The movement maintained its cohesion throughout the Cold War, even though some members were unfortunately involved in conflict with another.

It can be seriously debated whether the NAM actually served any major global security functions, or contributed to global peace. It has of course been criticized on this account by the rest of the world. Then at the Cuba Summit in 1979, the left orientation of the Movement became prominent. The Movement retained its relevance till the Cold War lasted. After its end and the break up of the Soviet Union, there were no need to retain an equidistance from the super powers and hence it lost its practical relevance. Yet, one should not under estimate its role in building solidarity amongst the developing world during almost three critical decades since its inception.

3.6 THE ASEAN CHARTER

The ASEAN process culminated recently in the ASEAN Charter, which was ratified by all ten states by Dec 2008. Among its principle objectives are;

(1) Respect for the independence, sovereignty and territorial integrity of member states

(2) Peaceful settlement of disputes

(3) Non-interference in member states' internal affairs

(4) Right to live without external interference[1].

This Charter statement is once again entirely in the spirit of the Five Principles of Panchsheel. Its ready acceptance by the ASEAN is a testimony of its continued validity. It is hoped that all those countries accepting the Charter will also go by its spirit and proceed along these principles in their bilateral and multilateral relations. The ASEAN Regional Forum (ARF), is already emerging as the region's pre-eminent security forum and it is hoped they will be able to develop its principles in a positive manner.

---

[1] http://news. bbc. co. uk/2/hi/asia-pacific/7783073. stm; accessed on 13 May 13.

3.7 ASIA'S UCCESSES IN DISPUTE RESOLUTION

What actually has been Asia's record in dispute resolution since the Second World War? At first glance the conclusion may well be, that it is mixed. There have been numerous conflicts in the region since then. Some conflicts still persist and have defied a solution. Yet, one has to accept that compared to the first half of this century in Europe, which is the appropriate framework for comparison in geo-political terms, Asia has been much less conflict prone. Casualties through war have been miniscule in comparison, violence has been much less and the potential for an escalation in the future is perhaps smaller.

Those wars in Asia in the last half a century after World War II that have led to massive death and destruction, have been foreign power led interventions. The first was the war in Korea. The others were the two Vietnam wars that lasted thirty years. No conflict since has been anywhere as destructive as these.

No deduction can of course be drawn entirely from this. It does not necessarily establish clearly a superiority of an Asian Way of dealing with difficult situations. Major challenges remain in Asia. Among a few are the Koreas, India-Pakistan relations in South Asia and in Afghanistan's periphery in the coming decades. But, today in the 21st Century, Asia has greater wisdom and stronger mechanisms for dealing with conflict situations. The mechanisms for dialogues and discussions, frameworks for informal consultations and an Asia wide security structure is beginning to slowly emerge. There is no space for discussing any of these in detail, but the structure of ASEAN provides a framework for building an Asian security architecture, which will truly have the Asian characteristics of conflict resolution, based essentially on the Five Principles of Peaceful Resolution (Panchsheel), the Bandung declaration and the ASEAN Charter.

Recent challenges in Asia have more to do with non-traditional security issues; natural disasters, large scale refugee movement and terrorism related issues. Here too the principles of Panchsheel as well as suitable regional cooperative mechanisms would be a better approach at resolving these conflicts. Among security issues, as land borders in Asia are getting steadily addressed, it is sea and oceanic spaces that are of greater jurisdictional and territorial concerns.

3.8 INDIA-CHINA RELATIONS AND THE PRINCIPLES OF PANCH-SHEEL

In many ways India-China relations actually prove the validity of the principles of Panchsheel in addressing the question of unresolved borders. If not in the early phase of this dispute, but later when its principles were properly evaluated and employed it has proved its advantages.

Finally, on May 1, 1970, Chairman Mao while shaking hands with the Indian Charge d'affaires in Beijing, Brajesh Mishra, told him, "We cannot go on quarrelling like this. We must become friends again. We will become friends again"[1]. This ended the state of tension and began a process of normalization of relations between the two countries. This process was in the complete spirit of Panchsheel. In spite of several changes and turbulences in subsequent decades, peace and tranquility prevails in the border areas. A number of major confidence building and cooperation agreements have been signed. Both sides remain engaged continuously in dialogue to find a resolution.

As would be natural in cases where no clear border demarcation exists, there are occasional transgressions by both sides. One such was experienced only last month in Ladakh at the Depsang plains in April/May 2013. Border meetings by designated military commanders, followed by a telephonic conversation between the high level Special Representatives ensured an early de-escalation. This ensured a visit by the Foreign Minister of India to Beijing within a week thereafter. A couple of weeks later the new Prime Minister of China, Li Keqiang, visited India in what was his first foreign visit as Premier.

---

[1] GS Iyer, "*Mao's Smile Revisited — Some Observations*"; Pap No. 413, Chennai Centre for China Studies, Dec 2, 2009; at http://www.c3sindia.org/india/1068; accessed on 16 May 13.

Meanwhile mutual trade is prospering, cooperation in multi-lateral forums is continuing and dialogue mechanisms to resolve outstanding issues are being pursued. I would argue that this has been possible mainly because both sides have adhered to the principles of Panchsheel in practice, even though this has not been openly stated. This has been possible through improving bilateral relations, participating in multilateral arrangements and through wider consultation in global fora. Bilateral trade between India and China has grown from a few hundred million dollars just fifteen years ago to about 66 billion dollars today. ①

Much work is still required in the realm of maintaining peaceful co-existence. This is where both sides are presently headed. An ambitious agenda lies ahead in the next few months. With all the basic foundational issues now in place between both countries, the new leaderships in both India and China are now moving to a new phase.

3.9 NEW POSSIBILITIES

On March 19, 2013 at Beijing, before departing for Durban in South Africa, President Xi Jinping, addressed a group of BRICS senior editors ahead of the meeting. There he unveiled five proposals for improving India-China relations. He said that first, China and India should maintain strategic communication and keep the bilateral relations on the "right track". Second, he said, "We should harness each other's comparative strengths and expand win-win cooperation in infrastructure, mutual investment and other areas." Next, he said both should strengthen cultural ties and constantly increase the mutually expanding friendship. Next, he identified coordination and collaboration in the interests of developing countries and tackle global challenges. The final and fifth proposal was that, "We should accommodate

---

① In 2012 the total bilateral trade in goods between both countries stood at 66.57 bn US$. This was a ten per cent drop from the previous year due to global economic slowdown. From the Indian Embassy in China web site at http://www.indianembassy.org.cn/DynamicContent.aspx? MenuId =3&SubMenuId =0; accessed on 16 May 13.

each other's core concerns and properly handle problems and differences existing between the two countries. " Xi, spoke of the traditional friendship between India and China, describing them as two largest developing countries of the world with a combined population of over 2.5 billion[1].

At Durban three days later in a meeting with Prime Minister Manmohan Singh, Xi Jinping said, "China and India should broaden exchanges and cooperation between their armed forces and deepen mutual military and security trust. " On the border issue, "China and India should improve and make good use of the mechanism of special representatives to strive for a fair, rational solution framework acceptable to both sides as soon as possible," Xinhua said[2].

Mr. Manmohan Singh on his part hoped that India and China "would respect each other's core interests and major concerns, deepen mutual strategic trust, strengthen coordination and cooperation on international affairs, and safeguard peace and stability in the region and the world at large. " He also appeared to reassure China about its recent concerns over India's possible role in the United States' "pivot" or rebalancing to Asia. Mr. Singh assured the President that it "adheres to an independent foreign policy" and "will not be used as a tool to contain China. " He also assured him concerning Tibet, by reiterating India's position saying that, it recognizes "the Tibet Autonomous Region is a part of the Chinese territory and that India will not allow Tibetans to conduct political activities against China in India". [3] Following up on this Premier Li Keqiang visited India from May 18-20.

3.10 BORDER ISSUES WITH PAKISTAN

The Principles of Panchsheel has unfortunately not worked between India and

---

[1] file:///Users/user/Desktop/IndiaChina/China% 20unveils% 205point% 20formula% 20to% 20improve% 20ties% 20with% 20India% 20-% 20Business% 20Line. webarchive; accessed on 17 May 2013.

[2] The Hindu, on — file:///Users/user/Desktop/India-China/India,% 20China% 20should% 20deepen% 20military% 20ties:% 20Xi% 20Jinping% 20-% 20The% 20Hindu. webarchive; accessed on 18 May 2013.

[3] Ibid.

Pakistan. India is committed to resolve the question of the Indian province of Jammu & Kashmir (J&K) in a peaceful and equitable manner based on the principles of Panchsheel. J&K is a legacy of British colonial policy and London left it unresolved at the time of its hurried departure from the sub-continent. Given goodwill and adherence to the principles of non-violence and Panchsheel, this issue too could have been resolved by now. But, Pakistan's recourse to the force of arms in 1947, 1965 and in 1999 at Kargil and continuous support to terrorism and involvement in internal affairs in India have not allowed positive relations between both countries to deelop. Official trade remains minimal. In spite of a South Asian free trade agreement in place; Pakistan cannot yet allow normal trade relations to take place with India.

Prime Minister Manmohan Singh had announced a principled position that while no new borders can be drawn by blood in the region; borders can instead be made irrelevant. This is through allowing free movement of goods and people (as long as they have no hostile intent) and building good relations between both countries under democratic leadership. But unfortunately, relations between India and Pakistan is exactly the opposite of that prevailing between India and China. But, here again, with the first democratically elected government in Pakistan succeeding a democratic government, which completed a full tenure of five years, there is new hope. Nawaz Sharif, the popularly elected leader of Pakistan, has already given very positive statements. Other than major domestic issues, he has pledged to prioritize free and open trade between both countries, clamp down on terrorism from Pakistan to India and facilitate all round cooperation. This will be truly in the spirit of Panchsheel and can alter future relations between these two major countries in South Asia which both have nuclear weapons.

3.11   CONCLUSION

We in Asia have great wisdom and a long and continuous history. The region has also seen much warfare and bloodshed. But, through these years have also benefited from the wisdom of Confucius and Buddha and from other leaders in more modern times who have inherited their ideals and principles. We believe much of these are incorporated in the Five Principles of Peaceful Coexistence or Panchsheel. This might be the Asian Way that we have been searching for. Given a period of peace and development in Asia over a few decades more, there can be a further all-round development in the Continent and a more harmonious world.

(Maj Gen Dipankar Banerjee, Founding Director of the Institute of Peace and Conflict Studies, New Delhi, India.)

CHAPTER 4   FIT or RPS? Which One Shall We Adopt to Deploy Renewable Energy

King Min WANG

Abstract: In 2009, Taiwan enacted the Renewable Energy Development Law and the renewable energy feed-in tariffs (FITs) for each type of renewable energy implemented. The two major objectives behind setting FITs for renewable energies include the achievement of renewable energy development targets and green industry development. Therefore, the calculation of an appropriate tariff level that provides appropriate incentives, captures renewable energy development targets and involves the most efficient method for renewable fund collection is the key factor to the success of the FIT policy. The purpose of this study is to explore the merits and shortcomings of Taiwan's FIT policy in relation to renewable deployment. We review the experiences of implementing FITs in several important countries of the world, and analyse the advantages and disadvantages of the FIT policy both theoretically and empirically and compare it with renewable portfolio standards (RPS) policy to find methods for improvement. The results indicate that accurate tariffs can never be found under risky and uncertain market conditions. Therefore, it is necessary to adopt some key factors in regard to RPS such as the bidding process and setting a cap amount in designing a successful FIT policy. The conclusion is that an FIT policy alone cannot achieve these goals and needs to be coupled with an RPS policy or its policy components to be able to develop renewable energy efficiently and effectively. Hopefully, the experience of the FIT renewable purchasing policy in Taiwan can contribute to the successful deployment of renewable energy in the world.

Keywords: feed-in tariffs, renewable portfolio standards, renewable energy

4.1 INTRODUCTION

Currently, the feed-in tariff (FIT) scheme and Renewable Portfolio Standards (RPS) are the most two popular procurement options for renewable energies (RE). The FIT scheme provides a guaranteed payment in dollars per kWh (i. e., a price-based scheme) for the full output of the RE system for a contract period of usually 10-25 years. This payment guarantee is usually coupled with assurance of access to the grid, and the tariff is often differentiated based on technology type, project size, locality of the resource and other project-specific parameters. By contrast, an RPS is a mandated target (i. e., a quota-based scheme), representing a minimum amount of generation to be supplied from RE sources. This can be fulfilled through ownership of renewable generation, the purchase of tradable Renewable Electricity Certificates (RECs), entry into long-term binding contracts, or a combination of these approaches (Kreycik et al., 2011). The minimum amount of RE must be delivered to customers, otherwise a penalty will be typically paid by the obligatory party. Although the procurement mechanism remains fundamentally a design choice, the procurement of RECs is the most widely adopted approach in the world.

The feed-in tariff (FIT) is currently adopted by more than 80 countries and jurisdictions and is the most popular renewable deployment policy (REN21, 2011). The main reason for its rapid adoption is due to the success of EU members such as Germany, Spain, Italy, etc. in developing their renewable energies through this policy. As a result, those original market-oriented countries (e. g., the UK, US, Australia, Japan, etc.) which have adopted the Renewable Portfolio Standards (RPS) have also begun to introduce the FIT as an additional instrument in accelerating RE development.

How to deploy and develop renewable energy in a stable and sustainable way is the current aim of Taiwan's energy policy. In 2009 Taiwan enacted the Renewable Energy Development Law and the renewable energy feed-in tariffs for each kind of renewable energy source implemented. Can the FIT scheme effectively and efficiently achieve and surmount the renewable target or is it only a cash-burning instrument to subsidize all renewable energy sources indifferently? The answer will be determined by evaluating the performance of the FIT policy implemented. In Taiwan, we encountered several obstacles in implementing the FIT and the difficulty in calculating an appropriate tariff level is the primary obstacle as in most other countries.

Setting accurate tariffs that provide appropriate incentives, capture renewable energy development targets and involve the most efficient method for renewable fund collection is the key factor in the success of the FIT policy. This study aims to investigate the merits as well as shortcomings of Taiwan's FIT policy in renewable deployment. First, we examine the FIT policy in Taiwan and review the FIT experiences of several important countries in the world. Furthermore, we analyze the advantages and disadvantages of the FIT policy and compare these with those of the RPS policy to find methods for improvement. Finally, some discussion and concluding remarks about the FIT policy are provided to contribute to the successful deployment of RE in the world.

4.2 TAIWAN'S FIT POLICY

The FIT policy prescribed by the Renewable Energy Development Law contains four essential elements (Bureau of Energy, 2011a.), namely, the RE subsidy target, tariff setting, government procurement and mandatory grid connection. Article six states that the total subsidized RE target of 6,500MW-10,000MW, equivalent to 11% of the generation mix shall be achieved by 2025 and the government shall announce the procurement amount of qualified REs biannually. Article eight obligates the utility, the Taiwan Power Company, to provide a mandatory grid connection service based on cost sharing to RE generators. Article nine authorizes the Ministry of

Economic Affairs (MOE) to convene a committee for setting the FITs annually.

The FITs have been calculated based on the levelized-cost approach in Taiwan. The tariff rates for each RE are set by amortizing the predicted installation cost and operation/maintenance (O&M) cost divided by the predicted average energy amount (kWh) generated in each year. However, the problem with the levelized approach in setting tariffs is the difficulty in collecting and predicting accurate information regarding (1) the installation cost level; (2) the internal rate of return of the capital recovery factor; (3) the O&M cost; and (4) the annual generation amount. In addition, other factors not contained by the levelized approach such as inflation rates, insurance fees, the overhaul and capital renewal cost and the risk premium for different REs have been the disputed issues in the tariff setting process in each year (Bureau of Energy, 2011b).

Table 4-1 presents the FITs for REs in Taiwan over the period from 2010 to 2013. As illustrated by the table, there are four scales for the roof-top PV and one ground-mounted PV system with tariff rates ranging between NTD7. 33 and NTD10. 32/kWh in 2011 (one US dollar was roughly equal to 29. 5 NTDs in 2011), NTD6. 76 and NTD9. 25/kWh in 2012, NTD5. 62 and NTD8. 18/kWh in 2013. In comparison to 2010, the PV FIT rate levels of 2011 are declining by around 30%. Similarly, in 2012 and 2013 it also registered an annual declining rate of about 10% and 12% respectively. For wind generation in 2013, the on-shore type has tariffs ranging from NTD 2. 63 to NTD 7. 36/ kWh and the off-shore type has tariffs of NTD5. 56/kWh, which is a slight increase over the previous year to reflect the cost of wind power plant construction. The tariffs for other renewables also change due to cost variation.

Table 4-1　FIT for REs in Taiwan 2013

RE category	Type	Scale (kW)	2013FIT (NTD/kWh)	2012FIT (NTD/kWh)	2011FIT (NTD/kWh)	2010 FIT (NTD/kWh)
PV	Roof-top	[1,10)①	8.18 (−11.54%)	9.25 (−10.35%)	10.32 (−29.34%)	11.19
		[10,100)	7.33 (−11.97%)	8.33 (−9.30%)	9.18 (−29.23%)	12.97
		[100,500)	6.90 (−13.39%)	7.97 (−9.68%)	8.82 (−31.98%)	
		500 and over	5.98 (−16.83%)	7.19 (−9.82%)	7.97 (−28.32%)	11.12
	Land-based	—	5.62 (−16.84%)	6.76 (−7.77%)	7.33 (−34.08%)	
Wind	On-shore	[1,10)	7.36 (0.00%)	7.36 (0.00%)	7.36 (1.17%)	7.27
		10 and over	2.63 (1.11%)	2.60 (−0.64%)	2.61 (9.67%)	2.38
	Off-shore	—	5.56 (0.00%)	5.56 (−0.00%)	5.56 (32.5%)	4.20
Small hydro	—	—	2.47 (5.79%)	2.33 (6.79%)	2.18 (5.85%)	2.06
Geothermal	—	—	4.80 (0.00%)	4.80 (0.00%)	4.80 (−7.33%)	5.18
Biomass	Nonanaerobic fermentation processes	—	2.47(5.79%)	2.33 (6.70%)	2.18(5.85%)	2.06
	Anaerobic fermentation processes		2.80 (3.77%)	2.70 (23.71%)		
Waste	—	—	2.82 (0.00%)	2.82 (5.08%)	2.69 (28.72%)	2.09
Others	—	—	2.47 (5.79%)	2.33 (6.79%)	2.18 (5.85%)	2.06

Note: The NTD:USD exchange rate is roughly 29.5/1. The numbers in parentheses are the annual variation rate.

Source: Bureau of Energy, 2013.

　　The most controversial issue in the implementation of Taiwan's FIT policy was the dispute regarding the PV tariff application year which should either be based on the commissioning date or contract signing date (Central News Agency, 2011). Initially, the government adopted the contract signing date for all RE tariff applications. Due to the dramatic and rapidly declining cost of PV, PV applicants purposely postponed the installation after signing the contract and waited for further

---

① [1,10) denotes the PV scale ranging from 1kW (included) to 10kW (not included).

cost decreases. A period of 2.5 years in length to grid connection after signing the application contract is legally allowed. Consequently, rushing to apply the PV installation increased many fold, created problems of RE fund depletion and generated criticisms of wind-fall profits. The government thus changed to adopt the commissioning date as the applicable year for the PV tariff. Moreover, the cost of PV varies frequently even within one year, and so the constant yearly FIT rate is again inappropriate. The FIT scheme for PV, therefore, has been revised to introduce a multi-phase bidding process to determine the suitable tariff level payable. Currently, the original FIT is still applicable to a PV system of less than 10kW without bidding, while other scales of PV systems are subject to a bidding process. The method of bidding requires the applicants to offer a discount to scale down the FITs available to each relevant category. In other words, the FIT is no longer a constant subsidy price, but acts as a price cap for bidding. The final real price paid will be determined by the qualifying bid rate (i.e., pay as you bid). In 2011, there are two phases for bidding (April and July) and the second phase has three stages starting from July and ending in September. 15 MW were released for the bidding process in phase one, of which 13.6 MW were selected in the end. In the second phase, 17.6 MW were released and 14.6 MW were selected. The details of the bidding results are presented in Table 4-2.

Table 4-2　2011 Phase 2 Bidding Results of the PV Tariff in Taiwan

PV type	Selected bids	Stage 1	Stage 2	Stage 3
Roof-top	Maximum offered discount	6.00%	6.20%	5.03%
	Minimum offered discount	2.25%	1.24%	1.25%
	Average offered discount	2.95%	3.21%	3.37%
	Total selected amount	2583kW	4840kW	7235kW
	Total number of selected bidders	40	38	87
Land-based	Average offered discount	0.31%	0.31%	NA
	Total selected amount	248kW	110kW	NA
	Total number of selected bidders	1	1	0
Phase two total selected capacity	14.658MW			

Source: Bureau of Energy, 2011c.

4.3 THE GLOBAL TREND OF FIT POLICY EVOLUTION

The problems of the yearly constant PV FIT encountered in Taiwan during its implementation of the FIT policy have similarly been experienced in many other countries (e. g., Germany, the UK, Australia, Spain, Italy, France, etc.). The UK changed its large-scale PV tariff in August 2011 due to drastically decreasing costs (Ofgem, 2011); Germany changed its yearly FITs and adopted new RE tariffs in July 2011 (Renewable Energy World, 2011); several of Australia's states also changed or stopped their PV tariffs in 2011 (Energy Matters, 2011a). Similar conditions also exist in other countries. The root of the problem lies in the calculation of the appropriate PV tariff and the prediction being unable to meet the uncertain and fast-changing market and technology conditions. Therefore, it is both necessary and helpful to transplant some key concepts of the RPS scheme such as the bidding process in determining the tariff level and setting a subsidized cap amount to control the total expenditure in designing a successful FIT policy. Following this revision trend, France indicated that its FIT policy for its large-scale PV system will be to switch to a bidding process (Renewables International, 2011). Australia ACT announced a reverse auction mechanism for its large-scale PV feed-in tariff in 2012 (Energy Matters, 2011b). California also applied a renewable auction mechanism (RAM) to determine its RE tariff (California Public Utilities Commission, 2011) in its FIT policy design in 2011. Among them, Taiwan has played the leading role in introducing a bidding process to its original constant FIT system for PV tariff setting at the beginning of 2011.

In order to establish a well-designed FIT policy for large-scale PV, a global trend is to revise the prototype FIT (German-style constant FIT) by introducing the key concepts of RPS policy, such as setting a procurement target cap, determining the tariff level by the bidding process or auction mechanism, and adding the RE obligation for particular parties in the FIT system. Alternatively, some countries (e. g., Korea) may choose to adopt RPS alone (Boo, 2011) or incorporate FIT-like elements, such as technology banding, price caps and floors, purchase guarantees and guaranteed price payments, etc. into RPS policies (e. g., the US, UK, Australia and Japan). As an exception to this trend, due to the Fukushima nuclear crisis, in order to accelerate the rate of RE infiltration into the generation mix and to fully deploy renewables as well as reduce the reliance on nuclear power, the National Diet of Japan introduced the Act on the Purchase of Renewable Energy-Sourced Electricity by Electric Utilities to switch from an RPS policy to a constant FIT system to take effect in July 2012 (METI, 2011). Although it has been argued that the FIT policies are not compatible with an RPS framework, detailed analysis and good design can indeed enable this incompatibility of the two systems to be avoided.

4.4   FIT AND RPS

FIT policies can be used as tools to help meet and promote pre-existing RPS objectives (Couture and Cory, 2009). That is, those countries which originally adopted RPS either switched to add FIT schemes or revised their RPS designs to boost RE development. Some countries, such as the UK and Australia have considered FIT-RPS interactions for their implementation mechanisms to help achieve the RE mandated target. To promote the less cost-competitive small-scale (with a capacity of between 5kW and 5MW) RE technologies, the UK government replaced the Renewable Obligation (RO) with FIT as the major mechanism of support for the small-scale PV, wind and hydro installations. For large-scale less cost-competitive REs in the market, a banding and weighting system for the Renewables Obligation was introduced. Similarly, Australia first introduced the Mandatory Renewable Energy Target (MRET) scheme for renewable electricity. In January 2011, the MRET was divided into two parts: a Large-scale Renewable Target (LRET) and a Small-scale Renewable Scheme (SRES). In addition, the Australian government revised its PV promotion program by introducing feed-in tariff schemes. By contrast, in the United States, an integrated approach has allowed the RPS policy to work in coordination with the FIT scheme (e. g., California, Washington, and Oregon).

That is, FIT policies could be offered to smaller scale projects while leaving the basic competitive solicitation mechanism for utility-scale projects intact (Couture and Cory, 2009).

The FIT scheme provides a guaranteed payment for the full output of the RE system by long-term contracts. In the scheme, apart from the FIT setting process, it typically includes a host of regulatory and technical provisions, interconnection rights, inflation adjustments, guaranteed power purchases, priority dispatches, eligibility requirements, etc. The guaranteed tariff is often differentiated based on technology type, project size, locality of the resource and other project-specific parameters. Hence, according to Couture and Cory (2009) and the above worldwide FIT-implemented experiences, a well-designed FIT policy needs to overcome at least the following challenges: (1) avoidance of default in exercising the contract; (2) updating the tariff frequently to reflect the market and technology conditions; (3) a high up-front installation cost of the RE system and the need for financing resources; (4) sufficient renewable funds to procure RE generation if a purchasing upper limit is not to be required; (5) frequently changing tariffs causing investor uncertainty and overall market risk; (6) tariffs capable of contributing positive economic growth and job opportunities; (7) streamlining the application and installation administrative approval process; and (8) tariff expenditure capable of liaising with the customer's electricity prices. A well-designed FIT policy includes the following advantages: (1) guaranteed profit for the RE investment; (2) cost-efficient procurement; (3) reduced default risk in project contracts; (4) being based on levelized cost to develop REs equally; (5) fostering more rapid development of new emerging and non-commercialized RE technologies; and (6) widely-supported by the majority of customers.

Strictly speaking, RPS policy is merely a mandatory target for RE supply. The obligatory party could usually fulfill the targets by three options of generating RE from own plants, purchasing RECs in the renewable markets or paying a penalty. Although competitive solicitations are most adopted in the US, the purchase of RECs in the renewable markets is simply the tool that most obligatory parties use to meet their RPS targets in other countries. Therefore, in this system, the government needs to establish a market platform on which REs or their derivative commodity, RECs, can be traded. Under the RPS system, the tariff for the REs will no longer be determined by the government or by a committee, but by market supply and demand conditions. As shown by Couture and Cory (2009), Wiser et al. (2004) and Kreycik et al. (2011), the advantages of RPS policy include the following: (1) the government relinquishes its tariff determination role and gives it to the market; (2) tariffs will be determined flexibly and frequently by the market; (3) the RE targets can be achieved using the approach that costs the least; (4) low cost REs can be developed rapidly; (5) the creation of RECs can enlarge the market transaction amount and provide sufficient liquidity to the market players; and (6) the REC market has the potential to be linked with the GHG emission trading system and generate synergy benefits. However, RPS policy appears to face a number of challenges in encouraging new and rapid RE development: (1) it is unable to encourage diversified and over-target development in REs; (2) volatile tariff levels increase the investment and mortgage risks; (3) an imperfectly competitive RE market results in unfair competition among market participants and also among different REs technologies; and (4) the establishment and the system of monitoring, declaration, and validation of obligation fulfillment are a demanding tasks for the market mechanism.

Both FIT and RPS policies have intrinsic shortcomings and merits. How to avoid the negative side effects and capture the positive components of these two policies is the key to their success in RE deployment. In Taiwan, we believe that currently FIT policy should be revised by introducing the RE cap amount and a bidding process for large-scale PV tariff determination. In the future, the author recommends that the two policies should act in parallel, but the way the two policies interact should be further studied and designed to help meet and surmount the RE development goal.

In the long term, when we will advance into the low carbon society and economy which must be based upon a low carbon power system to service the electricity demand, current FIT and RPS policies need to be fundamentally redesigned. In a low carbon power system, there are at least three aspects needed to be addressed and reformed. Firstly, due to the intermittent nature of most REs, a safe secure and reliable low carbon power system needs new smart technology innovation to overcome the problem of random and stochastic RE generation. The list of candidates in technology innovation, to name the least, are ranging from smart grid, smart meter, storage style generation, electric vehicle system, automatic generation control, energy management system, supervisory control and data acquisition to distributed generation system. Secondly, in the demand side, in order to curtail the magnitude of random and stochastic variations in electricity demand a new and effective demand side management must be implemented. Under the power demand side management the load will be controllable and mostly dispatchable to maintain the security of the power system and to smooth the function of the electricity market operation. Finally, it is the electricity market itself that should be reformed. Current electricity market, no matter deregulated or not, is built upon by a carbon intensive system. The generation mix is typically dominated by fossil-fuel burning units which are stable and controllable. A wholesale or retail electricity market can therefore be operated accordingly. However, in approaching to a low carbon power system when most generation units are replaced from REs, the current style wholesale market will shrink in its transaction volume and the level of price. The competitive mechanism of the market will face the challenge of collapse and the fossil fuel power plants will be under serious economic losses. Maintaining of current style FIT and RPS policies will not be sustainable economically. They must be revised and integrated into a single wholesale electricity market then. Therefore, the current wholesale electricity market needs to be reformed further to cope with the intermittent nature of REs.

4.5 CONCLUSIONS

Due to the daunting task of tariff setting each year, it takes three months for the tariff committee to calculate and predict the FITs in Taiwan. However, the FITs thus determined often cannot catch up with the market and technology-varying conditions and subsequently need to be revised or else are not applicable. In view of this situation, the Taiwan government has adopted FITs coupled with a bidding process to determine the subsidized tariffs for most PV systems since 2011. This innovation in FIT system design has lowered real FIT subsidies and removed some of the difficulty in the tariff setting task. Nevertheless, one of the dark sides of this change is that the constant FIT payable to the REs changes to unknown and uncertain levels. Although this introduces risk and uncertainty to the RE generators, a well-designed bidding process and tariff determination rule would reduce the magnitude of risk and uncertainty to a minimum.

By reviewing Taiwan's present FIT RE procurement policy, some items recommended for revision are put forward as follows:

(1) Currently, in phase two of the bidding process, there are three stages (July, August, and September) packaged together and applicants need to offer a sequential three-stage bid at the beginning of stage one. Once the bids are offered, subsequent changes are not allowed. This increases the risk to applicants. We suggest that subsequent changes to the bids at the second and third stages should be allowed provided that the administrative process and time required are manageable.

(2) Currently, the tariff setting in the bidding process follows the rule of pay-as-you-bid. The rule is suitable for an imperfectly competitive market but not for a perfectly competitive one. We argue that the tariff setting rule can gradually switch to a market clearing price (i. e., all applicants obtain the same tariff which is derived from the last qualified lowest discount bid). Under the market clearing price, the applicants can acquire their different producers' surplus depending on their production efficiency. In the long-term, due to the strong incentive to keep the producer's surplus, the applicants will tend to lower their production costs and offer relatively low bids. The results of this change will reduce the cost of RE procurement and enhance the RE's industrial competitiveness.

(3) To reduce the transaction cost, the current constant FIT without bidding policy for PV of 10kW and less could be revised to include larger scales (e. g., up to 20kW). The underlying principle is to leave the basic bidding process to a relatively large-scale RE.

(4) From the results of the bidding process, we find that an insufficient supply sometimes occurs. To overcome this problem, we recommend that a higher FIT cap price be cautiously set and the administritive process shortened and steamlined. On the other hand, the obligation concepts of RPS should be introduced to increase the demand for REs.

(5) It is recommended that the use of bidding in determining FITs is only suitable for RE technologies whose costs are changing rapidly, e. g., solar PV, but is impractical for those technologies whose costs are not changing rapidly such as wind power, hydro, or geothermal. In such technologies, with longer lead times and a more complex planning and siting procedure, a constantly changing price could significantly deter investors.

(6) At present, electricity customers in Taiwan have no choice in terms of choosing "green" or "gray" electricity. We recommend that a REC market or a voluntary green electricity market be designed and introduced into the electricity market in Taiwan.

(7) The current FIT policy applies the levelized cost approach in setting the tariff. This is suitable for the early stage of RE development. In the longer term, the benefit and value of REs to power systems and customers should be included in the process of tariff setting. The RAM mechanism adopted by California to reflect the time-of-delivery tariff or different locations could be a tentative project for Taiwan to consider.

The deployment and development of REs lies at the core of contemporary world energy policy. How to promote REs in a manner of environmental effectiveness, economic efficiency and social equity is challenging the wisdom of elite minds worldwide. FIT and RPS policies can be complementary or substitutive to each other; however, a complementary function is found in most cases because having just one policy has its intrinsic disadvantage and definitely needs to be rescued by the other policy. The trend around the world is moving towards the interaction of the two policies. RPS can be viewed as a necessary instrument to achieve the minimum RE targets, while an FIT policy can be used to surmount the targets and develop all REs equally. In the long term, these two policies should be able to act in parallel, but the way in which the two policies interact should be further studied.

References

[1] Boo, K. J., 2011. New and Renewable Energy a Key to Low Carbon Green Growth, paper presented at the International Conference on Green Trade, Chung Hua Institution for Economic Research, Taipei, June, 2011.

[2] Bureau of Energy, 2011a. The Renewable Energy Development Law. Bureau of Energy, http://www. moeaboe. gov. tw/opengovinfo/Laws (in Chinese).

[3] Bureau of Energy, 2011b. 2011 Renewable FITs and the Calculation Formula in the ROC. Bureau of Energy, http://www. moeaboe. gov. tw/opengovinfo/Laws/secondaryenergy/LSecondaryMain. aspx? PageId = l_secondary_31 (in Chinese).

[4] Bureau of Energy, 2013. 2013 FIT for Renewable Energies in Taiwan. http://web3. moeaboe. gov. tw/ECW/populace/content/Content. aspx? menu_id = 1955 (in Chinese).

[5] Bureau of Energy, 2011c. 2011 Phase 2 Bidding Results of PV Tariff in Taiwan. http://www. moeaboe. gov. tw/opengovinfo/Laws/secondaryenergy/LSecondaryMain. aspx? PageId = l_secondary_list (in Chinese).

[6] California Public Utilities Commission, 2011. Renewable Auction Mechanism. http://www. cpuc. ca. gov/PUC/energy/Renewables/hot/Renewable + Auction + Mechanism. htm.

[7] Central News Agency, 2011. The Control Yuan Corrects for FIT blunder. CNA news, 2011. 06. 08. http://n. yam. com/cna/politics/201106/20110608874855. html.

[8] Couture, T. and Cory, K., 2009. State Clean Energy Policies Analysis (SCEPA) Project: An Analysis of Renewable Energy Feed-in Tariffs in the United States, Technical Report, NREL/TP-6A2-45551, May 2009, National Renewable Energy Laboratory, USA.

[9] Energy Matters, 2011a. Victoria's Solar Feed In Tariff to be Slashed Soon, Energy Matters, Aug. 04, 2011, Energy Matters Pty Ltd, Australia, http://www. energymatters. com. au/.

[10] Energy Matters, 2011b. ACT Closes Micro Solar Feed In Tariff, Energy Matters, Jun. 01, 2011, Energy Matters Pty Ltd, Australia, http://www. energymatters. com. au/.

[11] Kreycik, C. E., Couture, T. D. and Cory, K. S., 2011. Procurement Options for New Renewable Electricity Supply, Technical Report, NREL/TP-6A20-52983, December 2011, National Renewable Energy Laboratory, USA.

[12] METI, 2011. Act on Purchase of Renewable Energy Sourced Electricity by Electric Utilities, Ministry of Economy, Trade and Industry (in Japanese).

[13] Ofgem, 2011. FIT Payment Rate Table with Retail Price Index adjustments and Fast Track Review amendments — Tariff rates are effective from 1 August 2011. The Office of Gas and Electricity Markets, London, UK, www. ofgem. gov. uk/.

[14] REN21, 2011. Renewables 2011 Global Status Report, Paris: REN21 Secretariat.

[15] Renewable Energy World, 2011. Germany Passes More Aggressive Renewable Energy Law, Renewable Energy World, July 25, 2011, RenewableEnergyWorld. com.

[16] Renewables International, 2011. France Announces Solar Feed-In Tariffs Retroactively, Renewables International, July 25, 2011, http://www. renewablesinternational. net/.

[17] Wiser, R., Porter, K. and Grace, R., 2004. Evaluating Experience with Renewables Portfolio Standards in the United States, Paper Prepared for the Conference Proceedings of Global Windpower, Chicago Illinois: March 28-31, 2004.

(King Min Wang, Energy and Environmental Research Center Chung-Hua Institution for Economic Research, Taipei, Taiwan)

CHAPTER 5 PACL: An Endeavour of Regional Harmonization of Contract Law in East Asia

Shiyuan Han

Abstract: This paper will make a description of PACL (Principles of Asian Contract Law). It will first describe how PACL as an idea is turning into some kind of reality. It will then talk about why should there be a PACL, especially when South Korea, Japan and China are now member states of the CISG. Then some basic problems of the PACL will be discussed, including the nature of the PACL, the working methods of the PACL, and Asian characteristics of the PACL if there is any. Finally, some prospects of the PACL will be mentioned.

5.1 INTRODUCTION

Following the development of the globalization of economy, it is an inevitable trend of the harmonization or unification of the relevant private law rules. This kind of harmonization or unification has both a global level practice and a regional endeavor. In Asia (especially in East Asia) there is a private initiative by scholars trying to harmonize rules of contract law, and the aim is a model law called Principles of Asian Contract Law (hereafter "PACL").

In this paper, first, how does the PACL become a continuous project from an idea (Part 2). Second, why a PACL is still necessary for East Asia while China, South Korea and Japan became a member state of the CISG (Part 3)? Third, what has been done about the PACL (Part 4). Fourth, some basic issues about the PACL will be described (Part 5). Finally, what is the future of the PACL (Part 6).

5.2   THE FIRST STEP TO A PACL

In East Asia a lot of scholars have been conscious of the necessity of the regional harmonization of private law in the region. For example Japanese professor Zentaro Kitagawa has expressed an idea of a model contract law in the middle of 1980s[1]. In 2004, at an international symposium in Qingdao China, professor Eichi Hoshino[2], professor Yongjun Lee[3], professor Songyun Kim[4] and I[5] talked about the harmonization of civil law in East Asia. My suggestion during the symposium is to borrow the experience of the PECL commission and to start a co-operation of comparative study and model law drafting between Chinese, Japanese and Korean

---

[1]   See Zentaro Kitagawa [北川善太郎], Zhongguo de he tong fay u mo fan he tong fa [*Chinese Contract Law and Model Contract Law*], translated by Chen Wang, in: Guo wai fa xue [Foreign Legal Theories], 1987 (3 and 4).

[2]   See Eichi Hoshino [星野英一], Ri zhong han min fa zhi du tong yi hua de zhu wen ti [*Issues on the Harmonization of the Civil Laws of Japan, China and South Korea*], translated by Tao Ju, in: Tao Ju ed., Zhong ri min shang fa yan jiu [Studies on Civil and Commercial Law of China and Japan], Vol. 4, Law Press China 2006, pp. 3-20.

[3]   See Young Jun Lee [李英俊], Dongya tong yi ma ma fa de gou xiang [*Ideas of an Uniform Sales Law in East Asia*], translated by Lulun Jin, in: Tao Ju ed., Zhong ri min shang fa yan jiu [Studies on Civil and Commercial Law of China and Japan], Vol. 4, Law Press China 2006, pp. 167-176.

[4]   See Songyun Kim [金相容], Zuo wei Dongbeiya pu tong fa de tong yi ma ma fa de li fa fang xiang [*The Direction of the Legislation of a Uniform Sales Law as Ius Commune in North-east Asia*], translated by Lulun Jin, in: Tao Ju ed., Zhong ri min shang fa yan jiu [Studies on Civil and Commercial Law of China and Japan], Vol. 4, Law Press China 2006, pp. 210-216.

[5]   See Shiyuan Han [韩世远], Cong PECL kan dong ya he tong fa xie tiao hua zhi lu [*A Path to the Harmonization of East Asian Contract Law: with an Inspiration of the PECL*], in: Tao Ju ed., Zhong ri min shang fa yan jiu [Studies on Civil and Commercial Law of China and Japan], Vol. 4, Law Press China 2006, pp. 198-209.

scholars. "A path to the harmonization of contract law or private law may be to start from scholars, from non-government initiatives and from model law." However, the idea has not initiated any action in the following several years.

In October 2009, I organized an international symposium named "Unification of Private Law in Europe and its Impact in East Asia" in Tsinghua University School of Law. A main purpose of the symposium is to improve the harmonization of private law in East Asia. The symposium not only invited European Scholars[1] to report the work of unification of contract law and tort law in Europe, but also invited a lot of Asian scholars, including professor Wang Zejian (China's Taiwan), Young Jun Lee (South Korea)[2], Sangyong Kim (South Korea)[3], Naoki Kanayama (Japan)[4], Naoko Kano (Japan)[5], Kunihiro Nakata (Japan)[6], Lei Chen (Hong Kong SAR) and a lot of scholars from Beijing. Just after the symposium, professor Wang Zejian, Yongjun Lee, Naoki Kanayama, Naoko Kano and I gathered in my research room in Tsinghau University School of Law. We discussed the possibility of a PACL co-operate project, got to a common view and reached an agreement (Beijing Agreement). According to the Agreement, Wang, Lee, Kanayama and Han should separately set up everyone's own research team and organize PACL fora in the coming years. This is the starting of the international/regional co-operation on the PACL in East Asia[7].

The set-up of the PACL project is based on the equal agreement among scholars

---

[1] Reports by European Scholars include: Christiane C. Wendehorst, *The Quest for a Coherent Civil Code: Comparing EC and PRC*; Bernhard A. Koch, *Tort Liability in the "Draft Common Frame of Reference" (DCFR) and in the Principles of European Tort Law (PETL)-Similarities and Differences*; Knut Benjamin Pissler, *In Search for Service Contracts in China*.

[2] Young Jun Lee, *Ideas on Harmonization of Law on Sale of Goods in East Asia-General Standard Contract*.

[3] Sangyong Kim, *Possibility of Restoration and Creation of Ius Commune in the North East Asian Region*.

[4] Naoki Kanayama [金山直樹], *Challenge to PACL*.

[5] Naoko Kano [鹿野菜穂子], *Recent Development of Japanese Consumer Law & Policy*.

[6] Kunihiro Nakata [中田邦博], *Contents and Performance of Contract and Consumer Law in Japan-The Role of Consumer Contract Law*.

[7] See Naoki Kanayama, *On the Meaning and Questions of a PACL* (in Japanese), in: Jurist No.1406, 2010(9), p.105.

from the three countries of East Asia. The three countries have their own different and special history of private law. It is difficult to say which country's law is better. Anyway, if the law is appropriate for the conditions of a country, then it is a good law. The PACL is aiming to be a set of rules and principles appropriate for Asian people.

5.3 WHY THE PACL

China as the second large economic body, Japan as the third large economic body, and South Korea will absolutely attract the view of the world by any kind of co-operation. We have to admit that the situation in East Asia is very complicated, considering the history, the feeling of people and the international relation. We also cannot ignore the important role of economic and commercial intercourse among the countries. For the past several years, the relation among the three countries is described as "cold in political side but warm in economic side".

Transactions among the three countries call for common rules. After China joined the CISG as one of the origin states, South Korea and Japan became member states of the CISG in the year 2004 and 2008. Since the CISG is now a common rule of the three countries, is it still necessary to have a PACL? This is a very natural question when we talk about the PACL.

The necessity of a PACL may be illustrated from the following points. First, the CISG covers only sales contract. For other kinds of contracts, it is still necessary to have a PACL as a set of common general rule. Second, even with sales contract, the CISG does not cover every aspect of a contract. For example, validity and transfer of ownership have not been regulated by the CISG. Third, the CISG is more than 30 years old. In the past 30 years the world changed quite a lot. New challenges call for new rules. Fourth, the CISG is a masterpiece of European and American scholars and specialists. It reflects mainly the experiences of western world. For East Asia people, it is still necessary for Asian scholars to product an Asian voice.

The PACL has some differences comparing with the CISG. The differences may be analyzed from two aspects, form and content.

First, it is clear that the PACL has some differences in form comparing with the CISG. The PACL is not a Convention. It does not have any binding force of law. It regulates the general part of contract law, including the validity of contract. From these points, the PACL may be a good supply to the CISG in practice.

Second, the differences in content of the PACL comparing with the CISG, if there is any, should be analyzed carefully. This will be good both for the PACL and the CISG. For the PACL, the drafter must show enough reasons to support the position. For the CISG, it may be a good point for re-thinking. For example, if the PACL's position is following the custom of Asia and different from the position of the CISG, we should re-think whether the CISG had sufficiently consulted the Asian custom.

5.4 WHAT HAS BEEN DONE ABOUT THE PACL

March 7-8, 2010, Keio University, Tokyo, the First PACL Forum, General Principle; Interpretation of Contract; August 25-26, 2010, Ho Chi Minh University, Vietnam, the Second PACL Forum, Formation of Contract; December 14-15, 2010, Seoul University, South Korea, the Third PACL Forum, Non-performance; May 21-22, 2011, Osaka, the Fourth PACL Forum, Validity of Contract; September 17-18, 2011, Tsinghua University, Beijing, the Fifth PACL Forum, Performance; December 17-18, 2011, Seoul University, South Korea, the Sixth PACL Forum, Non-performance; March 4-6, 2012, Keio University, Tokyo, the Seventh PACL Forum, General Maters, Performance and Non-performance; December 14-15, 2012, Seoul University, South Korea, the Eighth PACL Forum, Performance and Non-performance.

5.5 SOME BASIC ISSUES ABOUT THE PACL

5.5.1 The Nature of the PACL

A. Nongovernmental and private initiative

The PACL project has not been supported or authorized by any government. It is purely a private initiative not depending on politics. In principle, the participants have not obtained any financial support from the project. They took part in the meetings at their own expense. This does not mean that the national/regional teams may not find their own financial supports. Actually, professor Kanayama has obtained financial support from *the Foundation pour le droit continental* and Ministry of Education, Culture, Sports, Science and Technology of Japan. Professor Lee has obtained financial support from *the Humboldt Foundation*. I applied and obtained financial support from Tsinghua University. So it is clear that, the object of any financial support is the specific participant or national/regional team, not the PACL project as a whole. The PACL, as a common research result, belongs to all participants of the project (collective ownership by all members)[1], and not belongs solo to one person or one national/regional team.

B. Academic product

The PACL is a product of academic exchange and co-operation. The participants of the PACL are from different Asian countries or regions. They are mainly professors, and a few lawyers. They come together sharing a common academic ideal. The participants pursue academic democracy and freedom. They have different academic background, but they are not spokesperson of any specific legal family, either his own or any western legal family.

5.5.2　The Aimed Position of the PACL

Since the PACL is a nongovernmental private initiative and an academic product, it does not have any "binding force of law". It is only a kind of "model law" or "soft law"[2]. So the force of the PACL, if there is any, is not from *ratione imperii*,

---

[1]　This point has been discussed and affirmed during the 2012 Tokyo PACL Forum.

[2]　This point has been mentioned by professor Kanayama, see Naoki Kanayama, *On the Meaning and Questions of a PACL* (in Japanese), in: Jurist No. 1406, 2010(9), p. 103.

but from *imperio rationis*①. In Asia there is not any organization like EC or EU. People cannot pin their hope on any external authority. If the PACL can play any role in practice, it only can rely on its own force of persuasion.

Professor Michael J. Bonell has analyzed the UNIDROIT Principles in practice as: (1) Reception in academic and professional circles; (2) Model for national and international legislation; (3) Guide in contract negotiations; (4) Law chosen by the parties to govern their contract; (5) Rules of law referred to in judicial proceedings. The PICC's success in practice has gone beyond all expectations②.

As to the PACL, of course people may optimistically expect it has a similar function in practice. But, all these optimistic possibilities and glorious ideals depend on the crux of the matter — the quality of the final result. In other words, the PACL as a model law should not be a simple copy of the PICC or the PECL.

5.5.3　Work Methods of the PACL

A. Sketch of Work Methods of the PACL

Till now the work methods the PACL project adopted may be described as: three Chairmen and some national/regional teams plus voting-system. English is the working language from the very beginning. The three Chairmen are Shiyuan Han (China), Naoki Kanayama (Japan) and Young-June Lee (South Korea) (following alphabetical order). National/regional teams include Cambodia, China, China's Hong Kong SAR, China's Taiwan, Indonesia, Japan, Myanmar, Nepal, Singapore, South Korea, Thailand and Vietnam. During the PACL fora voting system has been used when there are different opinions.

---

① Professor R. Zimmermann has pointed out that, the DCFR is intended to be a reference text which, unlike the PECL, is to secure its authority not *imperio rationis* but *ratione imperii*, i. e., by virtue of the European Community endorsing or adopting it in one form or another ... See R. Zimmermann, *The Present State of European Private Law*, The American Journal of Comparative Law, Vol. 57, Spring 2009, Number 2, p. 491.

② See Michael Joachim Bonell, *The UNIDROIT Principles in Practice — The Experience of the First Two Years*, Uniform Law Review (1997) 34-45; *UNIDROIT Principles 2004 — The New Edition of the Principles of International Commercial Contracts adopted by the International Institute for the Unification of Private Law*, Uniform Law Review (2004).

The above methods have been used for three years and they do work, because some work results have been achieved by these methods. Anyway, the methods also have their own problems and have to be improved.

B. Efforts to Improve the Work Methods of the PACL

After an investigation of the work methods of the PECL Commission[1], I have made a proposal to improve the work methods of the PACL to the participants of the 2012 Tokyo Forum. The Main ideas of the proposal include the following points.

(1) Using Reporters instead of national/regional teams. The PACL project needs Reporters instead of national teams. Here **the Reporter plays an important role**. She/he is in charge of drafting the articles, comments and notes. When the task is given to a specific person, the Reporter, rather than a national team, it is much clearer what she/he should do. The participants of the PACL project are not really representatives of their own nations. It is not clever to let national teams against each other. Especially because of historical reasons in East Asia which are always very sensitive, so it is wise not to enlarge national teams. The final result of the project should not be a result of a kind of "political quarrels" between Asian nations. It is *imperio rationis* which will give PACL strength. The PACL project should follow rationalism rather than nationalism.

As a Reporter, she/he should be a specialist of contract law and comparative law, a professor good at English and able to take part in the PACL Forum frequently. The Reporter should be nominated by the PACL project (or the commission).

(2) Setting up a Drafting Group. The Drafting Group is composed by the Reporters. The Drafting Group may hold small meetings (comparing with the Forum, big meeting) if it is necessary. If the small meeting is separated from the big one, it will be much more efficient for the project, at least from the time and money's side. It is not necessary to hold the Forum three times a year. Both the small meeting and the big meeting may adopt "voting-system".

(3) Setting up an Editing Group. Some native speakers of English should be in

---

① See Lando and Beale ed., *Principles of European Contract Law*, Parts I and II, 2000, Preface.

charge of the Editing Group.

The above proposal has been discussed at the Forum, and a lot of ideas have been adopted. "National Reporter" has been re-labeled as "Jurisdictional Reporter" so as to take into account the status of Hong Kong SAR, Taiwan and Macau SAR. "Nominated Reporter" has been instituted to review the current drafts. Nominated Reporters are to work closely with the Original Drafters. Any disagreements between a Nominated Reporter and an Original Drafter should be set out in writing and considered by the Drafting Committee. Nominated Reporters are not bound by the current draft Articles because Nominated Reporters should take into account the Jurisdictional Reporters and coherence and level of detail across the whole 5 chapters of the PACL.

Without the Original Drafters' transcending the limit of nationalism and following rationalism or nationalism, it is impossible to introduce Nominated Reporter system. Now South Korea team's original draft is now reviewing by a Nominated Reporter from China's Taiwan. China team's original draft is reviewing by a Nominated Reporter from Singapore. By such a cross-examination, the quality of the draft will be improved.

5.5.4　Strategies of the PACL

A. A quick draft?

Comparing with the PECL, the work speed of the PACL is very quick. In the past three years there are totally eight PACL Fora. Five Chapters of the PACL have been drafted. My hope is to slow down the work, while most of the participants of the project are part-time contributors. With limited time and energy, it is difficult for them to follow the work speed. Before the Seoul Forum of December 2010, I have raised the issue to professor Kanayama and professor Lee[1]. By the end of the Forum,

---

[1]　The first meeting of the First Commission of the PECL is in December 1980. The main result of the First Commission is the parts of Performance, Non Performance and Remedies, which is published in the year 1995. So the PECL Commission had spent more than ten years on Performance and Non Performance. Comparing with the PECL, the speed of the PACL is astonishing.

when we three gathered together to discuss the future agenda, both of them expressed a wish for a quick draft. Professor Lee mentioned that, he himself as an old man of 70s wished to see the PACL to be finished as soon as possible. I do not know the reason why professor Kanayama supporting a quick draft. I guessed one possibility might be that he needed some work results to show his financial supporters.

There is an old Chinese saying, "slow work brings fine result" (Man gong chu xi huo. Soft fire makes sweet malt). Being anxious to achieve quick success may bring bad result. More haste, less speed. Till now the project has achieved five chapters, but they are only a rough result. In order to ensure the quality (the persuasiveness) of the PACL, they need a careful review in the future.

B. Brief principles or detailed rules?

The five chapters of the PACL were prepared by different drafters from different countries. Generally speaking, the drafts by the Japanese drafting team (including Interpretation of Contract, Formation and Validity) are comparatively simple; while the drafts by South Korean team (Non-performance) and by Chinese team (Performance) are much more detailed.

If the PACL, as a model law, is too simple[1], how is the value of them to judges or legislatures? How much will they attract the parties of contract? Even called "principles", actually the PECL's provisions are much more on general rules. And the PICC may show the same characteristic[2]; it is not limited to "principles". According to Article I. — 1:101(1) of the PACL, "these Principles are intended to be applied as *general rules* of contract law in the Asian Countries." The reality should correspond to its name.

---

[1] For example, the current draft of "Formation of Contract" by Japanese team contains only nine articles, while the counterpart of the Contract Law (1999) of China contains 35 articles. The provisions of the PACL here are much simpler comparing with the Chinese Contract Law, and it will not be attractive to Chinese Legislature, judges or contractual parties. It is recommended that this part of the PACL to be re-draft.

[2] PECL Article 1:101 (Application of the Principles) (1): These Principles are intended to be applied as general rules of contract law in the European Union. Similarly, the PICC declare at the Preamble the purpose of the Principles, "These Principles set forth general rules for international commercial contracts".

C. Restatement or innovation?

Restatement of law seems to be a product of American law. For a civilian, the "restatement" is no more than a systematic tidying-up of the existing legal rules and principles. It does not have much "new things". If we inspect the PECL as an example, on one hand, it may say that it is a kind of "restatement" of European contract law. From the style of the PECL: article, comment, illustration and note[1], it is clear that the American Restatement of Law has its impact on the PECL. On the other hand, the PECL is not only a "restatement" of law, it still has some "new things"[2]. Of course the PECL is successful. The success should not be separated from a path the PECL followed, namely "from restatement, overstep restatement".

Tuning back and focusing on the existing results of the PACL project, people may find a weak point of them, namely they are insufficient in restating the existing Asian laws. The restatement of Asian law must be based on a comparative study of the existing Asian laws and try to find their common core. Without an adequate comparative study, the PACL will be the water without the source[3].

Why should the PACL project try to find and to restate the common core of the existing Asian laws? One reason may be that, by this way can the PACL become a modern *lex mercatoria* or Asian *ius commune*. Generally speaking, merchants are familiar with their domestic laws. So in order for Asian merchants to accept the PACL, the closer are the rules of the PACL to the merchants' domestic rules, the

---

① See Ole Lando, *Principles of European Contract Law: An Alternative to or a Precursor of European Legislation?* The American Journal of Comparative Law, Vol. 40, 1992, p. 579.

② While comparing the PECL and the American Restatements, professor Zimmermann has pointed out that, "[t]he American Restatements, obviously, provided a source of inspiration for the draftsmen of the PECL." Compared to that with which the authors of the American Restatement were faced, the task undertaken by the draftsmen of the PECL has a more creative nature. "Divergences between the national legal systems had to be resolved, decisions implying value judgments and policy choices had to be taken, and sometimes unconventional solutions were adopted which the draftsmen of the PECL themselves describe as 'a progressive development from [the] common core.'" See Reinhard Zimmermann, *The Present State of European Private Law*, The American Journal of Comparative Law, Vol. LVII (2009) No. 2, p. 483.

③ Professor Won Lim Jee (池元林) has emphasized the importance of comparative study as a premise of the PACL. See Won Lim Jee, *On the Harmonization of Contract Law in Asia* (Japanese), The Horitsu Jiho [Law Times] Vol. 83, (2011) No. 8-9, p. 89.

better. Another reason may be that, comparative studies will make the final results of the PACL project unique and attractive. For example, the national reports, prepared by Asian scholars, will academic resources.

One thing must be pointed out. To emphasize the restatement of Asian laws does not mean that the author objects to innovation. For the participants of the PACL project, to have an ideal and to respect the reality are two things to be placed equal emphasis on. Here "to have an ideal" means to draft a set of rules and principles appropriate for Asian people. "To respect the reality" means to build the ideal of a PACL on the basis of the reality of Asian laws. An ideal PACL can only be obtained from restatement and overstep restatement of Asian laws.

5.5.5 Any Distinguishing Asian Feature of the PACL?

Since there are the CISG, the PECL, the PICC and the DCFR, the PACL, as a latecomer, should have something distinguishing to show the necessity of its existence. Is there any distinguishing Asian feature in the PACL? This is a question in heated dispute.

Someone thought that the "distinguishing Asian feature" of the PACL is no more than illusions[1]. I am not so pessimistic about the PACL. Actually, so long as the PACL is a product of comparative law study and is built on the basis of the existing Asian laws, there is no need to worry that there is not any distinguishing Asian feature. One example is the creditor's right of subrogation and right of revocation. When Chinese team prepared the "Performance of Contract" part, the participants found creditor's right of subrogation and right of revocation are two common cores of the laws of Japan, South Korea, and China (including Taiwan)[2]. The Chinese team prepared two articles on the common cores. Since there is no corresponding part in

---

[1]　See Naoki Kanayama, *From Comparative Law to PACL* (Japanese), in: NBL No. 973, 2012. 3. 15, p. 14.

[2]　For provisions on the creditor's right of subrogation, see Japanese Civil Code Article 423; South Korean Civil Code Article 404; Taiwan Civil Code Articles 242 and 243; Chinese Contract Law Article 73. For provisions on the creditor's right of revocation, see Japanese Civil Code Articles 424-426; South Korean Civil Code Article 404; Taiwan Civil Code Articles 244 and 245; Chinese Contract Law Articles 74 and 75.

both the PECL and the PICC, they may be taken as a kind of distinguishing Asian feature in the PACL. Another example is release of claim (this issue has not been dealt with by the PACL project yet). There is a noticeable difference of the idea of release between the West and the East. In the West, release is normally understood as a contract requiring an agreement of the two parties. The basic idea is that "favor should not be forced". In the East, as a contrast, release is a unilateral act.

Where to find the distinguishing Asian features of the PACL if there is any? The PACL is not only a set of rules and principles. The PACL should be viewed as a whole, and the black letter rules are only an integral part of the whole. So the above question may be divided into two parts. First, is there any distinguishing Asian feature in the black letter rules of the PACL? The answer should be "not so much". We should not be disappointed about the answer. Because too much distinguishing Asian features in the black letter rules of the PACL is not a good thing. It means the PACL runs in the opposite direction to the harmonization or unification of contract law in the world. Second, is there any distinguishing Asian feature in other parts of the PACL, including the commentary, the notes, the national reports etc. ? This part is the things behind the black letter rules of the PACL. It reveals the thinking, the understanding or the logic of the rules. It also reveals the practical experiences of the rules. This part of the PACL could and should have its distinguishing Asian feature.

5.6　THE PROSPECTS

What may one expect to be the result of our efforts? Will the principles of Asian contract law become rules written in the sand[①]?

The PACL is a part of the academic discourse in Asia. We are now reviewing and finalizing the articles of it and preparing comments and notes for it. It is not easy. But we are trying our best to finish it and to publish it. We are aiming to

---

　① This is the question faced by professor Ole Lando when he worked with his colleague to draft the PECL. See Ole Lando, *Principles of European Contract Law: An Alternative to or a Precursor of European Legislation?* The American Journal of Comparative Law, Vol. 40 (1992), 573, 584.

publish the Part I of the PACL as "Performance and Non-performance". The English version will be published by a European publisher. In Asia, Chinese, Japanese and Korean versions will also be published.

There will be no counterpart of EU in Asia in the near future. So it is impossible for the PACL to become a real law of Asia. Anyway, some Asian countries, including Japan and South Korea, are amending their national civil laws. The PACL may be a model for such kind of work. It is possible and practicable to realize harmonization of national contract laws in at least East Asia by following an Asian model law.

The PACL may also be expected to play a role in both arbitration and judicial trial.

(Shiyuan Han, School of Law, Tsinghua University, Beijing, China)

CHAPTER 6   Asian Contract Law and Its Legal Principles: Freedom of Contract vs. Social Justice

Tae Yong AHN

Abstract: This paper discusses certain fundamental principles of contract law in relation to the vision, direction, and characteristics of the Asian legal system. In particular, this paper will attempt to discuss the issue of freedom of contract vs. social justice in contract law and other relevant issues in connection with it. By looking into the question of the right place for the principle of freedom of contract and the principle of social justice in contract law, this paper attempts to shed some light on a bigger question of where Asian law stands now and where it is and should be heading.

For this, this paper discusses how each side espousing the principle of social justice and the principle of freedom of contract conceive the proper manner of codification of contract law and tries to show the way the social norms and fundamental values interact with contract law. Noting that both the short and vague codification style and the excessively detailed codification style are being advanced under social justice ideal, this paper submits that the enthusiasm for social justice should be properly counterbalanced by the appropriate understanding of the principle of freedom of contract and then discusses why freedom of contract should be given precedence over social justice.

This paper also criticizes moral control of contract law and analyzes the recent legislative and interpretative attempts for moral enforcement of a contract. This paper tries to suggest that moral enforcement of a contract is rather a social engineering project and is not necessarily required for fair and balanced resolution of contracting parties' interests. Finally, this paper points out that reform of contract law is not always a matter of substantive contract law and we need to pay attention to how ideals can be promoted and achieved by procedural and administrative aspects as well.

6.1 INTRODUCTION

It is often said that there are two distinct categories of legal systems in the world — the Common Law and the Civil Law. Indeed, this distinction holds true regarding many respects of overall differentiation among legal systems, while it has been proved to withstand the frequent criticism of overgeneralization.

Generally speaking, the countries which were the former British colonies follow the Common Law system, whereas the countries which were the former German, French, Dutch, Spanish or Portuguese colonies follow the Civil Law system. In Asia, Singapore, Hong Kong, and Myanmar, among others, which were the British colonies, maintain the Common Law system. The other Asian countries are generally put in the category of the Civil Law system. Especially, Japan, though never having been a colony of a Western power, adopted the European legal system for the reform of its pre-modern legal system, and as a result, Japan and its former colonies generally follow the Civil Law system.

Now, Asia stands at more than 60 years after the end of the Western colonization and World War II. During that period of 60 years, the economies of Asia advanced by leaps and bounds, which has been a wonder and an inspiration to the other parts of the world. Encouraged by its economic prowess, Asia then grabbed by the horns of the bull named social reform, and with those valiant efforts, the reform of legal system has been a constant agenda for many Asian countries.

Recently, Asia is prepared and also encouraged by the world to engage the world with a more proactive role, and by hosting huge investments both inbound and outbound, the legal culture of Asia has become ever sophisticated.

So, where does the Asian legal system stand in the landscape of the world legal systems? Is it a Common Law system or a Civil Law system or a separate and independent system? This question is of course of a solemn magnitude and is not a kind of topic that can be dealt with sufficiently in a short paper like this.

For the question of the place of the Asian legal system in the world, there can be many philosophical, jurisprudential, political, social and even anthropological debates that can go on infinitely. However, to deal with a question of jurisprudence of such grand scale, many small and basic questions need to be touched first. This paper's goal, though having relevance to some big questions concerning the vision, direction, and characteristics of the Asian legal system, is set to be modest.

In particular, this paper will attempt to discuss the issue of freedom of contract vs. social justice, and other relevant issues in connection with it, with all the implications of the discussion limited to the area of contract law. I hope that by looking into the question of the right place for the principle of freedom of contract and the principle of social justice in contract law, some light can be shed on a bigger question of where Asian law stands now and where it is and should be heading.

6.2　FREEDOM OF CONTRACT VS. JUSTICE

What are the distinct features of the Common Law system and the Civil Law system? According to a paper of the World Bank, a Common Law system exhibits the following features: (1) there are not always codified laws; (2) judicial decisions are binding; (3) extensive freedom of contract, and as a result, few provisions are implied into the contract by law; and (4) generally, everything is permitted that is not expressly prohibited by law. Thus, the World Bank advises that "it is therefore important to set out all the terms governing the relationship between the parties to a contract itself①. This often results in a contract longer than one in a Civil Law country.

With respect to the Civil Law System, the same paper notes that: (1) there are generally codified laws; (2) only legislative enactments are considered binding for all, and thus there is little scope for judge-made law, although in practice judges tend to follow previous judicial decisions; (3) in some civil law systems, writings of legal scholars have significant influence on the courts; and (4) less freedom of contract, and many provisions are implied into the contract by law and parties cannot contract out of certain provisions②. This often results in a contract shorter than one in a Common Law country.

Of course, these features of the Common Law system and the Civil Law system are understood to be only an indication of the general dispositions of a legal system, and are not meant to be an absolute definition of it. The difficulty to classify a legal system one way or the other is more pronounced nowadays when the interchanges between legal systems are much active and alive. In particular, I do not agree with the observation that while few provisions are implied into a contract by law under a Common Law system, many provisions are implied into a contract by law under a Civil Law system. In my view, gap-filling is the court's inalienable role in interpreting a contract, whether under the Common Law system or under the Civil Law system.

What about the observation that freedom of contract is regarded more highly in the Common Law system than in the Civil Law system? Well, this conceived confrontation of the Common Law system vs. the Civil Law system revolves around making, interpretation and enforcement of a contract, and it is played out in a legislative dimension that implicates something of a magnitude no smaller than Asia. Here, I take for an example an international project known as the PACL in which I have been involved since its early time. The PACL stands for the Principles of Asian

---

① http://ppp. worldbank. org/public-private-partnership/legislation-regulation/framework-assessment/legal-systems/common-vs-civil-law last visited on March 25, 2013.

② Ibid.

Contract Law[1]. Likewise its sister projects, the PACL sets its eye on achieving a common model of regional contract law with worldwide compatibility and internationally comparable quality, at the same time mindful of the particularities of Asia.

From my experience with the PACL, I observe that especially two huge theoretical questions have been pending from the inception of the project. One question is a rather methodological question. It is about whether the PACL should pursue the comparative law approach or the approach of reasonableness. One side argues that, without reliance on the facts of the comparative law studies in Asia, the PACL will have no root and source in the reality. This position considers the PACL as a restatement of the law. However, the opposing side counters that what the PACL really needs is the reasonableness exercise. This side aims at a common Asian contract law existing separately from national laws and social backgrounds of individual Asian countries. This side considers the PACL as an innovation, and even goes as far as to say that pursuing Asian uniqueness in Asian contract law is pursuing an illusion.

But I will not delve too much into this question, as that is not the topic of this paper. It would suffice to say that restatement and innovation, comparative law and reasonableness, are not readily separable; they often exist in amalgamation, as an undivided whole. Law as it should be is possible only when history and effectiveness of law should be considered together[2].

The second question, which is the proper topic of this paper, is about which of the principle of freedom of contract and the principle of social justice should be the supreme principle of the common contract law of Asia.

One side of the PACL group argues that, while the importance of the principle of

---

[1] This name for the project follows the example of the preceding international efforts of the similar calibration such as the PECL that stands for the Principles of European Contract Law.

[2] I fully agree with the observation made in the UNCITRAL Expert Group Meeting in February this year that "Reasonableness of a certain provision cannot stand alone without comparative law base of that provision. Reasonableness in and of itself cannot be something that ignores cultural and legal perception of Asian mind." *UNCITRAL Expert Group Meeting Handbook*, Feb. 25-26, 2013, Songdo Convensia, Incheon.

freedom of contract is fully appreciated, the role of social justice in administering the contract law in such political and historical environment like Asia is even more important, as the social, cultural, and economic particularities of Asia demand supervision by the principle of social justice over the principle of freedom of contract. The side espousing the supremacy of social justice even likes to refer to the historical uniqueness of Asia that underwent the imperialist colonization during the early modern times[1]. Although it is not easily understandable why such experience of colonization is relevant to the argument of superiority of social justice over freedom of contract, this argument may be understood as trying to suggest that the injustice caused by the colonial powers to the people of Asia and any vestiges of it should be redeemed by the role to be played by social justice in the area of contract law.

And understandably, there is the opposing side of the PACL group that rejects the proposed superiority of social justice over freedom of contract. This side understands that the principle of social justice is expected to correct the side effects resulting from the strict application of freedom of contract, but its role is supplementary at most. The principle of social justice cannot be elevated to the throne of contract law and be let to command every working of it. A contract is, at any rate, an arrangement freely reached between the parties without outside influence and intervention. The side espousing freedom of contract points out that, if the peculiarity of Asia in the experience of the colonial times is the reason why Asia should opt otherwise in this matter, it is to note that even the advanced legal systems like the United States were once colonized territories and yet they do not preach the superiority of social justice in contract law[2]. Asia needs to grow out of the mentality of victimhood, if any, and place her culture on the platform of interaction between equal and independently acting persons.

In Korea, too, there has been a heated theoretical debate on whether freedom of

---

[1]　Young-June Lee, "From Korean Contract Law to the PACL," submitted to the NBL Comparative Law Conference, Japan, June 2011.

[2]　Ibid.

contract is restricted or unrestricted as a matter of principle[1]. Some scholars, noting the revisions made to the traditional contract law since the 20th century, came to declare that the principle of freedom of contract has been compromised by the efforts to remedy the wrongs of the 19th century laissez-faire and this freedom should be understood in essence as a limited one. Others, however, criticized such revisionist theory, arguing that to accept the essentially limited nature of freedom of contract is to deny the foundation of a free society, and the distinction between the 19th century laissez-faire and the 20th century revised freedom of contract is at best a strained fabrication as there existed recognition of equity and fairness well in the 19th century contract law. Thus, the latter group argues that those restrictions deemed discovered only now were already inherent in the contract law itself whose true potential is revealed only lately[2].

I assume that similar discussions have been had in many national jurisdictions of Asia and worldwide.

6.3   MANNER OF CODIFICATION

Interestingly, from my experience with the PACL, this debate on social justice vs. freedom of contract spills over to a seemingly unrelated debate over the style of codification. It appears that the side arguing for the superiority of social justice likes to have the contract law rules that are brief and succinct, at the same time sufficiently vague to give enough leeway for the court to maneuver under the guide of social justice. If the rules are too rigid and too narrative, there will be less room within which the court can administer social justice in relation to the unique circumstances of each case. Therefore, they may argue that the choice of this style of codification is natural for the sake of social justice in contract law.

On the other hand, the side arguing for the central importance of the principle of freedom of contract prefers to have detailed contract law rules. Those espousing this

---

①   Young-June Lee, *The General Provisions of the Korean Civil Code* (2007), pp. 119-121.

②   Ibid.

approach believe that the more detailed the rules are, the more guidance people can derive from the rules in formulating their positions in contract making and implementation, and such should be the ideal way in which each party's respective interests are to be served through a means of a contract. Simply put, this side looks to the enhancement of party autonomy as the best solution to any contract problem, and considers that to contribute to this end, the contract rules should be preferably detailed.

In my opinion, there are at least two dimensions to this issue of the style of codification of contract law. The first is that certain aspects of social justice are rather absorbed into and reinforced by the principle of freedom of contract. For example, the regulation of an adhesion contract is well incorporated into contract law[1]. Regulation of such a contract is found both in the Civil Law system as well as in the Common Law System. It is accepted well by the traditional contract law because an adhesion contract itself is an anomaly from the perspective of the traditional contract law presumption that a contract is an agreement between free and equal contracting parties which prefers negotiated terms over pre-prepared terms.

Secondly, it can be the social justice side that demands more or rather extremely detailed rules in contract law, although that approach is not always appropriate and commendable. A case in point is the massive legislative experiment project undertaken by the European contract law scholarship, known as the DCFR (which stands for the Draft Common Frame of Reference). The DCFR covers the subjects of the civil law comprehensively and its articles are considerably detailed.

In fact, the legislative experiment of the DCFR thinks highly of the priority of social justice. The DCFR states that the provisions of the DCFR "are to be read in the light of any applicable instruments guaranteeing human rights and fundamental

---

[1] An adhesion contract refers to a standard form contract prepared by one party to be signed by another party who adheres to the contract with little choice about the terms. *Black's Law Dictionary* (Abridged 8th Edition).

freedoms and any applicable constitutional laws. "[1] In particular, the DCFR codifies non-discrimination[2] as part of protection of human rights which the DCFR considers to be "an overriding principle"[3]. Also, the DCFR does provide for an impressive array of mandatory rules, especially with respect to consumer protection, exclusion of or derogation from which by the parties' agreement is prohibited.

However, with the exceptions of consumer protection provisions and the rather experimental non-discrimination code[4], the DCFR's general concern of social justice is expressed through a provision like its Article II. — 7:301 which provides that a contract that contravenes fundamental principles in law is essentially void[5]. This intersection of "fundamental principles" is what is often considered as the gateway through which the basic human rights and the constitutional values can enter into the realm of the private law. In the civil code of Korea, Article 103 provides that "A juristic act which has for its object such matters as are contrary to good morals and other social order shall be null and void." I believe that many national contract laws have comparable provisions.

Not only that, the DCFR profusely uses in its provisions such ubiquitous abstract standards as good faith and fair dealing and reasonableness. For example, "A person who is engaged in negotiations has a duty to negotiate in accordance with good faith

---

① *The Principles, Definitions and Model Rules of European Private Law, Draft Common Frame of Reference (DCFR)*, Outline Edition (2009), I. —1:102 (2).

② Article II. —2:101 of the DCFR provides that "A person has a right not to be discriminated against on the grounds of sex or ethnic or racial origin in relation to a contract or other juridical act the object of which is to provide access to, or supply, goods, other assets or services which are available to the public."

③ *DCFR, op. cit.*, p. 14. "17. Protection of human rights. The DCFR itself recognises the overriding nature of this principle. One of the very first Articles provides that the model rules are to be read in the light of any applicable instruments guaranteeing human rights and fundamental freedoms. However, this is an overriding principle which is also reflected quite strongly in the content of the model rules themselves, most notably in the rules on non-discrimination in Books II and III and in many of the rules in Book VI on non-contractual liability arising out of damage caused to another."

④ Interestingly, the DCFR enforces non-discrimination only against discrimination based on sex or ethnic or racial origin in a contract to supply goods or services to the public. The non-discrimination of the DCFR is still experimental and is not allowed to be running across the board.

⑤ *DCFR, op. cit.*, II. — 7:301.

and fair dealing and not to break off negotiations contrary to good faith and fair dealing. This duty may not be excluded or limited by contract. "[1] For another example, if one party, but for a mistake, would not have concluded the contract and the other party "caused the contract to be concluded in mistake by leaving the mistaken party in error, contrary to good faith and fair dealing", such contract can be cancelled by the mistaken party[2].

These cases, one of which deals with contract making by a party who is unfaithful to the common purpose of the negotiation, and the other of which deals with contract making by a party who attempts to play a dishonest game on the other party, are both relevant to the circumstances where proper administration of social justice is called for. And the DCFR as a project by no means intended for its style of codification to be meager and scanty, but it does pay strong attention to the perspective of social justice. The link to social justice, as seen here, is not the style of codification, but the certain abstract principles that are explicitly permitted to guide the judgment of the court. That is, through such links as good faith and reasonableness, the court can administer social justice even under the detailed rules.

Let me introduce a case law in Korea in which the court brings the constitutional human rights principles on the decision of validity of a contract. This case[3] is concerned with the non-competition agreement which a company enters into with its employees. Such non-competition agreement used to provide that an employee should not disclose the trade secrets of the company nor engage in a business that may compete with the company during a certain period of time, even after the termination of employment with the company. Obviously the employee in the case argues that the non-competition agreement that he signed should be invalidated due to its violation of the constitutional human rights of freedom of profession.

The court observed that such agreement should be regarded reasonable and consistent with the constitutional freedom because the trade secrets involved in the

---

① *DCFR*, *op. cit.*, II. — 3:301 (2).

② *DCFR*, *op. cit.*, II. — 7:201.

③ Supreme Court of Korea, 13 June 1997, Case No. 97*Da*8229.

case were some special technology that should be regarded as a sort of "objectified intellectual property". Although the court in this case found that the agreement was not in violation of the constitutional freedom, the court essentially did apply the constitutional principle to the question of validity of a contract. After this decision, the lower courts went as far as to declare that under proper application of the constitutional freedom of profession and economic activity, among others, the duration of the non-competition and confidentiality should be limited to one year after the termination of employment[①].

Thus, when properly conceived, contract law is never a closed circuit value system. Further, social justice in contract law is realized through much higher connections that exist in the realm of the principles than through the choice of the style of codification. Therefore, vague and short rules, when intentionally intended for more active engagement of social justice, may only result in increasing arbitrariness in the court's discretion and thus uncertainty on the part of the parties, while the gateways for social justice are located somewhere other than in the casual provisions.

Thus, we should not turn the faucet of social justice too wide open by choosing vague and loose manner in the codification of contract law, because in that case, social justice does not only flow, but it can inundate. At the same time, pushing too detailed and intrusive rules into the contract law codification in the name of social justice, such as much detailed consumer protection rules, is not desirable either. The efforts to turn the contract law into a massive regulatory rule book that makes a contract look like rather a controlled purchase process for any transaction between any type and size of business and a consumer is an excess. Social justice in contract law is

---

① Suwon District Court of Korea, 7 June 2000, Case No. 2000*Kahap*95. The court held that "Considering among others that, if the duration of the non-competition agreement between a company and an employee should be extended too long, it will threat the economic survival of the employee by excessively restrict the freedom of profession and the freedom of economic activity of the employee who is in an economically weak position, and also considering that it may bring about the possibility of unfair monopoly by restriction of competition, the court is of the opinion that the duration of the non-competition and confidentiality should be limited to one year after the termination of employment."

not necessarily working that way and furthermore, there is another principle of contract law that deserves our first attention — the principle of freedom of contract to counterbalance too enthusiastic pursuit of the ideal of social justice in contract law.

6.4 PRIORITY OF PRINCIPLES

Social justice is expected to play its role in contract law through the connections by which the high-level guidance of contract law meets the bottom line values of the society. The principle of social justice may not be let running across every membrane of contract law. Such will end up with bringing the tyranny of social justice into the private law sector. If we acknowledge what a contract all about is the law's provision for construction of one's own life by self-determination and free interaction with others, there we see the ground for the transcendence of the principle of freedom of contract.

For example, the recently proposed the Common European Sales Law places the principle of freedom of contract as Article 1 and the principle of good faith and fair dealing as Article 2. Freedom of contract means that the parties are free to conclude a contract and to determine its contents unless prohibited by any mandatory rules. For all its concerns for social justice, the DCFR does not seem to have the mettle to place social justice ahead of freedom of contract[1]. Logically, where social justice takes precedence over freedom of contract, the freedom is meaningful only to the extent that it helps achievement of the purpose that is social justice. Such freedom may not be said to be a principle, as it becomes only a tool for something higher.

There is more practical reason why the highest place of the guiding principles of contract law should be reserved for freedom of contract. A most appropriate solution to a contract situation is often deliberated and selected by the parties themselves, rather than the court. A contract is a tool by which individuals can shape their lives by consent and agreement. At a profound level, a contract is thus an exercise of the

---

[1] *DCFR*, *op. cit.*, II. — 1:102(1) "Parties are free to make a contract or other judicial act and to determine its contents, subject to any applicable mandatory rules."

right of self-determination, and a myriad of contracts being made every day in turn shape how and where the society is moving as a collectivity. Even if a solution chosen by the parties may not seem wise on surface, that solution could be the best in the circumstances to which no one other than the parties themselves are privy. This society-wide accumulation of self-determination cannot be replaced and artificially managed even by the best exercise of the discretion of the court.

The political and cultural phenomenon in Asia distinctly known as the "benevolent totalitarianism" cannot equal in wisdom and intelligence to the sum of the countless of decisions made individually and collectively by the interested parties every day. The contract law should understand and reflect this truth.

The court can benevolently intervene to find the truth and bring out the most from each party to determine on their interests adequately. But the concept that the court should be given power and encouragement to rule *ex aequo et bono* ① as the embodiment and representative of social justice is wrong. In an arbitration, the arbitral tribunal can assume the power of an *amiable compositeur*, but only if the parties have agreed to give it such powers and only to the extent for resolution of a private dispute whose implication is limited to the parties themselves. A ruling of an *amiable compositeur* is acceptable so long as it does not violate the public order. In contrast, recognizing supremacy of social justice in contract law is like giving the court the power of an *amiable compositeur* to allow it to enthusiastically wade through the sea of private disputes and actively determine the scene in representation of the society's collective interests.

The law and the court should remain respectful and permissive to the parties' own choice of solution. The authority's intervention to bring down its final word on the problem in the private law area should be reserved as the backseat role. For example, in case of change of circumstances, things should be first left to the parties themselves to sort out the problem before social justice takes up the issue. In Korea, the increased use of court-supervised mediation is a positive indication that the above

---

① Latin for "according to the right and good" or "from equity and conscience".

mentioned truth, particularly in the contract law area, is now recognized and begins to be accepted in earnest.

The same approach is recommendable for legislative efforts as well. An example of this is the topic of whether specific performance should be recognized as a remedy for non-performance and if it should be recognized so, which remedy — specific performance or damages — should be the primary remedy. The Civil Law jurisdictions generally take the position that specific performance is the primary remedy for non-performance of a contract, whereas the Common Law jurisdictions see specific performance as an exception to the general remedy of damages.

I always observed feelings run high when the scholars discuss this issue in international fora. But, I like to point out some general consensus that can be derived from international efforts for model contract law. In the CISG (the UN Convention on Contracts for the International Sale of Goods (1980)) and other international model laws like the PECL and the DCFR, the trend has been to bring the remedy of damages to forefront while reducing the importance of specific performance. Nevertheless, in no such legislative efforts was the option of specific performance completely dropped from the list of available remedies. In fact, neither the court nor the law has a way to know which remedy is the best for a situation of a particular party; the answer to the question should be determined by the parties. Indeed, I observe that even in a Civil Law jurisdiction where specific performance is a default remedy, the aggrieved party itself knows intuitively whether a certain case is best suited for specific performance or for damages, and if specific performance is not effective in the circumstances, the party usually searches for alternatives.

Thus, any intervention into the choice of the remedy by the party is permitted only to the extent that the chosen remedy is not useful in the remedial effect but mainly results in harassing the other party. Once the boundary is set as such, the role of law should be that of offering an array of options for the party to choose from. This wisdom is not new, but should be given a renewed spotlight today.

Finally, the principle of freedom of contract is already in siege. The constraints on freedom of contract come from everywhere. Consumer protection, fair trade, economic human rights, social human rights, etc. have produced layers of regulations that can intervene into making and implementation of a contract and remedies for breach. This phenomenon of external regulation over contract law is not only true of the Civil Law system but also of the Common Law system.

I do not deny the significance of such external regulation over contract, but this does not mean that the supremacy of the principle of freedom of contract is to be compromised anyhow. Despite such external regulation, the principle of freedom of contract should maintain its self-respect and internal integrity. Once freedom of contract is disparaged by outsiders and also suffers self-criticism and sense of shame, there does not really remain a foundation for social justice to work on, because in that case there is not really a place reserved for contract law at all.

In this era of labyrinths of regulations, the importance of upholding the principle of freedom of contract is more emphasized. Further, more fundamentally, I like to consider that such regulations should be regarded as tentative stopgap measures to protect citizens in socially and economically weak position. We as the collectivity should rather strive to lift up the citizens to be equal in contracting positions than to leave them at a disadvantaged state and protecting them with special measures. We should better aim at educating the citizenry and reforming the social and economic conditions of the society so that the citizens will take due benefit out of the principle of freedom of contract as equal and independently contracting parties. To the extent that the traditional freedom of contract envisions exactly that ideal, the principle itself should not be lightly dismissed even in the modern day.

6.5   MORAL ENFORCEMENT OF CONTRACT

Morality in contract law is another big topic. We have already touched the issue of how fundamental values of the society can enter into the arena of contract law. The particular issue that I want to address in this section is, however, a more specific one. This issue could be called moral enforcement of a contract. It is about whether we should deal with a breach of contract and its consequence from moral perspective.

In fact, enforcement of any law has moral overtone. Law is enforced by coercion, but also by moral appeal, too. Many theorists consider that a contract is a promise. They tend to think that just as failure to keep a promise is morally wrong, failure to fulfill a contract is equally condemnable morally.

The first thing to discuss in this regard is whether contractual liability is strict liability or liability based on negligence. It is generally observed that the Common Law system espouses strict liability as opposed to the Civil Law system which espouses negligence liability for contract law. Basically, strict liability states that a party is contractually liable for remedies if he fails to comply with the contract whether or not such non-compliance resulted from his negligence. In contrast, negligence liability states that a party is contractually liable for remedies only if he fails to comply with the contract intentionally or because of his negligence.

Indeed, many Asian jurisdictions that follow the Civil Law system have the civil codes that embody the negligence liability principle. The recent trend in international contract laws, however, speaks otherwise. The CISG and other model contract laws such as the PECL, the DCFR, and the PICC① all adopted the strict liability principle for contract law.

To me, the basis of the negligence liability principle is morality. Moral judgment works strongly in the area of tort law. In tort, intention or negligence is required for liability and strict liability is rather an exception. Likewise, the negligence liability principle in contract law assumes that there should be some moral ground to condemn the obligor's non-performance, and such moral ground comes from the negligence or the intention of the obligor.

Actually, the negligence liability principle exaggerates the moral significance of a breach of contract. By shifting the burden to prove non-existence of negligence to the obligor, the obligee can make a *prima facie* case of a breach of contract any time when there is a provable objective fact of non-performance. Further, a wide range of facts that are arguably not directly translated into the obligor's negligence do not

---

① The PICC refers to the UNIDROIT Principles of International Commercial Contracts.

exempt the obligor's liability even under the negligence liability principle. Under the Korean law that adopts the negligence liability principle in contract law, such a fact that a third party supplier did not supply the parts to the seller and as a result the seller could not comply with the delivery deadline is not a workable defense.

While it is acknowledged that there can still be some difference of degree between the negligence liability principle and the strict liability principle in the scope of defenses permissible for non-performance (that the negligence liability principle would be more lenient in terms of the possible scope of such defenses), it is also true that the scope of defenses permissible under the negligence liability principle becomes growingly similar to that of the impediment or force majeure defenses under the strict liability system.

However, attempts to strengthen morality in the enforcement of a contract do not stop there. Moral enforcement of a contract proceeds to even a new height in certain variations. The DCFR determines that if the breach of contract was intentional, reckless or grossly negligent, the obligor is liable for all the losses resulting from such breach of contract irrespective of whether the obligor was able to foresee such losses at the time of the contract[①]. In contrast, in case of no negligence or simple negligence, the obligor is liable only for the losses that he foresaw or could reasonably have foreseen at the time of the conclusion of the contract. Obviously, this is a penalty based on morality judgment of the obligor.

Similar approaches can be seen in some national jurisdictions in Asia. For example, the New Civil Code of Cambodia provides that " Where the non-performance is the result of [the obligor's] malicious intent or bad faith conduct, the court may, based on the obligee's demand for damages, order that the obligor pay to the obligee as damages the profit or benefit obtained by the obligor from the conduct comprising the non-performance. "

I rather like to understand that if a malicious aspect of non-performance particularly undermines the social norms, such case should rather be treated as a tort

---

① *DCFR*, *op. cit.*, III. — 3:703.

rather than non-performance of a contract. Anyhow, however, the Cambodia's approach to order disgorgement of the profit/benefit obtained by malicious non-performance is still a moderate version of moral judgment.

Compared with that, the deprivation of the foreseeability restriction in the scope of damages in case of intentional, reckless or grossly negligent non-performance is quite a serious initiative for moral enforcement of a contract. In my understanding, deprivation of foreseeability restriction in the scope of damages is supposed to occur in tort law, only for an intentional tort and its equivalents. Such tort law approach is understandable from the nature and the purpose of tort law. However, taking the same approach in contract law is an odd deviation.

It is to note that the general consensus in international model contract law is that the scope of damages for non-performance is determined by the extent that the obligor foresaw or could have foreseen at the time of the conclusion of the contract. Such consensus has a good reason. A contract is an exchange, and the economic interests of the parties in the exchange were determined at the time of the conclusion of the contract.

I can understand that deprivation of foreseeability restriction can be considered if the non-performance was made with a malicious intent, as seen in the case of the New Civil Code of Cambodia, like plotting to cause a larger damage to the other party by withholding the required performance at the time when the other party was most vulnerable. By riding roughshod over the social norms and offending the sense of dignity of the society as a whole, the obligor's behavior attaches a totally new dimension to an otherwise simple breach of contract case.

However, depriving foreseeability restriction for a mere intentional, reckless, or grossly negligent non-performance is an attempt of excessive social engineering that is inappropriate for the proper purpose and functioning of contract law. From that perspective, it would not be much exaggeration to say that the project for morality enforcement of a contract can be likened to, or at least connected in spirit with, the project for supremacy of social justice.

Sometimes, there can arise certain events that compel the party to breach the contract unavoidably. The breach was made with knowledge and intention, but the damages are enough at the level that the other party expected at the time of entering into the contract. Increasing damages simply for knowledge and intention is to disregard all happenstances that may arise during the course of the life of a contract and punish the breaching party under the sweeping statement that "you broke the promise."

As an issue of Korean contract law doctrine, a similarly inappropriate approach has been enforced by the court. With respect to determination of the scope of damages, the courts have interpreted the relevant provisions of the civil code as implying that foreseeability should be determined at the time of non-performance, rather than the time of conclusion of the contract. As a result, special damages, i. e. damages resulting from special circumstances, should be payable if the obligor was able to foresee such special circumstances as of the time when the obligation became due. For example, if the buyer intended to resell the product to a third party for a profit, and the seller did not know about this at the time of conclusion of the contract but came to know about it by the time when the obligation to supply became due, the seller should pay the increased damages due to the unrealized resale as the special damages. While the Korean scholars seem to generally agree with the court's position, it is undeniable that a strong moral overtone is superimposed that is not necessarily required for fair and balanced resolution of contract disputes.

6.6   CONCLUSION

In the above, I generally defended the principle of freedom of contract. I defended the cardinal importance of that principle in contract law because if we allow the principle of freedom of contract to relinquish its position to other principles such as social justice, the minimal foundation upon which social justice can be realized at all may disappear.

The approach suggested in this paper may make those advocating social justice a little uncomfortable. Their concern for social justice has been accepted in some leading international contract law efforts and many national contract laws are trying to learn from their suggestions.

For those who feel particularly strong about realization of social justice in contract law and want to give it a more prominent role, I suggest that how the legal process over contract disputes is managed is equally important or perhaps more important than how substantive rules are imbued with certain ideology. For example, adoption of the inquisitorial system in the legal procedures may further dissipate undesirable overrunning of freedom of contract in case that it is abused or misused by the parties.

The inquisitorial system is a system of proof-taking whereby the judge conducting the trial determines on its own the scope and the extent of the inquiry into the case and the questions to be asked to the witnesses[1]. In contrast to the inquisitorial system is the adversary system which refers to a procedural system involving active and unhindered parties contesting with each other to put forth a case before a judge as an independent decision-maker[2]. Generally speaking, the Civil Law tradition is friendly to the inquisitorial system while the Common Law tradition is friendly to the adversary system.

The inquisitorial system has the virtues of clarifying obscure facts, discovering unrepresented truths, and supplementing the imbalance in the parties' litigation skills and resources. Such virtues are valuable not only in a proceeding between a business and a consumer, but also in a proceeding between a business and a business, and a consumer and a consumer as well. The inquisitorial system is often useful even in international arbitrations where well-resourced corporations clash with each other and some of the best legal mouthpieces are mobilized for representation. Thus, while the inquisitorial system itself is not automatically anonymous with social justice, it is still axiomatic to say that a neutral adjudicator's own investigation of the case in addition to the parties' representation can lead to more uncovering of the facts and better informed determination of the matter.

---

① *Black's Law Dictionary* (Abridged 8th Edition)
② Ibid.

The inquisitorial system stops spillover of exploitation of freedom of contract into the legal proceedings and curb freedom of contract to where it should belong. By the role played by the inquisitorial system, a dispute is often returned to the realm where the principles of good faith and reasonableness control the fate of the case. The strength of freedom of contract is still preserved while the advantage of social justice can be drawn on in adjudicating the case. The inquisitorial system can contribute in this manner without unpleasant violation of the private law sector. The bottom line is that the battle is not always fought and determined in the substantive law.

Finally, at the end of all this, for all the good things to come, education, training, and staffing of the adjudicators, arbitrators, and mediators is pivotal in achieving and maintaining the balance and the right places among the ideals discussed so far. We cannot discuss reform of law and enhancement of legal culture without paying attention to the quality of the administrators of justice themselves. Speed, fairness, and transparency are the symptoms of well-administered judicial process. If we agree that we cannot speak of realization of social justice without realization of these values as the ideals of legal procedures, we need to approach the issue of contract law reform or reform of any law for the matter from a more holistic perspective.

(Tae Yong AHN, Attorney-at-law, Seoul National University, Seoul, South Korea)

CHAPTER 7   Beijing, Hong Kong and Shanghai in Asia and the world

Peter J Taylor

7.1   INTRODUCTION

In a recent paper on leading Chinese world cities, Karen Lai (2012) makes two key points about understanding cities in globalization. First, she departs from the traditional hierarchical-competitive approach for understanding intercity relations[1] and "foregrounds a relational perspective on intercity linkages and highlights complementary roles" (Lai, 2012 p. 1277.). However, she adds the important caveat that hierarchical processes are not thereby dismissed, rather she "emphasises the complex co-existence of competition and collaboration" (ibid)[2]. Second, she does not follow the recent spate of quantitative studies measuring intercity relations and prefers to conduct "intensive research (using) qualitative data" (p. 1279) to ascertain 'how or why certain urban and economic processes take place in … cities' (p. 1280). However, again her position includes a caveat, this time to the effect that

---

[1]   Recent examples for China cities include Shi and Hamnett (2002), Yusuf and Wu (2002), Zhao (2003) and Wang et al. (2007).

[2]   For a similar argument see also Sassen (1999), Beaverstock et al. (2005), Taylor (2012, 2013) and Wójcik (2013).

quantitative researchers "have produced important results on city rankings and network structures" (p. 1279), implying a complementary relation between the two approaches. This suggests a critical realist methodology where extensive research provides input to intensive research (Sayer 1992), which is confirmed by the way she starts her substantive contribution by drawing on previous quantitative results from Taylor (2006, p. 1281).

We agree with both of Lai's qualified positions and we build upon them here in a very specific manner. In our interpretation of critical theory methodology the extensive research does not have to stop once it has provided ideas that only intensive research can properly examine; rather we view a spiral process where quantitative measures can return to refine further the network structures as suggested through the qualitative evidence and interpretation. In this case we identify from Lai's (2012) results and discussion a specific need for moving the focus of quantitative research from individual cities as the basic units of analysis to city-dyads. This brings actual intercity relations to the fore as a new focus in world city network analysis. Lai's primary findings concern how Shanghai relates to Beijing and Hong Kong; whereas there have been many commonplace views generating competitive narratives for these city-dyads (pp. 1275-76), she finds more evidence for complementarities, termed "dual-headquarter strategy" (p. 1282) and "parallel markets" (p, 1286) respectively. The Beijing-Hong Kong dyad is not part of Lai's central concern but obviously features explicitly in her interpretation of the meaning to Hong Kong of being a Chinese "autonomous area" (i. e. one step removed from Beijing's political power). In this paper we build upon Lai's (2012) initial use of quantitative results showing a simple ranking of China's three leading cities (Table7-2); using a new world city network approach featuring city-dyad connectivities, we present an extensive investigation of Beijing-Hong Kong, Beijing-Shanghai and Hong Kong-Shanghai to complement her intensive research. Drawing on Sassen's (1991, pp. 3-4; 1994, p. 18) initial interpretation of "global cities" as "strategic places", which we link to Sheppard's (2002) concept of "geographical positionality", wherein he identifies Sassen's global cities as an example (p. 324), We investigate how Hong Kong, Shanghai and Beijing have been positioning themselves in the world city network. Because city networks operate through mutuality it follows that instead of the rise of Shanghai and Beijing implying a decline in Hong Kong, the latter can continue to prosper through repositioning itself within the world city network. The geographies of these processes are shown through measures of the relative degrees of business connectivities between the three leading Chinese cities and other major world cities. In this manner we take Lai's (2012) ideas forward to show in detail geographical outcomes of city repositionings empirically. Overall, the basic finding is that these leading China cities are strategically much more important in the world city network than their simple rankings suggest. This has both (i) important implications for how we understand the ways in which China and non-China cities link the Chinese space-economy to the global economy, and (ii) potentially profound consequences for how scholars treat the role of China in contemporary globalization

This is a theoretically-informed empirical paper in which the argument is presented in five parts. We begin by outlining the interlocking network model of world cities that directs the data collection and underpins the analyses. Initial quantitative descriptions of Chinese cities and city-dyads that include Chinese cities are used to illustrate the model. The main substantive analyses are then laid out in the following order. We begin by displaying the disproportionate connectedness of Beijing, Hong Kong and Shanghai, which appears to be particularly emphasized through our focus on city-dyads. This confirms the specific importance of Hong Kong being not far behind London and New York in its connectivity. In the next section we concentrate on the differences between the other two leading China cities; we are able to delineate quite distinctive patterns in the connectivities of their respective city-dyads. In the final substantive section we trace changes from 2000 to 2010 in levels of connectivity between the three China cities plus London and New York to discover their various repositionings in the world city network. In a short conclusion we provide some hints for turning our findings into questions for a new research programme for more intensive investigations.

7.1.1 World city network analysis

There is now a considerable literature on the role of cities as key nodes in an increasingly globalized economy. One expression of this can be found in recent large edited volumes: Scott (2001), Brenner and Keil (2006), Taylor et al. (2007, 2011, 2013) and Derudder et al. (2012) muster over 300 chapters between them but still represent only the tip of this particular iceberg. Amongst this body of research, the Globalization and World Cities (GaWC) Research Network (www. lboro. ac. uk/ gawc) has pioneered a relational approach to understanding cities in globalization as a world city network. In developing a theoretically grounded measurement of world city network formation, we have drawn explicitly upon Sassen's (1991) seminal writings on the "global city" as the prime production site and market for financial, professional and creative services for corporate business. Specifically, major firms across the world have become increasingly dependent on advanced producer services, such as financial services, accountancy, advertising, law, and management consultancy which offer customized knowledge, expertise and skills to their corporate clients. In this process, many of these service firms have become transnational enterprises in their own right as they have expanded into a growing global market to both service their existing customers and acquire new clients (Aharoni and Nachum, 2000; Harrington and Daniels, 2006). According to Sassen (1991, p. 126) "global cities" have "a particular component in their economic base" that gives them a "specific role in the current phase of the world economy": they are the business service centres that have a key enabling role in economic globalization.

7.1.2   Data and Methods

While world city network analyses are based upon Sassen's global city thesis we depart from her approach in identifying more than just a select number of cities in the servicing of global capital. In this we follow Manuel Castells' (1996, p. 380) argument for a network society that encompasses a "global network" of cities that "cannot be reduced to a few urban cores at the top of the hierarchy". For the purpose of the large-scale empirical analyses reported here, the key point is that service firms have benefited immensely from the technological advances in telecommunications, allowing them to extend the geographical reach of their service provision. Thus while advanced producer service firms have always clustered in cities, in contemporary globalization they have been able to do their work through multiple offices in large numbers of cities around the world. This enables them to protect their brand integrity and offer a "seamless" service to their corporate clients operating in international markets (i. e. as opposed to previous instruments such as using 'correspondence banks' for clients' financial transactions). Each firm has its own strategy in terms of the location and number of cities in its office network, as well as the size and functions of individual offices. We employ an interlocking network model that treats the work done in these offices on projects that require multiple office inputs as "interlocking" the cities in which they are housed. Thus these intercity relations through servicing practices consist of both electronic and embodied flows (for example, online exchange of information and sharing of knowledge, as well as face-to-face meetings involving business travel). It is these "working flows", combined across numerous projects in many firms, that constitute the world city network as specified in the GaWC model (Taylor, 2001, 2004).

Specification of the model begins with formal representation as a city-by-firm matrix Vij, where vi,j is the "service value" of city i to firm j. This service value indicates the importance of a city within a firm's office network, which depends on the size and functions of a firm's office (or offices) in a city. From this service values matrix the city-dyad connectivity CDCa-i between cities a and i is defined as follows:

$$\text{CDC}_{a-i} = \sum_{i} v_{ai} \cdot v_{ij} \qquad (\text{where } a \neq i) \qquad (1)$$

This measures the potential working flows between any two cities within the world city network. It is based upon the assumption that the more important an office, the more working flows it generates, therefore flows between two cities with many large offices will be appreciably greater than flows between two cities with fewer large offices. For pedagogic and comparative reasons, in our analysis below, measures of CDCa-i are presented as percentages of the largest CDC, and therefore range from 0% (for pairs of cities that have no firms in common) to 100% for

London-New York (the most connected city-dyad). This makes our results independent from the number of firms and cities in the analysis.

The global network connectivity (GNCa) of city a in this interlocking network is then derived from equation (1) by aggregating all the city's connectivities across the network:

$$ \mathrm{GNC_a} \ = \ \sum_{i} \mathrm{CDC_{a-i}} \qquad (\text{where } a \neq i) \qquad (2) $$

For the same reasons given for equation (1), GNC measures are expressed as percentages of the largest computed connectivity in the data. Thus in our analysis below, measures of GNCa range from 0% (indicating cities where the firms have no offices) to 100% for London (the most connected city).

To operationalize the interlocking network model requires data on the city office networks of large multi-locational advanced producer service firms. We carried out a data collection in 2010 on the location strategies of major firms in a number of key service sectors: financial services, accountancy, advertising, law and management consultancy. Firms were chosen by their ranking in lists of the largest firms in each sector; for financial services, the top 75 firms and for other service sectors we included the top 25 firms, giving a total of 175 firms. Cities were chosen on the basis of a number of overlapping criteria, whereby the selection is in part based on cities identified in previous GaWC research with additional cities based upon city size (all cities with populations over 2 million) and function (all capital cities of states with populations over a million). 526 cities were thus selected. (For more details on firm and city selections see Taylor et al. (2011)).

Assigning service values for the 175 firms' use of the 526 cities focused on two features of a firm's office(s) in a city as shown on their corporate websites: first, the size of office (e. g. number of practitioners), and second, their extra-locational functions (e. g. regional headquarters). The resulting multifarious compilation of information on firms was codified into service values ranging from 0 to 5 as follows. The city housing a firm's headquarters was scored 5, a city with no office of that firm was scored 0. A typical office of the firm resulted in a city scoring 2; reasons for moving away from this score were (ⅰ) with something missing (e. g. no partners in a law office), the score reduced to 1, (ⅱ) with particularly large offices the score was raised to 3, and (ⅲ) with important extra-territorial functions (e. g. regional headquarters) a score of 4 was recorded. All such assessments were made firm by firm. The end result is a 526 cities x 175 firms matrix of 92,050 service values ranging between 0 an 5, which can be used as the input to the interlocking network model as summarized in equations (1) and (2).

7.1.3 Introducing China cities in world city network analysis

In previous studies of the world city network most of the focus has been on global network connectivity and Table 7-1 illustrates the results from Equation (2) featuring the top 20 China cities in terms of this measure. World rankings are also shown and the main point of this table is to show the global importance of China's three leading cities, Hong Kong, Shanghai and Beijing in that order, followed by a long tail including many cities with limited connectivity into the world city network. In this paper we concentrate on just these three cities; this becomes inevitable when we turn to the city-dyad analysis illustrated by Table 7-2(a). Here the results from using equation (1) are shown focusing on the top 20 city-dyads that include a China city. In this case all dyads feature just the three main China cities (this would have remained the situation if we had included the top 250 city-dyads!) and they display much higher world rankings than shown in Table 7-1. This is a first sign of the very strong integration of these cities into the world city network — 7 of the top 20 city-dyads across the world feature a Chinese city. In addition the city-dyads linking China's three major cities all appear in this list. But in some ways this actually under reports the role of the three cities in the world city network.

In Table 7-2(b) the top twenty city-dyads featuring China cities are listed in terms of their city-dyad relative connectivity (CDR). This is a city-dyad's connectedness relative to the two individual city's connectivity, indicated by the product of their global network connectivities:

$$CDR_{a-i} = CDC_{a-i}/(GNC_a \cdot GNC_i) \qquad (\text{where } a \neq i) \qquad (3)$$

This measures the relative concentration of the two cities' potential working flows in this particular dyad. High values indicate many firms choosing to locate offices, often important offices, in both cities suggesting extra business being conducted through this particular city-dyad; such city-dyads are relatively over-connected, we can think of them as "punching above their weight" in interlocking the world city network; it indicates an enhanced "strategic-ness". The obverse is low values of CDR indicating few firms choosing to locate in both cities. Here we focus on the former. As with the other measures, these values in Table 7-2 (b) are presented as percentages of the highest value. The basic message of this table is the over-connectedness of city-dyads including a China city: although the China cities are only 3 of the top 20 cities in terms of global network connectivity (Table 7-1), they feature in over half the top 38 highest over-connected city dyads. The three all-China city-dyads are ranked from 4th to 6th, which is a remarkable show of concentrated potential working flows. China's three leading cities certainly display all symptoms of being strategic places as conceived by Sassen. It is with this over-connectedness that we begin our detailed investigation of the way in which China is integrated into the world city network through its three leading cities.

7. 2   THE DISPROPORTIONATE CONNECTEDNESS OF BEI-JING, HONGKONG AND SHANGHAI

In Table 7-3 we have arrayed all the cities that are members of the top 40 city-dyads in terms of relative connectivity against the leading 20 cities as measured by global network connectivity. We know from Table 7-2 (b) that Hong Kong, Shanghai and Beijing feature prominently in these results; the new table provides the detailed geography of where concentrations of potential working flows are to be found across the world.

Since the global network connectivity of a city is constituted by the sum of its dyad connections (equations 1 and 2) it follows that cities with higher levels of global network connectivity will likely have more high dyad connectivities. This is clearly shown in Table 7-3 where the frequencies of relative over-connectedness tend to decrease as we go down the city rankings by global network connectivity. But this is by no means a simple definite tendency, and the exceptions are particularly relevant. The extreme counter case contrasts Dubai and Frankfurt: the former city is ranked 9th for GNC but does not feature at all in over-connected dyads whereas the latter ranked 19th is a member of 8 such dyads. Clearly our city-dyad analysis is picking up patterns that are missed in a focus on total global network connectivity. It seems that more firms locating in Dubai do not thereby generate strong links to other leading cities whereas less firms locating in Frankfurt are more geographically strategic to create several strong links to other major cities. Of course, Dubai is a city that has experienced massive commercial real estate development similar to China cities but this parallel built environment growth hides a very different contribution to world city network formation. In stark contrast to Dubai, the three China cities are strongly over-connected, including all featuring among Frankfurt's strategic links.

Table 7-3 also shows that relative over-connection has a local geographical dimension. This confirms the "regionality" within the world city network (Taylor et al. 2012): there are concentrations of strong inter-city connections in world-regional (e. g. Europe, Pacific Asia) and large-national (e. g. USA, China) space-economies. Thus the first ranked city-dyad is Chicago-Los Angeles and Paris' strongest link is with London, Sydney's with Singapore, and Madrid's with Paris. Again this tendency is not universal: Frankfurt is actually most over-connected to Beijing! However, this general feature obviously accounts for the degree of over-connection in the all-China dyads. But this does not translate into a simple set of relations, and it is here that we begin to add geographical detail to Lai's (2012) discussion. For a start, Hong Kong is most over-connected to Singapore, followed by Shanghai and Beijing. Shanghai is most over-connected to Hong Kong, followed by Beijing but the latter city ranks Shanghai before Hong Kong in over-connectedness. This suggests a rather subtle localism operating across the all-China city-dyads. In addition, we should note Tokyo's Pacific Asian strategic localism: it is most over-connected to the four other Pacific Asian cities in the table but with the three China cities ranked above Singapore. This particular localism is reinforced by London not featuring at all, and New York only in 40th place behind Los Angeles. Finally, we should not neglect Hong Kong's particular importance in this table: it is the most over-connected partner for three other cities, which is the most for any city in the table, two of which are not in China (Tokyo and Singapore) clearly suggesting not just Hong Kong as generally China's "gateway city" (Taylor et al., 2002) but specifically as the hinge city between China and the rest of Pacific Asia.

The results from Table 7-3 are summarized in Table 7-4 where cities are ranked in terms of over-connected city-dyad membership. Global network connectivity ranks are also shown and confirm Frankfurt as the biggest "riser" through the new analysis and Dubai as the biggest "faller". In terms of the three China cities: Hong Kong strongly continues in its position just below London and New York; Shanghai rises above Singapore to be 4th; and Beijing rises second most places to 7th above Paris. Thus the key finding is that in terms of strategic potential working flows the China cities appear even more important than recent studies of global network analyses have indicated (Derudder et al., 2010; Hanssens et al., 2011; Taylor et al., 2011), and their flows strongly feature both intra-China and global connections.

7.3 CONTRASTING CONNECTIONS: SHANGHAI AND BEIJING

Hong Kong is the established and continuing leading China city in the world city network but the relative positions of Shanghai and Beijing are still being constructed. In Table 7-5 differences between their respective city-dyads are explored to add further to our knowledge of the geographies of their network positioning. For this exercise the top 50 cities in terms of GNC are included so as to go beyond Table 7-3 by presenting the geographies of Shanghai and Beijing's connectivity strengths amongst the other 48 leading cities.

The following findings can be gleaned from this table.

(1) Although Beijing and Shanghai have similar numbers of cities tending towards each of them (25 and 23 respectively), Shanghai has more cities in the top

20 (11 to 7) and these are generally ranked higher including both London and New York. This is consistent with Shanghai having a larger GNC than Beijing but more crucially it shows Shanghai developing commercially as the more strategic place.

(2) The main geographical difference between Shanghai and Beijing's city-dyads is that the latter include all Pacific city links (including two Australian cities) except for Hong Kong. This finding suggests a regional propensity for firms in western Pacific non-China cities to favour links to China's capital city. This is consistent with Wang et al. 's (2011) discussion of "power and market" in how multinational firms choose where to locate their main China office, possible with political considerations trumping commercial advantages.

(3) This political dimension is further supported by the tendency for capital cities to be linked more strongly to Beijing where there is more than one city from a country —Washington over New York, Delhi over Mumbai — and with city-states — Singapore and Dubai. The position of Washington being ranked first for Beijing over Shanghai is largely the result of leading law firms and their strategic need to be located in political cities.

(4) European cities are generally more strongly linked to Shanghai, 13 compared to 6 for Beijing, and the latter include the European capital Brussels, the "Eurasian capital" Moscow, and more specialist financial centres notably Frankfurt, Zurich and Dublin.

(5) There is a more even distribution amongst US cities, 6 to 4 in Shanghai's favour but the latter consist of the top 5 US cities in terms of GNC plus Miami (7th ranked in US) the main link to Latin America.

(6) There are four Latin American cities in these data and they break 3 to 1 in favour of Shanghai, with Sao Paulo and Shanghai having particularly strong links.

(7) The only African city in these data, Johannesburg, is strongly linked to Beijing, possibly indicating a dependent relationship. Perhaps confirming the political nature of this link, Chinese service firms such as the China Construction Bank and the Bank of China feature strongly in its construction.

We can conclude that the distribution of Shanghai and Beijing's city-dyads have a clear structural pattern reflecting regional, political and GNC size influences.

7.4 CHANGING CONNECTION: 2000 TO 2010

Finally, we can take a tentative look at how city-dyad connectivities have been changing. This has to be cautious because although we have been collecting data to create service value matrices from 2000, the methodology has been slightly modified as we have better understood the processes. The main difference is in terms of selection of firms and cities; the former has risen from 100 in 2000 to 175 in 2010, the latter from 315 to 526. It is the selection of firms that is most important for our results and in what follows we have reduced 2010 results by a factor of 100/175 to create approximate comparable measures. For more details on these data differences see Derudder et al. (2010).

In Table 7-6 we present results showing changes over the first decade of the twenty first century for just ten major city-dyads, the three China city-dyads, their changing relations with London and New York, and the latter two cities' dyad as a base against which to compare. Taking each China city in turn, we can make the following statements about recent changes in their main world city network links:

(1) Shanghai. This city records the largest growth in CDCs with each of the other cities under consideration. The biggest increase is with Beijing. This clearly shows the degree of growing importance of Shanghai's strategic-ness in the world city network.

(2) Beijing. This city records the second largest growth in CDCs with the other cities, at a level approximately half that of Shanghai. Note however that the strong link to Shanghai confirms the mutuality between the two cities: Shanghai's growth is feeding into Beijing and vice versa in a manner similar to that previously reported for London-Frankfurt relations (Beaverstock et al., 2005).

(3) Hong Kong. This city shows CDC growth with the other China cities but records a reduction in CDC with London and New York. This should not be interpreted as Hong Kong declining in importance following its reincorporation into

China in 1997. Rather we have a reorientation of the city's position within the world city network: increases in potential working flows to Shanghai and Beijing more than making up for the smaller negative trend with London and New York. This is supported by the non-China city-dyad in Table 7-6; the London-New York CDC has declined at about the same rate as these cities' individual relations with Hong Kong. No one would suggest London and New York have declined in importance but rather their orientations have moved slightly away from a North Atlantic fulcrum to other parts of the world where the world city network is intensifying, notably China where compensations in CDCs are shown with Shanghai and Beijing in Table 7-6. In other words, Hong Kong's links are trending like London and New York's; its repositioning is maintaining a very important strategic-ness within the world city network.

This change analysis confirms the previous 2010 findings that the leading three China cities have exceptionally developed as key strategic places within the world city network, albeit empirically with different relations towards other major world cities. These different geographies are not trivial; they imply inter-city mutuality for the process of integrating the Chinese economy into the global economy.

7.5 CONCLUSION

In the world cities literature there is only one city-dyad that has been widely researched: London-New York (Wójcik, 2013), which even has its own name, NYLON (Smith, 2012). Thus Lai's (2012) intensive study of China's three leading cities as city-dyads is relatively unusual. In the introduction we suggested that this new paper might be seen as an extensive complement to Lai's research in a research spiral of advancing understanding. It is the nature of extensive research that it cannot answer "why questions", rather it shows patterns such as the findings in our tables above. Such results should not be over-interpreted. Thus this conclusion will briefly consider where our research might be leading in terms of further intensive study. In other words it is not so much about our findings as "answers", rather this work should be evaluated by our findings bringing new questions to the fore.

Our contribution should be evident at two levels, the general and the specific. For the former what our study has shown is that China cities are properly to be understood as part of a world city network. Lai's (2012) three city dyads are just as much part of this global structure as Chicago-Los Angeles, or indeed NYLON. From any single country focus, the world city network is not "out there" featuring "foreign cities" to compare to a so-called "national urban system"; rather we are dealing with a transnational process, an interlocking network formation (Hoyler, 2011). Lai frames her study in terms of "China's financial centre network", which is fine as long at it does not get filed away under "China Studies". What she is describing are new emerging centralizing tendencies in the world city network challenging previous centralizing (NYLON). Of course, she is fully aware of this wider context, some of her fieldwork was carried out in London and she explicitly refers to the extra-China work experiences of her interviewees (p. 1280). The results in this paper show the need for a transnational framework in studying contemporary city-dyads, that is to say filing under "Global Studies".

Beyond framing research there are the specific findings that require further intensive investigation about why and how the world city network makers, leading advanced producer service firms, are developing their intercity office networks the way they are. Here are six findings that we believe deserve further analysis: (1) There is the interesting contrast between the China cities and Dubai in terms of major dyad links despite similarities in their capital investments in real estate (where the high cranes are). Has this made China cities more resilient and if so exactly how? (2) Beijing's dyads appear to be more political than Shanghai's. What specifically is this political process within world city network formation? (3) Beijing is particularly well connected to other western Pacific cities. Does this indicate initial signs of dependency relationships and if so what forms might this take? (4) Shanghai has stronger relations with more important cities across the world than Beijing. Does this make Shanghai's position more resilient and what might this mean? (5) Shanghai has more rapid growth in connectivity than the other two China cities. How sustainable is this — are we at the beginning or near the end of the process? (6) Hong Kong appears to have been successfully repositioning itself. What exactly does this mean for the firms operating through Hong Kong? Positing these questions points towards a new research agenda for developing a new understanding of the role of Chinese cities in a globalizing world. In sum we trust other studies will treat our findings as a foundation upon which to build theoretically-informed and policy-relevant knowledge.

References

[1] Aharoni, Y. and Nachum, L., 2000. Globalization of Services: Some Implications for Theory and Practice. London: Routledge.

[2] Beaverstock, J. V., Hoyler, M., Pain, K. and Taylor, P. J., 2005. Demystifying the euro in European financial centre relations: London and Frankfurt, 2000-2001, Journal of Contemporary European Studies, 13(2), pp. 143-157.

[3] Brenner, N. and Keil, R. (Eds), 2006. The Global Cities Reader. London: Routledge.

[4] Castells, M., 1996. The Rise of the Network Society. Oxford: Blackwell.

[5] Derudder, B., Taylor, P. J., Ni, P., De Vos, A., Hoyler, M., Hanssens, H., Bassens, D., Huang, J., Witlox, F., Shen, W. and Yang, X., 2010. Pathways of change: shifting connectivities in the world city network, 2000-08, Urban Studies, 47(9), pp. 1861-1877.

[6] Derudder, B., Hoyler, M., Taylor. P. J. and Witlox, F. (Eds), 2012. International Handbook of Globalization and World Cities. Cheltenham, UK: Edward Elgar.

[7] Hanssens, H., Derudder, B., Taylor, P. J., Hoyler, M., Ni, P., Huang, J., Yang, X. and Witlox, F., 2011. The changing geography of globalized service provision, 2000-2008, The Service Industries Journal, 31(14), pp. 2293-2307.

[8] Harrington, J. W. and Daniels, P. W. (Eds), 2006. Knowledge-based

Services, Internationalization and Regional Development. Aldershot, UK: Ashgate.

[9] Hoyler, M., 2011. External relations of German cities through intra-firm networks — a global perspective, Raumforschung und Raumordnung, 69(3), pp. 147-159.

[10] Lai, K., 2012. Differentiated markets: Shanghai, Beijing and Hong Kong in China's financial centre network, Urban Studies, 49(6), pp. 1275-1296.

[11] Sassen, S., 1991. The Global City: New York, London, Tokyo. Princeton, NJ: Princeton University Press.

[12] Sassen, S., 1994. Cities in a World Economy. Thousand Oaks: Pine Forge Press.

[13] Sassen, S., 1999. Global financial c + enters, Foreign Affairs, 78(1), pp. 75-87.

[14] Sayer, A., 2002. Method in Social Science: A Realist Approach. London: Routledge.

[15] Scott, A. J. (Ed.), 2001. Global City-Regions: Trends, Theory, Policy. Oxford: Oxford University Press.

[16] Sheppard, E., 2002. The spaces and times of globalization: place, scale, networks, positionality. Economic Geography, 78(3), pp. 307-330.

[17] Shi, Y. and Hamnett, C., 2002. The potential and prospect for global cities in China: in the context of the world system, Geoforum, 33(1), pp. 121-135.

[18] Smith, R. G. (2012) NY-LON, in: B. Derudder, M. Hoyler, P. J. Taylor and F. Witlox (Eds) International Handbook of Globalization and World Cities, pp. 421-428. Cheltenham, UK: Edward Elgar.

[19] Taylor, P. J., 2001. Specification of the world city network. Geographical Analysis, 33(2), pp. 181-194.

[20] Taylor, P. J., 2004. World City Network: A Global Urban Analysis. London: Routledge.

[21] Taylor, P. J., 2006. Shanghai, Hong Kong, Taipei and Beijing within the world city network: positions, trends and prospects. GaWC Research Bulletin

No. 204 (www. lboro. ac. uk/gawc/rb/rb204, accessed 1/7/12).

[22] Taylor, P. J., 2012. On city cooperation and city competition, in: B. Derudder, M. Hoyler, P. J. Taylor and F. Witlox (Eds) International Handbook of Globalization and World Cities, pp. 51-63. Cheltenham, UK: Edward Elgar.

[23] Taylor, P. J., 2013. Extraordinary Cities: Millennia of Moral Syndromes, World-Systems and City/State Relations. Cheltenham, UK: Edward Elgar.

[24] Taylor, P. J., Derudder, B., Hoyler, M., Ni, P. and Witlox, F., 2012. New regional geographies of the world as practised by leading advanced producer service firms in 2010, Transactions of the Institute of British Geographers, doi: 10. 1111/j. 1475-5661. 2012. 00545. x

[25] Taylor, P. J., Derudder, B., Saey, P. and Wilox, F. (Eds), 2007. Cities in Globalization: Practices, Policies and Theories. London: Routledge.

[26] Taylor, P. J., Hoyler, M., Beaverstock, J. V., Faulconbridge, J. R., Derudder, B., Witlox, F., Harrison, J. and Pain, K. (Eds), 2013. Global Cities (four volumes), London: Routledge Major Works

[27] Taylor, P. J., Ni, P., Derudder, B., Hoyler, M., Huang, J. and Witlox, F. (Eds), 2011. Global Urban Analysis: a Survey of Cities in Globalization. London: Earthscan.

[28] Taylor, P. J., Walker, D. R. F., Catalano, G. and Hoyler, M., 2002. Diversity and power in the world city network, Cities, 19(4), pp. 231-241.

[29] Wang, D. T., Zhao, S. X., Gu, F. F. and Chen, W. Y., 2011. Power or market? Location determinants of multinational headquarters in China, Environment and Planning A, 43(10), pp. 2364—2383.

[30] Wang, T., Zhao, S. X. and Wand, D., 2007. Information hinterland — a base for financial centre development: the case of Beijing versus Shanghai in China, Tijdschrift voor Economische en Sociale Geografie, 98 (2) pp. 102-120.

[31] Wójcik, D., 2013. The dark side of NY-LON: financial centres and the global financial crisis. Urban Studies, doi: 10. 1177/0042098012474513.

[32] Yusuf, S. and Wu, W., 2002. Pathways to a world city: Shanghai rising in an era of globalisation, Urban Studies 39(7), pp. 1213-1240.

[33] Zhao, S. X. B., 2003. Spatial restructuring of financial centers in mainland China and Hong Kong: a Geography of finance perspective, Urban Affairs Review, 38(4), pp. 535-571.

Table 7-1 Top 20 Chinese cities for Global Network Connectivity

China rank	World rank	City	GNC*
1	3	Hong Kong	73.0
2	7	Shanghai	62.7
3	12	Beijing	58.4
4	43	Taipei	41.7
5	67	Guangzhou	34.1
6	106	Shenzhen	25.8
7	188	Tianjin	16.8
8	223	Kaohsiung	14.3
9	245	Nanjing	13.5
10	252	Chengdu	13.1
11	262	Hangzhou	12.5
12	267	Qingdao	12.3
13	275	Dalian	12.0
14	291	Macao	10.9
15	319	Chongqing	8.9
16	323	Xi'an	8.7
17	325	Suzhou	8.6
18	337	Wuhan	8.0
19	346	Xiamen	7.5
20	348	Ningbo	7.5

* GNC is global network connectivity and is presented as percentage of the most connected city (London).

Table 7-2(a)　Top 20 city-dyads that include China cities

China rank	World rank	City-dyad	CDC*
1	2	Hong Kong and London	75.0
2	3	Hong Kong and New York	69.0
3	6	London and Shanghai	62.1
4	10	New York and Shanghai	58.7
5	14	Beijing and London	55.6
6	19	Beijing and New York	52.3
7	20	Hong Kong and Singapore	51.6
8	31	Hong Kong and Shanghai	47.5
9	32	Hong Kong and Paris	47.2
10	37	Hong Kong and Tokyo	44.9
11	39	Beijing and Hong Kong	43.9
12	44	Shanghai and Singapore	41.1
13	45	Paris and Shanghai	40.4
14	46	Dubai and Hong Kong	39.8
15	47	Chicago and Hong Kong	39.7
16	50	Hong Kong and Sydney	39.2
17	52	Beijing and Singapore	38.8
18	54	Shanghai and Tokyo	38.4
19	56	Beijing and Shanghai	38.0
20	57	Hong Kong and Milan	37.0

＊CDC is city-dyad connectivity and is shown as % of the most connected city dyad (London-New York) — see equation (1).

All China city-dyads are emboldened.

Table 7-2(b)   Top 20 city-dyad over-connections that include China cities

China rank	World rank	City-dyad	CDO*
1	3	Hong Kong and Singapore	97.4
2	4	Hong Kong and Shanghai	96.4
3	5	Beijing and Shanghai	96.4
4	6	Beijing and Hong Kong	95.7
5	7	Hong Kong and London	95.5
6	9	Hong Kong and New York	93.0
7	10	New York and Shanghai	92.1
8	12	London and Shanghai	91.9
9	14	Beijing and Singapore	91.6
10	16	Beijing and Frankfurt	90.2
11	17	Shanghai and Singapore	90.1
12	19	Hong Kong and Tokyo	89.6
13	21	Beijing and Tokyo	89.3
14	25	Shanghai and Tokyo	89.2
15	26	Frankfurt and Hong Kong	89.1
16	29	Beijing and London	88.5
17	33	Beijing and New York	88.2
18	35	Hong Kong and Paris	88.0
19	37	Paris and Shanghai	87.6
20	38	Frankfurt and Shanghai	87.1

* CDO are measures of city-dyad over-connections presented as %s of largest over-connection (Chicago-Los Angeles). Only cities in the top 20 of global network connectivity are included.

All-China dyads are emboldened.

Table 7-3 The main dyad partners of the top 20 cities

GNC rank	City	Dyad-partners with rankings									
1	London	2 New York	7 Hong Kong	12 Shanghai	13 Singapore	18 Paris	22 L. Angeles	24 Chicago	28 Frankfurt	29 Beijing	
2	New York	2 London	8 L. Angeles	9 Hong Kong	10 Shanghai	11 Chicago	15 Singapore	23 Frankfurt	31 Paris	32 Beijing	40 Tokyo
3	Hong Kong	3 Singapore	4 Shanghai	6 Beijing	7 London	9 New York	19 Tokyo	26 Frankfurt	33 Paris		
4	Paris	18 London	20 Frankfurt	31 New York	33 H. Kong	35 Shanghai	37 Madrid				
5	Singapore	3 Hong Kong	13 London	14 Beijing	15 New York	17 Shanghai	27 Tokyo	38 Frankfurt			
6	Tokyo	19 H. Kong	21 Beijing	25 Shanghai	27 Singapore	30 Sydney	34 L. Angeles	40 New York			
7	Shanghai	4 Hong Kong	5 Beijing	10 New York	12 London	17 Singapore	25 Tokyo	35 Paris	36 Frankfurt		
8	Chicago	1 L. Angeles	11 New York	24 London							
9	Dubai										
10	Sydney	30 Singapore									
11	Milan										
12	Beijing	5 Shanghai	6 Hong Kong	14 Singapore	16 Frankfurt	21 Tokyo	32 New York				
13	Toronto										
14	Sao Paulo										
15	Madrid	37 Paris									
16	Mumbai										
17	Los Angeles	1 Chicago	8 New York	14 Tokyo	22 London						
18	Moscow										
19	Frankfurt	16 Beijing	20 Paris	23 New York	26 H. Kong	28 London	29 London	36 Shanghai	38 Singapore		
20	Mexico City	20 Paris									

The top 40 city-dyads are included as measured by city-dyad relative connectivity — see equation (3)

Table 7-4   Top 20 GNC cities ranked by top 40 dyad memberships

City	Dyad memberships [*]	Membership rank [**]	GNC rank
New York	10	1	2
London	9	2	1
Hong Kong	8	3	3
Shanghai	8	4	7
Singapore	8	5	5
Frankfurt	8	6	19
Beijing	7	7	12
Paris	7	8	4
Tokyo	6	9	6
Los Angeles	4	10	17
Chicago	3	11	8
Sydney	1	12	10
Madrid	1	13	15
Toronto	0 (59)	14	13
Mumbai	0 (67)	15	16
Milan	0 (100)	16	11
Sao Paulo	0 (109)	17	14
Moscow	0 (120)	18	18
Dubai	0 (132)	19	9
Mexico City	0 (174)	20	20

* for cities with zero membership in the top 40, their highest ranked dyad membership is given in brackets to be used in ranking.

* * for cities with dyad membership that have equal totals, they are ranked by their lowest average of ranks from Table 7-3.

Table 7-5　Relative strengths of Shanghai and Beijing in city-dyads with other top 50 GNC cities

Cities tending towards Shanghai	Difference*	Cities tending towards Beijing	Difference*
Munich	1.09	Washington	−0.86
Milan	1.04	Seoul	−0.73
Madrid	1.01	Dublin	−0.66
Sao Paulo	0.81	Kuala Lumpur	−0.52
Santiago	0.70	Johannesburg	−0.50
Mumbai	0.69	Frankfurt	−0.48
New York	0.61	Melbourne	−0.34
London	0.53	Moscow	−0.30
Lisbon	0.52	Dallas	−0.24
Stockholm	0.51	Atlanta	−0.23
Warsaw	0.51	Singapore	−0.23
Prague	0.46	Philadelphia	−0.22
Miami	0.46	Brussels	−0.20
Istanbul	0.37	Zurich	−0.19
Boston	0.32	Delhi	−0.16
Barcelona	0.30	Dubai	−0.16
Paris	0.24	Taipei	−0.13
Vienna	0.23	Bangkok	−0.12
Los Angeles	0.17	Mexico City	−0.10
Buenos Aires	0.15	Sydney	−0.09
Hong Kong	0.11	Jakarta	−0.08
San Francisco	0.09	Tokyo	−0.03
Toronto	0.07	Düsseldorf	−0.00
Amsterdam	0.01		
Chicago	0.00		

* Difference is computed as (CDRshanghai − i — CDRBeijing-i). These values are very small and therefore they are multiplied by 10,000 for presentation.

Top 20 GNC cities are emboldened.

Table 7-6   Changes in city-dyad connectivity (2000-10)

City-dyads	CDC % change
Beijing-Shanghai	69.40
Hong Kong-Shanghai	39.58
Beijing-Hong Kong	20.54
London-Shanghai	37.91
London-Beijing	16.73
London-Hong Kong	−11.04
New York-Shanghai	38.84
New York-Beijing	20.22
New York-Hong Kong	−14.85
London-New York	−12.65

(Peter J Taylor, Globalization and World Cities Research Network, Northumbria University, Newcastle, UK.)

CHAPTER 8   Regional Trade Agreements and US-China Trade Relations

Jeffrey J. Schott

8.1   INTRODUCTION

Almost two decades ago, United States and Chinese leaders agreed at the Asia-Pacific Economic Cooperation (APEC) Summit in Bogor, Indonesia to achieve free trade and investment in the region by 2010 for developed countries and 2020 for developing countries. The deadlines for those ambitions ventures might have seemed distant to the APEC leaders in November 1994, but the first marker is already long past and the second fast approaching.

APEC gets a grade of "A" for its vision of regional economic integration and an "incomplete" for its execution. Nonetheless, progress towards an Asia-Pacific free trade region over this period has been notable, even if much of it has taken place outside the scope of APEC deliberations. Bilateral and regional free trade agreements (FTAs) have proliferated in the region. The United States and China have been active participants in a variety of arrangements, with one notable exception: neither has pursued an FTA initiative involving the other. But both are still essentially committed to doing so under APEC's broad umbrella and continue to work haphazardly toward that end in APEC fora.

Although the United States and China are pursuing separate strategies with regard to economic integration in the Asia-Pacific region, their paths could converge in the future to their mutual benefit. Both countries already have an extensive network of FTAs in place or under negotiation with countries in Asia and the Pacific and are committed to the long-run APEC goal of creating a Free Trade Area of the Asia-Pacific or FTAAP (see tables 8-1 and 8-2). The United States has FTAs in effect with its NAFTA partners, Canada and Mexico, as well as bilateral deals in the region with Australia, Chile, Colombia, Peru, Panama, Singapore and South Korea. Combined, these pacts account for 38 percent of the US's sotal trade. In addition, the United States has an FTA with five Central American countries and the Dominican Republic, and is one of eleven countries participating in the Trans-Pacific Partnership (TPP) negotiations, which is crafting a comprehensive free trade regime and new rulebook for trade and investment in goods and services (see Schott, Kotschwar and Muir 2013). Japan announced in March 2013 that it wants to join the TPP talks and could well do so in the second half of 2013. If it does, South Korea is likely to follow suit.

China has an FTA in place with the Association of Southeast Asian Nations (ASEAN) — seven of which are also APEC members[1]— as well as bilateral agreements with Chile, Japan, New Zealand, Peru and Singapore. Together, these trade pacts account for 20 percent of China's total trade. China also has negotiations underway with Australia, Japan and South Korea, which account for another 20 percent of China's total trade (table 8-2). In addition, China is preparing to broaden and deepen its Asian integration through the negotiation of the Regional Comprehensive Economic Partnership (RCEP). The RCEP talks, which include ASEAN, Australia, India, Japan, Korea and New Zealand, as well as China, is a

---

[1] This includes: Brunei, Indonesia, Malaysia, Philippines, Singapore, Thailand and Vietnam.

large deal in the making; Chinese trade with RCEP members was over $ 1 trillion in 2011, about 32 percent of total Chinese trade.

8.2 US-CHINA TRADE IN THE REGIONAL CONTEXT

Tables 8-3 and 8-4 illustrate the relative importance of bilateral trade between the United States, China and the TPP-11 countries over the past decade. For the United States, the TPP-11 is an important trading bloc, representing nearly 40 percent of total US exports and about 30 percent of its imports. Bilateral US merchandise trade with the TPP-11 totals about $ 1.2 trillion annually, almost double the value of trade a decade ago. US trade with China has grown even more dramatically. In 2000, US exports to China accounted for just 2 percent of total US exports, while US imports from China were less than 10 percent of total US imports. In 2011, those shares had risen to 8 percent and 18 percent respectively (see table 8-3). However, US imports from China still dominate exports; the US trade deficit with China has hovered around $ 300 billion for the past few years and is a focal point of US public debate on trade policy.

The United States is one of China's most important trading partners; Chinese exports to the United States have increased six-fold since 2000 and now account for 17 percent of total exports. Imports from the United States increased from just $ 22 billion in 2000 to over $ 100 billion in 2011, and now account for roughly 8 percent of total Chinese imports (see table 8-4). Nearly a third of Chinese exports are destined for the TPP-11 and just over 20 percent of its imports come from the group. However, the vast majority of this trade involves Chinese exports to the United States. If the United States is excluded from the TPP-11 group, Chinese exports to the TPP-11 as a share of total exports drops from 23 to 10 percent. Chinese imports from the TPP-11, however, are not only a US story. Even excluding the United States, the TPP-11 still accounts for 15 percent of total Chinese imports.

Despite the importance of bilateral trade, and the numerous obstacles that continue to constrain the growth of cross-border flows of goods and services, bilateral FTA negotiations are not on the radar screen of policymakers in either country for a variety of economic and political reasons. The bilateral option deserves more analysis to gauge its long-term potential to boost output and trade in each country. At this point, suffice it to say that pursuing regional initiatives seems likely to be the more feasible path to liberalizing barriers to bilateral trade in goods and services.

8. 3   TPP AND THE INTRA-ASIAN APPROACH: PARALLEL TRACKS TO REGIONAL INTEGRATION

While the intra-Asian and TPP strategies pursued by China and the United States share the same vision for region-wide integration, they differ starkly in terms of the breadth and depth of the obligations undertaken to liberalize trade and investment in goods and services. Intra-Asian pacts tend to focus on dismantling barriers to merchandise trade through gradual liberalization of tariffs. More comprehensive coverage of trade topics like services and investments, intellectual property rights, government procurements and disciplines on state-owned enterprises are, for the most part, given short shrift or excluded from intra-Asian pacts. That said, recent pacts like New Zealand's FTAs with China and Malaysia broadened coverage in services and included disciplines on a range of domestic policies. China's current FTA negotiations with South Korea, a country that already has concluded high standard agreements with the United States and the European Union, could go even further. These recent initiatives among Asian countries provide significant precedents for the nascent RCEP negotiations, which, if adopted, could narrow the gap between the intra-Asian and Asia-Pacific integration pacts in terms of substantive coverage.

The following sections outline the scope and coverage of the TPP and RCEP agreements and evaluate their role in the path towards regional integration.

8.3.1 The Trans-Pacific Partnership

The TPP negotiations aim to craft a high-standard, 21st century trade accord that is far more comprehensive and legally binding than the trade arrangements forged among Asian countries. More precisely, the TPP seeks to establish a new set of trade rules and commitments that (1) dismantle barriers to trade in goods and services; (2) develop a new trade rulebook on issues like labor, environment, investment, competition policy, and state-owned enterprises (SOEs); and (3) develop a more coherent approach across sectors with regard to regulatory policies that affect flows of trade and investment (Schott, Kotschwar and Muir, 2013).

Since negotiations began in March 2010, the TPP has expanded its membership: first in October 2010 when Malaysia joined the talks, followed soon after in December 2010 when Vietnam gained full member status, and then in October 2012 when Canada and Mexico were accepted into the pact. Most recently, on March 15, 2013, Japan announced its intention to seek TPP membership, and South Korea will likely to follow suit if Japan joins the talks.

However, once TPP negotiations are concluded adding new members will be far more complex. Unlike accession to the WTO that allows partial reforms, the TPP generally calls for full trade liberalization and requires compliance with its comprehensive rulebook. These additional requirements explain why accession clauses in FTAs have almost never been invoked. Adding new members affects the nature of competition in the preference area and the balance of concessions between signatory countries. Such knitting does not work for simple economic and political reasons. On the economic side, expanding the geographic area of a free trade zone effectively dilutes remaining protection for domestic industries and is thus strongly resisted. On the political side, the rules of origin, different in each agreement, are meant to restrain competition and to provide side payments to domestic companies. National legislatures are reluctant to reduce such protection without additional compensation from trading partners.

That said, the TPP agreement will likely include an accession clause to enable other Asia-Pacific countries to join the agreement if they are willing to accept and enforce its obligations. However, its use is likely to be very limited. While some candidate countries might be willing to adhere to all of the provisions of the existing pact, and might be accepted without the need to revise or augment the terms of the agreement, such basic "docking" onto the TPP would be very unlikely for large economies like China or Indonesia, whose entry would probably require a renegotiation of specific components of the deal with existing TPP members.

8.3.2 The Regional Comprehensive Economic Partnership

In the medium-term, China will likely pursue regional economic integration through the RCEP, in addition to its bilateral and trilateral FTAs. The RCEP aims to broaden and deepen the ASEAN + 1 pacts with six countries (Australia, India, Japan, Korea, New Zealand and China) by the end of 2015. Like the TPP, the RCEP aims to cover extensive areas of economic activity such as trade in goods and services, rules on intellectual property rights and regulatory policies. However, RCEP aims at softer commitments than the hard law obligations under construction in the TPP. Unlike the TPP, the RCEP will provide special preferences for poorer countries, plus additional exemptions for less developed countries.

Essentially, the goals of the RCEP closely resemble those of the ASEAN Economic Community (AEC), which seek deeper integration among ASEAN members by the end of 2015. However, ASEAN members have missed or side-stepped important deadlines along the way, especially on services, and are far from achieving their integration goals. RCEP could help accelerate progress on the AEC. Perhaps more importantly, RCEP will provide China a platform to continue incremental reforms that, in the future, would allow it to participate in more comprehensive regional and global pacts.

That said, the RCEP is not competing with the TPP. First, the RCEP and TPP have different timeframes. Negotiations on an RCEP are just starting in 2013. In contrast, TPP negotiations will be close to completion by the end of 2013. Second, there is overlapping membership between the pacts; 6 of the 16 RCEP countries (Australia, Brunei, Malaysia, New Zealand, Singapore and Vietnam) are also participating in the TPP talks, and Indonesia, Japan, the Philippines, South Korea, and Thailand have expressed interest in joining. For those eleven countries, it will be easier to implement RCEP standards if they already have committed to more comprehensive TPP obligations. It is conceivable that, perhaps by the start of 2016, a majority of TPP and RCEP countries will be signatories of both pacts. The main outliers will be the United States and China.

8.4 WHITHER CHINA?

It is hard to conceive of a comprehensive Asia-Pacific trade arrangement that does not eventually include China. While China is currently not participating in the TPP negotiations, it is an ever-present concern of those countries that are crafting the trade pact or that seek to join the TPP talks.

TPP participants already have extensive trade and investment ties with China and expect those flows to increase markedly in the future. They also expect China to become involved in new trade talks with the TPP countries as they proceed toward the long-term APEC goal of free and open trade and investment in the Asia-Pacific region. China, in turn, has a vested interest in maintaining good access to TPP markets that, when countries that could well join the talks in the coming year (Japan and South Korea possibly in 2013) are included, account for more than 50 percent of Chinese merchandise exports and over 40 percent of its imports. It has committed to the regional trade integration strategy endorsed by APEC leaders; indeed, its participation is essential to the long-term viability of such an initiative.

In the short run, however, China is likely to pursue and deepen its ties with Asian neighbors before engaging with the TPP countries. Such restraint is basically due to China's political priorities as well as a lack of readiness and willingness to pursue a comprehensive trade accord. Contrary to the frequent accusations in public debate, I see little evidence to support the notion that China is being excluded as part of a broader containment strategy. But the continued talk of such a strategy requires a brief rebuttal.

By crafting a high-standard, 21st century trade accord that is far more comprehensive and legally binding than the trade arrangements forged among Asian countries, some observers have concluded that TPP participants deliberately want to set the bar very high in terms of FTA obligations in order to exclude China from their integration arrangement. Others take this argument further and claim that the United States is trying to keep China out of the TPP and is trying to "contain China" in order to retard its economic and political influence in the region. Charges that the United States seeks to "contain" China seem to ring true to those accustomed to hearing US officials berate unfair Chinese trade practices. US trade officials clearly prefer to talk about US trade enforcement actions against China—and will emphasize trade litigation even more now that the new Interagency Trade Enforcement Center is up and running—rather than including China in "free trade" talks in the Asia-Pacific region.

However, the containment thesis falls flat for several reasons. First, and most obviously, a trade agreement simply cannot "contain" a large country, either economically or politically. Second, US officials need a cooperative China to confront the myriad problems facing the world economy and the security challenges posed by Iran and North Korea as new and aspiring nuclear nations in Asia. The United States and China need to work together and therefore must manage the inevitable frictions that arise as the breadth and scope of their commercial relations expand. Third, no one else in Asia wants to contain China either. The trade and investment integration in the Asia-Pacific region achieved over the past few decades benefits all the TPP participants, even as it poses competitiveness challenges for their manufacturing industries. The proper response is to use trade arrangements, in conjunction with domestic economic reforms, to boost productivity of local industry and thereby be better positioned to compete against Chinese firms at home and abroad.

In any event, China is not ready to implement and enforce the types of obligations under construction in the TPP negotiations and thus the issue of blocking its entry to the talks is moot, for now. But the gap between China and the prospective TPP accord is not unbridgeable due to the extensive reforms undertaken pursuant to (1) China's WTO accession and (2) its participation in numerous preferential trading arrangements.

China's accession to the WTO required significant reforms; most have been implemented true to the letter if not the spirit of WTO obligations, though there have been notable disputes over Chinese subsidies and intellectual property policies. Nonetheless, its border barriers are less restrictive than most developing countries. But China is not ready to undertake TPP requirements with regard to the transparency of government policies that affects trade and investment; its opaque and often discriminatory domestic policies and regulations, its distortive production subsidies, and its management of its exchange rate are clear barriers to TPP entry.

China has concluded bilateral trade pacts with 4 of the 11 TPP participants (Chile, New Zealand, Peru, and Singapore), has a broader deal with the ASEAN members, and has negotiations in progress with Australia. To be sure, these FTAs are of varying quality in terms of the scope of coverage and depth of reforms, though the recent pact with New Zealand broadened coverage in services and included disciplines on a range of domestic policies. Going forward, the FTA negotiations with South Korea, which started in May 2012, should also propel Chinese reforms, even though the deal is unlikely to be as comprehensive as the Korean FTAs with the United States and the European Union. But this parallel initiative, as well as possible trilateral talks with Japan and South Korea, should help prepare China for more substantial ties with TPP signatories in the medium term.

Whether China ultimately opts to join the TPP as the pathway to APEC's long-sought FTAAP is still an open question. I suspect that China and the United States, each for its own political reasons and economic objectives, might pursue a hybrid approach that bridges elements of the TPP and intra-Asian approaches to trade integration. Such an arrangement could establish the FTAAP as an umbrella for the hard and soft integration pacts in the region and link the two economic powers without diluting the vitality of the TPP on trade and investment among its signatories.

In sum, China has made progress regarding convergence with prospective TPP norms. However, it still would need to implement significant trade and domestic policy reforms to be able to comply with the comprehensive set of obligations expected to be adopted by TPP signatories. It will not be ready to do so before the initial TPP accord is signed and implemented. But the expectation of most TPP participants is that, over the next decade or so, China will join the TPP partners in some broader Asia-Pacific trade regime that hastens the achievement of the APEC goal of an FTAAP.

8.5 PROSPECTIVE PAYOFFS FROM REGIONAL INTEGRATION

The United States and China stand to gain significantly from regional economic integration. Tables 8-5 and 8-6 summarize the prospective income and export gains from regional integration under the TPP track, the intra-Asian track and a hybrid approach as reported by Petri, Plummer and Zhai (2012). The TPP track includes the TPP in its current form (TPP 11) and a TPP 13, which includes Japan and South Korea in the agreement. The intra-Asian track describes the RCEP, or ASEAN + 6 approach, while the hybrid approach consolidates the TPP and intra-Asian tracks to cover all 21 APEC economies.

In the near term, the United States gains the most in terms of income and export gains, under the TPP 13 track and FTAAP hybrid tracks (see table 8-5). After an initial boost in income and exports, the positive effects of the TPP 13 remain relatively flat past 2020. On the other hand, the payoff of the FTAAP hybrid track grows substantially over time, increasing income by $267 billion and exports by $576 billion above the baseline scenario in 2025. The RCEP agreement has negligible effects on the US economy in the near term, though there would be minimal losses over the long-run.

If the TPP agreement is concluded — either with its current 11 members, or including Japan and South Korea — China would experience minor income and export losses in the near term; however, those losses would reach almost $50 billion in income and $60 billion in exports by 2025 (see table 8-6). Concluding the RCEP agreement will have negligible effects for China in the near term, but will significantly boost income and exports over the long run. Similar to the United States, China would see the largest gains from participating in a hybrid FTAAP. In the long run, the hybrid approach would boost China's exports by $1.5 trillion and increase its income by nearly $700 billion over the 2025 baseline.

8.6 THE PATHWAY TO THE FTAAP: A HYBRID APPROACH

The pathway to toward economic integration in the Asia-Pacific region is still uncertain. One of the most prominent options under review is the TPP. Some TPP architects envision building an eventual FTAAP on the comprehensive foundations of the TPP accord, with other APEC countries joining the pact in coming years through an accession process similar to that provided in the World Trade Organization (WTO) for new members. The clarity of the accession clause is its main attraction. In the WTO context, candidate countries negotiate protocols of accession, which codify their acceptance of existing WTO obligations and set out the scope and depth of trade liberalization that will be bound in their national schedules.

That said, the TPP is unlikely to be the template for a prospective FTAAP. As noted above, China and other big countries are likely to face significant obstacles in using the TPP accession process. Other APEC members may also be reluctant to follow the TPP script. No wonder that several options for crafting the FTAAP are still under review. As a practical matter, however, the two main integration arrangements in the APEC region — TPP and RCEP — will substantially inform the APEC debate. But neither is likely to command support across the region.

More likely, the pathway to an FTAAP will follow a hybrid approach that links together elements of the TPP and intra-Asian approaches to trade integration. Countries involved in both integration "tracks" could become key architects of a broader Asia-Pacific trade pact that bridges the intra-Asian and TPP-style disciplines.

Overlapping membership between the two regional integration schemes should make it easier to link the two in a hybrid arrangement providing free and trade and investment across the entire Asia-Pacific region. Under such a scenario, the hybrid pact — the FTAAP — would be an umbrella providing reciprocal obligations applying to all TPP and RCEP countries, while the more comprehensive and legally binding TPP provisions would remain in force among the TPP signatories. Importantly, the United States and China would deepen their commercial relationship without the strain of trying to fit China into the TPP or the cost of diluting the TPP to accommodate China.

A prospective middle ground between the TPP and RCEP approaches is beginning to evolve in recent initiatives taking shape in Northeast Asia. South Korea and China launched FTA talks in May 2012, and in 2013 a parallel negotiation between China, South Korea and Japan was launched. Although a bilateral or trilateral trade pact among these countries would comprise obligations far less comprehensive than those negotiated in the Korea-United States FTA, these initiatives could produce a deal in the large middle zone between the two sharply distinctive integration paths of the Asia-Pacific region. Korean officials assume that Chinese commitments will cover a broader range of trade and investment in goods and services than previous Chinese pacts with ASEAN, Chile, and New Zealand. For example, they point to the trilateral China-Japan-Korea (CJK) investment pact signed in May 2012 as evidence of Chinese willingness to commit in incremental steps to increasingly substantive economic reforms in regional trade pacts. If Japan is accepted as a participant in the TPP talks and Korea joins soon after, in addition to their new ventures with China, those Northeast Asian countries and their economic accords could become important drivers of both intra-Asian and Asia-Pacific arrangements.

In sum, closer US-China economic relations could well evolve over the coming decade in the context of broader Asia-Pacific economic integration. Both countries should continue to pursue comprehensive FTAs with their TPP and RCEP partners. Then, they should seek to bridge those new initiatives with an FTAAP that provides an umbrella of reciprocal obligations applying to all Asia-Pacific countries and to US-China trade.

References

[1] Petri, Peter A., Michael G. Plummer and Fan Zhai., 2012. The Trans-Pacific Partnership and Asia-Pacific Integration: A Quantitative Assessment. Policy Analyses in International Economics 98. Washington: Peterson Institute for International Economics.
[2] Schott, Jeffrey J., Barbara Kotschwar and Julia Muir., 2013. Understanding the Trans-Pacific Partnership. Policy Analyses in International Economics 99. Washington: Peterson Institute for International Economics.

Table 8-1   United States: bilateral FTA partners

Status [*]	FTA Partner	Agreement	US merchandise trade, 2011 (billion US $)			
			Exports to	Imports from	Trade balance	Total trade
A	Israel	US-Israel FTA (1985)	14.0	23.3	-9.3	37.2
A	Canada	US-Canada (1989), NAFTA (1994)	280.7	319.1	-38.4	599.8
A	Mexico	NAFTA (1994)	197.5	265.3	-67.8	462.9
A	Jordan	US-Jordan FTA (2001)	1.5	1.1	0.4	2.5
A,B	Chile	US-Chile FTA (2004), TPP (launched 2010)	15.9	9.7	6.1	25.6
A,B	Singapore	US-Singapore FTA (2004), TPP (launched 2010)	31.4	19.4	12.0	50.7
A,B	Australia	US-Australia FTA (2005), TPP (launched 2010)	27.5	10.4	17.2	37.9
A	Guatemala	DR-CAFTA (2006)	6.2	4.4	1.8	10.6
A	Honduras	DR-CAFTA (2006)	6.1	4.7	1.4	10.8
A	Nicaragua	DR-CAFTA (2006)	1.1	2.7	-1.6	3.7
A	El Salvador	DR-CAFTA (2006)	3.4	2.6	0.8	5.9
A	Bahrain	US-Bahrain FTA (2006)	1.2	0.5	0.7	1.8
A	Morocco	US-Morocco FTA (2006)	2.9	1.1	1.8	3.9
A	Oman	US-Oman FTA (2009)	1.4	2.3	-0.9	3.7
A,B	Peru	US-Peru FTA (2009), TPP (launched 2010)	8.3	6.5	1.8	14.9

Continued

Status*	FTA Partner	Agreement	US merchandise trade, 2011 (billion US $)			
			Exports to	Imports from	Trade balance	Total trade
A	Costa Rica	DR-CAFTA (2009)	6.1	10.4	−4.3	16.5
A	Colombia	US-Colombia FTA (2012)	14.3	23.7	−9.4	38.0
A	Dominican Republic	DR-CAFTA (2007)	7.3	4.3	3.0	11.7
A	Panama	US-Panama TPA (2012)	8.2	0.4	7.8	8.7
A	South Korea	KORUS FTA (2012)	43.5	58.6	−15.1	102.1
B	Brunei	TPP (launched 2010)	0.2	0.0	0.2	0.2
B	Malaysia	TPP (launched 2010)	14.2	26.5	−12.3	40.7
B	New Zealand	TPP (launched 2010)	3.5	3.3	0.2	6.8
B	Vietnam	TPP (launched 2010)	4.3	18.5	−14.1	22.8
Total			700.8	818.7	−117.9	1,519.5
US total trade with the world			1,298.8	2,262.6	−963.8	3,561.4
Total / US total trade (%)			54.0	36.2		42.7

Notes:
1. "A" denotes date of entry into force; "B" denotes the date negotiations were launched.
2. Totals are adjusted to avoid double counting of bilateral trade.

Sources: USTR, 2013, www. ustr. gov. ; IMF Direction of Trade Statistics, 2013.

Table 8-2　China's bilateral and regional trade agreements, as of March 2013

Status[a]	FTA partner	Agreement	Merchandise trade, 2011 (billions of US dollars)			
			Exports	Imports	Trade balance	Total trade
A	Association of South-east Asian Nations[b]	China-ASEAN (2005)	170.1	193.0	−22.9	363.1
A	Chile	China-Chile FTA (2006)	10.8	20.6	−9.8	31.4
A	Costa Rica	China-Costa Rica FTA (2011)	0.9	3.8	−2.9	4.7
A	Hong Kong	China-Hong Kong Closer Economic Partnership Agreement (2003)	268.0	15.5	252.5	283.5
A	Macao	China-Macao Closer Economic Partnership Agreement (2003)	2.4	0.2	2.2	2.6
A	New Zealand	China-New Zealand (2008)	3.7	5.0	−1.3	8.7
A	Pakistan	China-Pakistan FTA (2009)	8.4	2.1	6.3	10.5
A	Peru	China-Peru FTA (2010)	4.7	7.9	−3.2	12.6
A	Singapore	China-Singapore FTA (2009)	35.6	28.1	7.5	63.7
Subtotal			**469.0**	**248.1**	**220.9**	**717.1**
B	Australia	China-Australia FTA (2005)	33.9	82.7	−48.8	116.6
B	Gulf Cooperation Council[c]	China-GCC FTA (2004)	46.9	86.8	−40.0	133.7
B	Iceland	China-Iceland FTA (2007)	0.1	0.1	0.0	0.2
B	Japan, South Korea	China-Japan-Korea FTA (2013)	231.2	357.3	−126.1	588.5

Status[a]	FTA partner	Agreement	Merchandise trade, 2011 (billions of US dollars)			
			Exports	Imports	Trade balance	Total trade
B	South Korea	China-Korea FTA (2012)	82.9	162.7	-79.8	245.6
B	Norway	China-Norway FTA (2008)	3.8	3.6	0.2	7.4
B	South African Customs Union[d]	China-SACU FTA (2004)	14.4	32.4	-18.1	46.8
B	Switzerland	China-Switzerland FTA (2010)	3.7	27.3	-23.6	31.0
Subtotal			**333.9**	**590.3**	**-256.3**	**924.2**
C	ASEAN, Australia, India, Japan, Korea, New Zealand	Regional Comprehensive Economic Partnership (2012)	479.8	661.4	-181.6	1,141.2
C	India	China-India FTA (2003)	40.9	23.4	17.5	64.3
Subtotal			**479.8**	**661.4**	**-181.6**	**1,141.2**
Total			**843.8**	**861.8**	**-18.0**	**1,705.6**
Memorandum: China (world trade totals)			1,898.4	1,620.8	277.6	3,519.2

a. "A" denotes date of entry into force; "B" denotes the date negotiations were launched, and "C" denotes the date an agreement currently under consideration was proposed.

b. ASEAN comprises Brunei, Cambodia, Indonesia, Lao, Malaysia, Myanmar, Philippines, Singapore, Thailand and Vietnam.

c. GCC comprises Bahrain, Kuwait, Oman, Qatar, Saudi Arabia, and the United Arab Emirates.

d. SACU comprises Botswana, Lesotho, Namibia, South Africa, and Swaziland.

Note: subtotals are adjusted to avoid double counting of bilateral trade.

Sources: Ministry of Commerce of the People's Republic of China, 2012, http://english. mofcom. gov. cn; UNComtrade Database, 2012, http://comtrade. un. org.

149

Table 8-3 United States bilateral merchandise trade ($ billions)

Reporter	Trade partner	Trade flow	2000	2001	2002	2003	2004	2005	2006	2007	2008	2009	2010	2011
United States	China	Exports	15.3	18.0	20.6	26.7	32.6	38.9	51.6	61.0	67.2	65.1	85.7	96.9
		As a share of total US exports (%)	2.2	2.7	3.3	4.1	4.5	4.8	5.6	5.8	5.7	7.0	7.6	7.5
		Imports	107.6	109.4	133.5	163.3	210.5	259.8	305.8	340.1	356.3	309.5	383.0	417.3
		As a share of total US imports (%)	8.6	9.3	11.1	12.5	13.8	15.0	15.9	16.9	16.5	19.3	19.5	18.4
	TPP-11[1]	Exports	300.8	276.4	271.1	276.3	306.9	338.1	375.3	400.1	434.2	342.6	418.4	489.3
		As a share of total US exports (%)	42.2	41.5	43.1	42.4	42.1	42.1	40.4	38.2	37.1	36.6	37.3	37.7
		Imports	431.8	407.6	408.2	430.1	488.3	545.5	601.4	621.7	648.1	480.7	596.2	678.7
		As a share of total US imports (%)	34.3	34.5	34.0	33.0	32.0	31.5	31.3	30.8	29.9	30.0	30.3	30.0
	European Union	Exports	156.1	151.0	135.9	142.2	156.6	168.4	197.5	226.6	251.9	202.7	217.7	241.9
		As a share of total US exports (%)	21.9	22.7	21.6	21.8	21.5	20.9	21.2	21.7	21.5	21.6	19.4	18.6
		Imports	234.7	233.8	240.0	261.3	292.3	319.6	341.4	364.0	376.7	286.7	326.3	375.5
		As a share of total US imports (%)	18.7	19.8	20.0	20.0	19.2	18.5	17.8	18.0	17.4	17.9	16.6	16.6
	World	Exports	712.2	666.0	629.6	651.3	728.3	804.0	929.4	1,046.2	1,169.6	936.5	1,121.8	1,298.8
		Imports	1,258.1	1,180.1	1,202.3	1,305.1	1,525.3	1,732.3	1,919.0	2,017.1	2,164.8	1,601.9	1,966.5	2,262.6

1 TPP-11 excludes Brunei due to the unavailability of data, and the United States.

Note: Imports are reported on a cost, insurance, freight (CIF) basis, while exports are reported as free on board (FOB).

Source: World Integrated Trade Solutions, 2013, http://wits. worldbank. org.

Table 8-4 Chinese bilateral merchandise trade ($ billions)

Reporter	Trade partner	Trade flow	2000	2001	2002	2003	2004	2005	2006	2007	2008	2009	2010	2011
China	United States	Exports	52.2	54.4	70.1	92.6	125.1	163.2	203.8	233.2	252.8	221.3	283.8	325.0
		As a share of total Chinese exports (%)	20.9	20.4	21.5	21.1	21.1	21.4	21.0	19.1	17.7	18.4	18.0	17.1
		Imports	22.4	26.2	27.3	33.9	44.7	48.7	59.3	69.5	81.6	77.8	102.7	123.1
		As a share of total Chinese imports (%)	10.3	11.2	9.7	3.8	8.6	8.1	8.3	8.0	7.8	8.5	8.0	7.6
	TPP-11[1]	Exports	71.3	75.3	97.8	128.4	175.3	228.4	291.7	350.1	391.1	347.0	444.7	519.9
		As a share of total Chinese exports (%)	28.6	28.3	30.0	29.3	29.6	30.0	30.1	28.7	27.3	28.9	28.2	27.4
		Imports	45.6	51.3	58.4	77.3	107.0	122.4	142.6	175.3	209.6	207.6	295.8	372.2
		As a share of total Chinese imports (%)	20.9	21.8	20.8	19.9	20.5	20.2	19.9	20.1	20.2	22.6	22.9	23.0
	European Union	Exports	41.1	44.6	53.0	79.0	108.6	145.6	190.0	245.6	293.4	236.4	311.4	356.2
		As a share of total Chinese exports (%)	16.5	16.7	16.3	18.0	18.3	19.1	19.6	20.1	20.5	19.7	19.7	18.8
		Imports	31.3	36.4	39.8	55.0	70.5	74.0	90.6	111.0	132.6	127.8	168.4	211.2
		As a share of total Chinese imports (%)	14.4	15.5	14.2	14.2	13.5	12.2	12.6	12.8	12.8	13.9	13.1	13.0
	World	Exports	249.2	266.1	325.6	458.2	593.3	762.0	968.9	1,220.1	1,430.7	1,201.7	1,577.8	1,898.4
		Imports	217.9	234.8	280.2	387.7	522.6	604.8	718.1	870.3	1,040.1	919.1	1,289.1	1,620.8

1 TPP-11 excludes Brunei due to the unavailability of data.

Note: Imports are reported on a cost, insurance, freight (CIF) basis, while exports are reported as free on board (FOB).

Source: World Integrated Trade Solutions, 2013, http://wits. worldbank. org.

Table 8-5   United State's prospective income and export gains

	2015		2020		2025	
	$ billion	Share (%)	$ billion	Share (%)	$ billion	Share (%)
Income gains:						
TPP 11	2.5	0	17.6	0.1	23.9	0.1
TPP 13	7.8	0	58.8	0.3	77.5	0.4
RCEP	0	0	-1.6	0	-0.1	0
FTAAP hybrid	7.9	0	59.6	0.3	266.5	1.3
Export gains:						
TPP 11	8.4	0.4	50.3	2.1	54.8	1.9
TPP 13	17.0	0.9	118.6	5.1	124.2	4.4
RCEP	0	0	-3.4	-0.1	-3.7	-0.1
FTAAP hybrid	18	0.9	119.5	5.1	575.9	20.5

Source: Petri, Plummer and Zhai, 2013, www. asiapacifictrade. org.

Notes:

1. All figures in constant 2007 dollars.

2. Income gains include FDI effects.

3. Export gains indicate a change in exports.

4. TPP 13 includes the current 11 members plus Japan and Korea.

5. RCEP = ASEAN + 6.

6. FTAAP hybrid = consolidation of the TPP and Asian tracks to cover all 21 APEC economies.

Table 8-6   China's prospective income and export gains

	2015		2020		2025	
	$ billion	Share (%)	$ billion	Share (%)	$ billion	Share (%)
Income gains:						
TPP 11	-1.6	0.0	-12.4	-0.1	-20.2	-0.1
TPP 13	-2.4	0.0	-27.6	-0.2	-46.8	-0.3
RCEP	0.0	0.0	94.4	0.8	249.7	1.4
FTAAP hybrid	13.0	0.2	86.4	0.7	678.1	3.9
Export gains:						
TPP 11	-2.7	-0.1	-20.6	-0.6	-24.9	-0.5
TPP 13	-4.4	-0.2	-47.2	-1.4	-57.4	-1.2
RCEP	0.0	0.0	358.8	10.7	638.3	13.9
FTAAP hybrid	83.9	3.5	310.9	9.2	1,505.3	32.7

Source: Petri, Plummer and Zhai, 2013, www. asiapacifictrade. org.

Notes:

1. All figures in constant 2007 dollars.

2. Income gains include FDI effects.

3. Export gains indicate a change in exports.

4. TPP 13 includes the current 11 members plus Japan and Korea.

5. RCEP = ASEAN +6.

6. FTAAP hybrid = consolidation of the TPP and Asian tracks to cover all 21 APEC economies.

(Jeffrey J. Schott, Peterson Institute for International Economics, Washington D. C. US)

CHAPTER 9   ON NORMATIVE DUALISM

— Some Preliminary Thoughts on Chinese Approaches to Order and Disputes

Yu Xingzhong

Abstract: Using one system of norms to positively maintain order but another system of norms to eliminate chaos is basically, one of essential, Chinese traits. This can be described as normative dualism. The dualist practice has been proven to have a long-lasting influence. Though it originated more than three thousand years ago, dualism is still being cherished in contemporary China after a series of revolutions and reforms. Unfortunately, in the normative framework, laws are submissive to those unwritten rules. This paper discusses this feature of Chinese normative system by examining its phenomenological attributes, which separate "*Li*" from "*Xing*", and its profound philosophical foundation of dialecticism that distinguishes *Yin* from *Yang*, namely the positive from the negative and right from wrong. The paper has three parts: the first part lays a foundation for the discussion of normative dualism; the second part explains the idea of normative dualism and its Chinese representation, while the last part discusses the judge-centered legal mentality that reinforces the normative dualism.

9.1 INTRODUCTION

Using one system of norms to positively maintain order but another system of norms to eliminate chaos is basically, one of essential Chinese traits. This can be described as normative dualism. To many, this Chinese practice simply does not make sense because of the redundant nature of it, as judging based on their own cultures. The dualist practice has been proven to have a long-lasting influence. Though it originated more than three thousand years ago, dualism is still being cherished in contemporary China after a series of revolutions and reforms. It is not a secret that despite the set of laws, regulations procedures and rules borrowed from the West, Chinese society is regulated, but by numerous internal instructions, policies and speeches of the Communist Party and its leaders, rather than public announcements. The new dualism does not significantly differ from the old one in essence. The difference is that the New *Li* (internal decisions, policies, etc.) has replaced the Old Li and the New *Fa* (law) has replaced the Old Fa. Unfortunately, in the normative framework, laws are submissive to those unwritten rules.

This paper discusses the feature of Chinese normative system by examining its phenomenological attributes, which separate "*Li*" from "*Xing*" and its profound philosophical foundation of dialecticism that distinguishes *Yin* from *Yang*, namely positive from negative and right from wrong.

9.2 MORALIZATION OF LAW

Unlike Jewish people who have successfully constructed their communities according to the beliefs revealed by the Yahweh and illustrated by Moses, which stressed the nourishment of soul — the highest of human faculties, or the modern Westerners since the Papal revolution who went through such earth-shaking changes as the Renaissance, the Reformation, Enlightenment and Bourgeois Revolutions, in which rationality — the most fundamental of the human faculties — finally triumphed in every corner of society. Chinese people, as not being enlightened by the holy light, are those whose "soul" has never been cultivated by a prophet,'[1] or saved for utilitarian rationality, eventrally push themselves into pursuit of cultivation of heart — the middle level of human faculties — and social harmony. The nourishment of the soul introduces a religious social framework where religion supreme, and laws are commandments that existed along with morality which echoed sacred teachings. Over the past thousands of years, This did not occur in China. In fact, reliance on rationality led to a legal social framework where law replaced religion as the supreme criterion, with morality revolving around legal values such as rights and obligations; the pursuit of cultivation of the heart produced a moral social framework where morality was predominant and directly addressed work, communication and exchange. Laws become mere punishments while religion is left to the darkest corner and reduced to superstition and ancestor worship.

Laws, as product of human rationality, have three forms: 1) inchoate and intuitive manifestn of the normative dimension of rationality, embodied by sporadic and contingent rule-making and rule-observing behavior, usually termed customary law, 2) systemized knowledge of rules backed up by coercive power and 3) the legal civil order in which law reigns.

None of these forms of law, however, can adequately describe the place of law in the Chinese moral civil order. Chinese law, as the moralized law, resembles laws with inchoate and intuitive manifestation of rationality as well as systematized knowledge of rules, but does not comfortably fit in either.

Law in the Chinese moral civil order tended to be subordinate to morality and thus the law was, moralized. The moralization of law means that law is substantively informed by morality and that the role of law is secondary to the role of morality in social, political and economic activities. In terms of dispute resolution, mediation, instead of litigation, was widely used in traditional China. Traditionally, Confucian ideology extos non-confrontational nature of community life and discourages litigation. Confucius said, "In hearing cases, I am as good as others, but the best

---

[1]　See Max Weber, THE RELIGION OF CHINA, translated by Hans H. Gerth, (New York: The Free Press 1951) p. 142.

situation is not to have any lawsuits at all. "[1] Confronted with disputes, gentlemen were encouraged to yield, not to pursue their interest. Because to do so would disturb social harmony. That was probably due to the fact that most Chinese lived in closed communities scattered around the country. Government officials, village elders, relatives and friends were all potential mediators. When a dispute occurred, the first resort was mediation and litigation would be brought as the last resort only when mediation failed. In Almost all types of cases, including property disputes, divorces and sales, and even minor criminal cases, could be dealt with through mediation. Very often a dispute would follow the simple process beginning with private settlement, and if that fails to solve it, mediation by village elders would follow; if that also fails, the case would be brought to the magistrate's court for mediation.

When the People's Republic of China (PRC) came into being in 1949, attempts were made to abandon China's traditional culture and institutions, but mediation was kept alive for solving contradictions among the people and for political and social control purposes. People's mediators and people's mediation committees were introduced to do the job. Under the dispute resolution framework established by the PRC government, mediation is carried out according to certain principles. These principles including lawfulness, voluntariness and equality of the parties whose rights to sue are protected. Types of mediation include mediation by grassroots governments, the people's mediation committees, mass organizations such as enterprise, trade unions, institutions and women's federations, and grassroots legal service institutions. Most mediation cases are carried out in five steps: accepting disputes, making preparations for investigation, carrying out the mediation, reaching an agreement and implementing the agreement. While mediation has many advantages, such as being inexpensive, non-confrontational and flexible, it also has drawbacks. For instance, it is not rights-oriented, accommodates external influence, and non-final. Very often the demarcation between right and wrong is blurred and when mediation fails, problems become even more serious and difficult to address.

---

[1] Confucius, *Analects*.

9.3   NORMATIVE DUALISM

From Han Dynasty (206 B. C. — 220 A. D.) onward, Confucianism became the only influential legal ideology, and law and legal ideas were transformed in terms of Confucian values. The Confucianization of law from the Han fostered a distinctive mode of legal thinking that was a synthesis of previously existed views of different schools of thought. That mode of legal thinking was traditionally called the fusion of Rites and law. It had been the only legal ideology in imperial China.

At the institutional level, one striking feature of the Chinese moral civil order is the use of both *Li* (Rites) and *Fa* (law) to embody and safeguard central values of the conceptual categories of that civil order. Perhaps the single important difference between Western and Chinese legal traditions can be characterized as the following: in the West, both order and disorder are dealt with by one coercive external system of norms. Law in the West both protects and punishes. Whereas in China law was designed as a negative force to punish disorder while the glorious task of maintaining order was given to *Li*. "*Li* prohibits while law punishes."[1] The Tang Code made this quite clear by saying that "morality and Rites are roots for governance while law and punishments are instruments for governance."[2] Using a system of norms to positively maintain order but another system of norms to negatively punish disorder is a unique Chinese experience. Many western scholars misunderstood China because they were not ready to accept this difference. For them that unique Chinese experience simply does not make sense because of the redundant nature of it, judged from the point of view of their own cultural traditions. This needs further clarification.

During the formative years of the Chinese moral civil order, two things were

---

[1]   *See* Sima, Qian and trans. Watson, Burton, RECORDS OF THE GRAND HISTORIAN: HAN DYNASTY. (Research Center for Translation, The Chinese University of Hong Kong and Columbia University Press 1993).

[2]   *See* TANGLU SHUYI, Partial English translation see Johnson, Wallace, trans., The Tang Code: Volume One: General Principles. (Princeton: Princeton University Press 1979).

considered important for the state craftsmanship: sacrificial ceremonies and military endeavors. It is from these two important activities that *Li* and *Fa* were respectively originated.

There is no doubt that the first group of *Li* was sacrificial rituals. ① As sacrificial activities were often conducted by aristocrats, *Li* gradually evolved into norms for aristocratic interactions. By Zhou dynasty, *Li* became fairly detailed rules governing not only behaviors of aristocrats but also commoners. Because of this, some scholars call Zhou dynasty a period ruled by *Li*.

Concurrently, as recorded in many historical sources, *Fa*, or rather its earliest form *Xing*, originated from war. This can be seen in three ways. First, the word *Xing* was used to denote both war and punishments. According to Zuo Zhuan, Shang Shu and other sources, *Xing* was used to refer to wars among the tribes, very often on prisoners of war or to punish rebels. Then it was used by the ancestors of the Han people to deter minority tribes. (de yi rou zhongguo, xing yi wei si yi) (Zuo Zhuan, xigong 25 nian) One contemporary historian, Lu Simian supported this latter point. He said, "*Xing* was created to cope with foreign tribes. " ② Second, the official who was responsible for legal affairs was also responsible for military affairs.

---

① The Chinese character Li signifies a sacrificial ceremony and much of ZHOU LI concerns rituals. Thus, Radcliffe-Brown firmly believed that Li was some kind of religion. Max Weber talked very little about Li. By contrast, Unger's discussion of Li is far more detailed and interesting. He is partially correct in saying that Li stands for abstract principles, rather than specific rules. For the term Li usually refers to three things: ZHOU LI, YI LI, and LI JI. ZHOU LI, also known as ZHOU GUAN, is a collection of institutes of the Zhou Dynasty, something like an administrative code in the modern sense. It recorded the responsibilities and powers of the offices of six major governmental departments, the head of which were called ministers of Heaven, Earth, Spring, Summer, Autumn and Winter. The Autumn minister was the one charged with the responsibility of adjudication. YI LI represents mainly norms for interactions among princes and ministers and other aristocrats, which contained 17 chapters with specific rules concerning greeting, copulation, marriage, hunting, funerals, drinking and imperial tributes. LI JI, sometimes called the philosophy of Li discusses ideas, principles and standards of Li and the ways through which a gentleman attains his internal refinement. Li in this sense is abstract and Unger is correct on this point. *See* RADCLIFFE-BROWN, STRUCTURE AND FUNCTION IN PRIMITIVE SOCIETY add page numbers that correspond with Chapters VII and VIII (New York: The Free Press 1965). *See* ROBERTO UNGER, LAW IN MODERN SOCIETY 93-96 (The Free Press1976).

② *See* LU SIMIAN, ZHONGGUO TONGSHI (A GENERAL HISTORY OF CHINA) (Kaiming Shuju, 1944).

The legendary Chi You who was blamed for making five punishments, and Gao Yao, the super judge, were such person. Third, the early instruments for punishing criminals were weapons used in war.

The separation of *Xing* from War is believed to have something to do with the prisoners of war during that time. Large numbers of prisoners were turned into slaves of the Han people and *Xing* was used on them. Although they were slaves, they no longer belonged to tribes for whom war was still effective.

This difference of the origin of *Li* and *Fa* is of great significance for understanding why there were two systems of behavioral norms in China. It also makes the so-called transformation era in the Warring States period meaningless in terms of the normative order. Essentially, *Li* was used to maintain order, the major participants of which were aristocrats and Han people, while *Fa* was mainly used to punish disorder, the causes of which were either other tribes or slaves.

The ancient Chinese developed a concept called *Yin/Yang*, which is a belief that there exist two complementary forces in the universe. One is *Yang* which represents everything positive or masculine and the other is *Yin*, which is characterized as negative or feminine. One is not better than the other. Instead, they are both necessary and a balance of them is highly desirable.

This thinking is different from the duality of most religion where one state overcomes the other e. g. good over evil. In the concept of *Yin/Yang*, too much of either one is bad. The ideal is a balance of both.

It was believed that the Yellow Emperor once said "Heaven was created by the concentration of *Yang*, the force of light; earth was created by the concentration of *Yin*, the forces of darkness. *Yang* stands for peace and serenity; *Yin* stands for confusion and turmoil. *Yang* stands for destruction; *Yin* stands for conservation. *Yang* brings about disintegration; *Yin* gives shape to things..." (From Huangdi Neijing)

The *Yin/Yang* doctrine served as the philosophical foundation of many branches of learning and institutions, including normative institutions. In Han dynasty Dong Zhongshu (179—104 BC), the main architect of Confucianism after Confucius and the ideological orthodox of imperial China, incorporated the *Yin/Yang* doctrine into his Confucian theory and legitimized the place of *Yin/Yang* in Chinese official doctrines and ideology.

He specifically said this when discussing the roles of *De* and *Xing*: "The Law of Heaven and Earth resides in *Yin* and *Yang*; *Yang* is the virtue (*De*) of Heaven while *Yin* is the punishment (*Xing*) of Heaven." (*Yin Yang Yi*, in *Chun Qiu Fanlu*) "Spring and summer belong to *Yang* and it is the time to practice governance by virtue; autumn and winter belong to *Yin* and it is the time to carry out punishments." (Sishi Zhifu)

9.4   MIXED FORMS OF LAW

Moralization of law can also be seen from forms of law the Chinese moral civil order stressed. Some people think that ancient China only had statutory laws and that no case law ever existed. In fact, it might be more accurate to say that ancient China had mixed forms of law. By mixed forms of law I mean two things. First, all branches of law are arranged in one single comprehensive code, rather than in separate laws. *Fa Jin*, which was the first comprehensive code of China and allegedly compiled by Li Kui in Warring States period, contained six chapters of rules covering substantive and procedural laws. The Tang Code (653 A. D.) had 12 chapters incorporating 502 articles, including laws governing matrimonial matters, granary management and trial procedures. *Da Qing Lu Li* had 30 chapters incorporating 436 articles and 1047 sub statutes. It made no distinction between substantive and procedural laws.

Secondly, mixed forms of law also mean that statutory law is not the only form of Chinese law. Apart from statutes, there were also officially approved cases which had same and sometimes even higher legal effect as statutory law. In the West Zhou and Spring and Autumn period the practice of adjudication was summarized as being dependent on "exemplary stories rather than laws." In the West Han Dynasty, there were those famous cases "decided according to the classics." In subsequent dynasties, there were *Jueshibi*, *Gushi*, *Fali*, *Duanli* and *Li*. All these contributed to the continuity of case law as part of the Chinese legal tradition. Because the exemplary cases were usually approved by the emperors, they were more important and effective than statutory laws. That is why "following the exemplary case instead of law" became one of the principles of adjudication.

Moralization of law is also reflected in the legal institutions. Chinese legal systems have been known as having no independence from political and administrative manipulation. ① Not only is it characterized by lack of autonomous legal courts which administered law exclusively, but also by the non-existence of a legal profession which specialized in prosecution and defense on behalf of the parties involved. The dynastic judicial systems coincided exactly with the levels of bureaucracy, which was a hierarchy of ascending importance from county courts at the bottom through prefectural and provincial courts in the middle to the central judicial organs in the capital at the top. The administrative officials of different ranks served as judges of the different levels. The principle adopted was that the more serious the offense, the more important the body with the power of final disposition②.

This type of judicial system, that is, the bureaucratic hierarchy where administrators were concurrently judges had two implications on the legal process. First, lack of independence also meant that participation in the legal process was open to all bureaucratic officials. In fact, every imperial official was a possible source of justice for commoners. Although only certain officials were endowed with the power to adjudicate, all officials were responsible for keeping harmony and ensuring the administration of justice. Therefore, if one felt wronged, he could always find a proper or alternative authority to which he could appeal. Substantively, the Chinese legal system reflected a profound mistrust of the notion that rules and procedures could guarantee justice, which in turn reflected a justified mistrust of the capacity of

---

① *See generally* D. BODDDE & C. MORRIS, LAW IN IMPERIAL CHINA (1967); Geoffrey MacCormack, TRADITIONAL CHINESE PENAL LAW(Edinburgh University Press 1990).

② *See* WILLIAM ALFORD, *Of Arsenic and Old Laws: Looking Anew at Criminal Justice in Late Imperial China*, 72 CALIFORNIA LAW REVIEW1180 (1984); WEJEN CHANG, QINGDAI FAZHI YANJIU, (Institute of History and Philology Academia Sinica 1983).

human beings to properly administer justice at all in this world. Yet, the Chinese regarded truth as unitary and knowable; the search for truth was not limited to available procedures and means. Professor Randle Edwards noted that "the reluctance of China's rulers to enforce statutory limits on legal review reflects a sense that genuine justice should be served at whatever cost to administrative regularity and efficiency."[1] Therefore, sometimes the search for justice involved looking beyond this world. In many Chinese courtroom dramas and tales, we find the administration of justice extended to the world of deities and the world of ghosts and souls.[2] The lessons of these courtroom stories are obvious: justice can be sought not only on earth, but also high above in Heaven, and under the earth in the world of ghosts and souls. Wherever it may be, justice must be and will be served if someone is seriously wronged.

9.5　JUDGE-CENTERED LEGAL MENTALITY AND THE ENFORCEMENT OF NORMATIVE DUALISM

Moralization of law is also reflected in the judge-centered legal mentality. As morality cannot be independent of its ontological carrier, the best way to see it at work is to have it embodied in somebody's actions and words. Therefore, concern for a typical moral man became the obsession of the moral civil order. With regard to the legal system, expectation of a just moral judge-official ran higher than expectation of a rational legal procedure. From the legendary ancient judge Gao Yao to one-time judge Confucius and to the well-respected Bao Zhen in Song Dynasty, the Chinese

---

① *See* RANDLE EDWARDS, "Civil and Social Rights: Theory and Practice in Chinese Law Today" in HUMAN RIGHTS IN CONTEMPORARY CHINA, edited by Randle R. Edwards, Louis Henkin and Andrew J. Nathan (New York: Columbia University Press 1986).

② *See generally* Ching-Hsi Perng, DOUBLE JEOPARDY: A CRITIQUE OF SEVEN YUAN COURTROOM DRAMAS (The University of Michigan1978); GEORGE A. HAYDEN, CRIME AND PUNISHMENT IN MEDIEVAL CHINESE DRAMA: THREE JUDGE PAO PLAYS (Harvard University Press 1978).

gambled their stake of justice on the "blue Heaven"① type of judges, showing little enthusiasm in the implementation of the rational legal procedure.

The "blue Heaven" type judges were not tightly bound by specific rules. Trained in the literary classics and traditional moral principles, they served the emperor by performing the designated responsibilities of their training. General knowledge of existing law was compulsory for them. In the Han, Tang and Song dynasties, a legal examination was part of the imperial examination and the ability to write a good judicial decision was one of the four standards for selecting officials②. These judges, although not very concerned about the legal process, did have guidelines for adjudication: they were bound by time honored moral principles to which both the ruling class and the ruled subscribed. They were expected to investigate cases personally, to be able to tell even slightest differences in the merits and twists of subtle cases. But for them the authoritative ideal was not the "rule of law" but "the rule of virtue."

Western legal systems are usually portrayed as being an autonomous legal order which includes methodological autonomy. Methodological autonomy refers to a distinctively legal mode of reasoning or analysis that characterizes the legal process. While the very existence of such a mode of legal reasoning is now being questioned by critical legal scholars in the United States, the Chinese never had the slightest notion of it. Although works like *Yi Yu Ji*, *Tang Yin Bi Shi*, and *Mingong Shupan Qinminji* discussed the valuable experience of the trial method and processes and stressed methodological and logical significance, traditional Chinese magistrates and legal authorities failed to imagine any mode of legal reasoning different from common sense deduction or induction.

Model judges in ancient China did not have an autonomous legal method and their reasoning was more ethical than legal. In making a judicial decision they might not only rely on the black letter law. They had to take into consideration many factors

---

① "Blue Heaven" was a term adopted by the populace to address righteous officials who were responsible for adjudication.

② *See supra* note 5 at 700-703, 705-707.

including the conventional moral standards, the interest of parties involved, and even the natural environment. Their adjudicative method may best be summarized as a way of practical reasoning. This way of judicial decision-making gave a judge more discretion. In making decisions the judges relied more heavily on their wisdom, learning and experience and other substantive factors than on formal and procedural requirements. For that reason, ancient Chinese justice was labeled "Solomonic" Cadi-justice[1].

Here is a story widely known in China which has subtle connection with Solomonic justice. Two women claimed to be the mother of a child. The case was brought to a clever judge who was going to decide to whom the child should belong. After hearing both women's accounts of their own stories, the judge thought for a little while and said, "Honestly, I cannot tell which of you is the real mother. Why don't you two have a tug-of-wall game, see who wins and the winner will have the child. Then a circle was drawn on the court floor. The child was placed within the circle and the two alleged mothers stood by either side of the child and each grabbed an arm of the child. The tug-of-wall began. Suddenly a woman cried out and let go the child's arm. Obviously she lost her game, but the judge decided that she was the real mother. Why? Because the real mother could not bear to see her child suffering. So she let go the child's arm. Even if the woman is not the real mother, the decision is still a right one because it is certainly desirable to put a helpless child under the care of a kind-hearted woman than in the hands of a cruel one.

Model judges in China were not those who strictly applied the law or observed the procedures, but those who made the best use of their intelligence to find criminals and to redress wrongs. The judge's wisdom and imagination solved cases. For instance, in the Tang dynasty, in one case a mother sued the son for not being dutiful. The law stipulated that punishment for an undutiful son was death or life imprisonment. This undutiful son was the only child of the accusing woman. Imprisonment of the son would leave the woman without anyone to care for her, a

---

[1] *See* MAX WEBER, *supra* note 1 at 102, 149.

circumstance against humanity. But paying no attention to the woman's accusation was not lawfully right. The judge finally sentenced the son to imprisonment, — imprisonment in his own home to serve his mother[1]. The following case recorded in Zheng Ke's Mirrors for Adjudication may better illustrate the method of practical reasoning[2].

In the Western Han dynasty, a wealthy man had an undutiful daughter and a toddler son. When he was dying, the wealthy man made his will, leaving all his property to his daughter, but only a sword to the son. The will made it clear that because the son was too young to have the sword at the moment it should remain in the daughter's custody until the son reached fifteen years of age. When the son reached fifteen, he asked for the sword, but his sister refused to give it to him. The son then brought a suit to the Prefect He Wu. Having read the will and investigated the case, He Wu reasoned thusly:

"The woman being undutiful and her husband greedy, the young son's life itself was even in danger, let alone having the property inherited, therefore the property was given to the daughter and her husband just let them take care of it. The sword is but a token. When the boy reached fifteen, he would have intelligence enough to be himself. The father knew that the daughter and the son-in-law would not give the son the sword, which would end up with the involvement of government officials who would see justice done eventually. How far thinking this old man was!"[3]

Accordingly, the property and the sword were returned to the son. In this case, the judge decided against the black letters of the wills by relying on his own understanding of human feelings and sentiments, namely by practical reasoning. For them, what was important was not to carry out the will as it was written, but to see justice done for the weak and the young. When rules and laws hindered the judge's

---

[1] *See* 10 MINGGONG SHUPAN QINGMING JI (A Collection of Fine Decisions by Renowned Song Judges) (Zhonghua Shuju 1987).

[2] The case was quoted and discussed in LIANG ZHIPING, FAYI YU RENQING (THE SPIRIT OF LAW AND HUMAN SENTIMENTS) 149-154 (Haitian Publishing House 1992).

[3] The case was quoted and discussed in LIANG ZHIPING, FAYI YU RENQING (THE SPIRIT OF LAW AND HUMAN SENTIMENTS) 149-154 (Haitian Publishing House 1992). at 150.

pursuit for justice, the judge was expected to have discretion over the cases. In short, a blue-Heaven type judge was not ultimately concerned with law, but with justice.

This reminds us of Ronald Dworkin's Herculean judge[1]. A Herculean judge, when confronted with hard cases, makes his decisions according to his understanding of history, moral tradition and legal principles of society. A Herculean judge believes that there is a consistency between the legal culture and moral principles of a society and it is his duty to find out that consistency by which he can discard wrong precedents and follow the correct ones in his decision making. A Herculean judge knows how to choose among possible competing solutions to a hard case based on competing legal theories and political moralities. He is a discretionary judge, but he is not totally unbridled — he is bound by his duty to remain faithful to the past, and his acceptance of the non-rule standards derived from legal theory, political morality, culture and social ideals of his community[2].

Clearly, we see striking similarities between a blue-heaven judge and a Herculean judge. Both are discretionary, but bound by larger concerns of morality, tradition and culture. Both are concerned about finding out correct answers to difficult problems more than merely following whatever is available as legal rules. Both are flexible, pragmatic, and concerned with ultimate justice. We should not, however, get carried away by these similarities as to fail to acknowledge more fundamental differences between the two. Hercules as an independent and professional judge works quite differently in a highly complex legal system from a blue-heaven judge who was primarily a bureaucrat working in a network of literati officials. A blue-heaven judge is in no way as committed to justice and law as a Herculean judge is because his many other obligations prevent him from being so.

(Yu Xingzhong, Anthony W. and Lulu C. Wang, Professor in Chinese Law, Law School, Cornell University, US)

---

[1] See RONALD DWORKIN, *Hard Cases*, *in*, TAKING RIGHTS SERIOUSLY 81-132 (Harvard University Press 1977).

[2] Ibid.

CHAPTER 10　How Labor Market Developments Affected Labor Costs in China?[①]

Wenlang Zhang and Gaofeng Han

Abstract: Labor markets in China have experienced remarkable changes in the past decade. In this paper we use above-scale industrial firm-level data of 2001-2008 to study how labor market developments have affected labor costs of firms across regions, and different levels of technology and ownership in China. Our estimates suggest that, labor market tightness has had some impact on the labor costs of Hong KongMacau-Taiwan (HMT) firms and private enterprises, particularly in coastal arcas, but ovcrall the impact is limited. Our research also shows that labor migration has had some impact on the labor costs and employment of HMT and private firms in East China.

　　Our analysis suggests that China has not yet seen an absolute shortage of labor, but there have been structural problems in the labor market. Demand for young low-end workers and skilled workers has outpaced supply, while the opposite is true for

---

　　①　The authors thank Dong He for his guidance, Junsen Zhang and the participants of the seminar at the People's Bank of China and the Hong Kong Institute for Monetary Research 4th Conference of the Chinese Economy for their thoughtful comments. Errors are our own. The views of this paper only those of the authors and do not necessarily represent the views of the Hong Kong Monetary Authority.

better educated workers such as young college graduates. As the majority of the employees of HMT and private enterprises are at the low-education end, wage pressures for these firms have increased accordingly. As such, it is necessary to remove the barriers that hinder rural labor forces from working in urban areas and to develop vocational and technical education. It is also useful to upgrade production chains to reduce the relative demand for low-end workers and increase that for better-educated workers to reduce skill mismatch in labor markets.

Keywords: Labor market tightness, Labor migration, Labor costs.

10.1 INTRODUCTION

China's labor market has experienced remarkable changes in the past decade. First of all, as shown in Figure 10-1, total working-age population has been growing at a decelerated pace and is expected to start declining in 2017 according to projections by the United Nations, while the young working-age population (15-29 years old) is expected to start shrinking in 2012[1]. Secondly, while China experienced a "flood of migrant workers" and substantial underemployment in state-owned enterprises (SOEs) in the 1990s, in recent years, there have been reports of shortages of labor, particularly in coastal areas. Minimum wages have been rising at a fast pace from an average of RMB368 in 2005 to RMB1060 in 2011. The aggregate demand for labor was lower than supply in cities before 2010, but has outpaced supply in recent years, with the demand-to-supply ratio rising steadily to above unity in 2011 (Figure 10-2). A survey by the National Bureau of Statistics (NBS) also shows that migrant workers' wages increased significantly, by about 21% on average in 2011, while cross-province migrant workers have accounted for a progressively declining share of total migrant workers in recent years. This suggests more workers prefer to work in inland provinces (the major source of migrant workers), reducing the supply of labor in coastal areas in relative terms.

---

① According to the NBS, the working-age population (15-59 years old) started to decline in 2012.

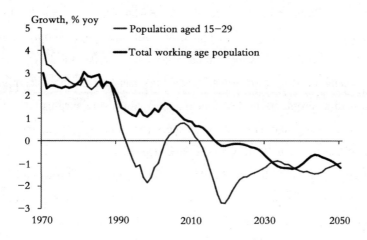

Figure 10-1　Working-age Population

Sources: CEIC and United Nations.

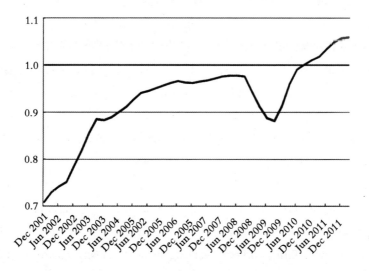

Figure 10-2　Labor Demand-Supply Ratio

Source: CEIC.

Against this backdrop, some commentators have argued that China has moved from a period of unlimited labor supply to a new era of labor shortage. For instance, Cai et al. (2007) argue that China passed the Lewis turning point as early as in 2004, while Cai (2010) and Cai and Wang (2008) also claim that there is no more surplus labor in China. On the other hand, Kwan (2009) and the International Monetary Fund (IMF, 2012) argue that China still has ample supply of labor, and the IMF (2012) further argues that China is unlikely to reach the Lewis turning point until 2020. Meng (2012) also argues that China has surplus labor supply, but that there are structural problems in the labor market that prevent surplus labor from being fully employed. Wang and Hu (2012) expect the labor supply in the non-farming sector to continue to grow steadily in the next decade.

Accordingly, discussions on the driving forces of wage growth in China have been inconclusive. Cai et al. (2007) ascribe rising migrant wages to labor shortages, while Li et al. (2012) argue that wage growth in China has been driven by improvements in labor productivity and demographic transition, but that wage pressures will rise along with shrinking demographic dividends going forward. On the other hand, Ge and Yang (2011), based on urban household survey data, find that wage growth has been mainly driven by improvements in human capital and external demand, while the migrant labor supply has not had a significant impact on wages.

The inconclusive nature of these studies can be partly ascribed to the data used to test different hypotheses. It is not easy to estimate employment and labor costs in China given on-going structural changes in the economy as well as the difficulty in collecting data on employment and wages for many private and small sized firms. The official data on employment and wages at a macro level may not serve the purpose well when it comes to studying labor market developments, particularly for the employment and wages of migrant workers. For instance, Knight et al. (2010) argue that the approach by Cai and Wang (2008) is not persuasive as their analysis is based on assumptions about farm workers' working man-days using macro-level data, and the results are pretty sensitive to these assumptions.

As such, to have a better understanding of China's labor market developments, it is necessary to analyze the problems at a disaggregate level using micro-level data rather than at an aggregate level using macro-level data. In the research below we use above-scale industrial firm-level data for 2001-2008 to study the extent to which labor market developments have affected the labor costs of firms across regions, and different levels of technology and ownership. Our estimates suggest that, overall, the impact of labor market tightness and the changes in the migrant labor force on labor costs has been limited, but the effect has been more significant on the labor costs of Hong Kong-Macau-Taiwan (HMT) firms and private enterprises, particularly in coastal areas.

Our analysis suggests that China has not yet seen an absolute shortage of labor, but there have been some structural problems in the labor market. For instance, the demand for young low-end workers and skilled workers in urban areas has increased at a much faster pace than supply, while the opposite is true for better educated workers such as young college graduates. As the majority of employees of HMT and private enterprises are less educated, wage pressures for these firms have increased accordingly. On the other hand, the unemployment rate for young college graduates has been much higher than that of low-end workers of a similar age. To solve these structural problems, it is necessary to remove the barriers that hinder rural labor forces from working in urban areas on a permanent basis, and to develop vocational and technical education. It is also useful to upgrade production chains to reduce the demand for low-end workers and increase that for better-educated workers to lessen skill mismatch in labor markets.

The remainder of this paper is organized as follows. In the second section, we estimate the impact of labor market tightness on the labor costs of firms across regions, with different levels of technology and different ownership. In the third section, we study how the changes in migrant labor forces have affected labor costs and employment of industrial firms in coastal areas. The fourth section discusses policy implications and the last section concludes.

10. 2　HOW SIGNIFICANT HAS BEEN THE IMPACT OF LABOR MARKET TIGHTNESS ON LABOR COSTS IN CHINA?

According to efficiency wage and bargaining models, the real labor cost depends on labor market tightness as well as firms' productivity, given reservation wages

(Blanchard and Katz, 1999). While empirical studies suggest the reservation wage is shaped by workers' previous earnings, laboratory experiments show the reservation wage is also affected by the minimum wage because the presence of the minimum wage law may change workers' fairness concern which in turn affects individual reservation wages (Falk, et al., 2005). Therefore, the real labor cost can be expressed as a function of its own lagged value, labor market tightness, real minimum wages, and firms' productivity. Following Brucker and Jahn (2010), we add time trend as a control variable, and the labor cost equation is estimated as follows for industrial firms across regions, with different levels of technology and different ownership:

$$w\ gqnt = \beta 0 + \beta 1 w\ gqnt - 1 + \beta 2 \varphi nt + \beta 3 mw\ gt + \eta 1 x\ gqn\ t + \eta 2 t + \varepsilon gqnt$$

$$(3)$$

where the subscribes g, q, and n represent region, technology level and firm ownership respectively; w is the log real labor cost, mw is the log real minimum wage, x_t is firms' log real output, and t the time trend. The labor demand-to-supply ratio φ is measured as urban job openings by ownership divided by total labor supply in urban areas. While the short-term effect of labor market tightness on labor costs is captured by β_2, the long-term effect is captured by $\beta_2/(1 - \beta_1)$[1].

The generalized method of moments (GMM) approach is used to estimate the above dynamic panel model with annual data from 2001-2008. The nominal labor costs (which include a basket of labor compensation, such as salaries, benefits etc.) and output are from China Annual Survey of Industries (CASI); Provincial minimum wages, and the urban sectoral job openings and labor supply used to construct φ are from the CEIC[2]. We use the national level CPI to deflate labor costs and output, and

---

[1] Wage growth should be stationary to estimate the long-term effect. This is not a concern here as the equation is estimated with the GMM which transfers the equation into a first-difference form. Due to data limitations, the labor demand-to- supply ratio is constructed only according to firm ownership.

[2] CASI, originally from the NBS, contains 1.8 million financial and production records for above — scale industrial firms. We aggregate the labor costs, employment and output based on firm ownership, technology level, and location.

the provincial CPI to deflate the minimum wage[1]. The firm-level real labor costs and output are aggregated according to a firm's location, technology level, and ownership.

We divide China into four regions: East China, Central China, West China and Northeast China[2]. For level of technology, following the OECD (2011), we divide firms into four groups ranging from low-tech to high-tech. High-tech industries mainly include electronic and communication equipment, while low-tech industries include food-beverage-tobacco, textiles-leather-footwear, and wood-paper products. There are four types of ownership in the analysis, namely SOEs, foreign enterprises, HMT firms and private firms. The equation is in first-order differences when estimated with the GMM, and the instruments include lagged independent variables (except the minimum wage) and lagged log exports[3]. The detailed regression results are presented in Appendix 1, where J-statistics suggest that the over-identifying moment conditions are satisfied.

Our estimates indicate that the impact of labor market tightness is only statistically significant for labor costs of HMT and private firms in some areas, and it is insignificant for SOEs and foreign enterprises in all regions, as shown in Table 10-1 (which is abstracted from Appendix 1). The parameter β_2 has the right sign and relatively significant t-statistic for HMT and private firms in East China, private firms in West China and HMT firms in Northeast China. It has either a wrong sign or insignificant t-statistics for other firms. As the affected firms accounted for only about

---

[1] Using provincial CPI to deflate the minimum wage can partly capture the effect of minimum wage variation resulting from the local price change. However using national level CPI to deflate the minimum wage will not cause much change to our results.

[2] East China includes almost all the coastal provinces (Beijing, Tianjin, Hebei, Shandong, Zhejiang, Jiangsu, Shanghai, Fujian, Guangdong, and Hainan); Central China includes Shanxi, Henan, Hubei, Hunan, Jiangxi, Anhui; West China includes Inner Mongolia, Xinjiang, Shaanxi, Gansu, Qinghai, Ningxia, Chongqing, Sichuan, Guizhou, Yunnan, and Guangxi; Northeast China includes Heilongjiang, Jilin, and Liaoning.

[3] The maximum of two years of lags is used for the instruments. While most regressions only need a one-year lag for the instruments, two years of lags for lagged labor costs and exports for private firms in East, two years of lags for lagged labor costs, labor market tightness, output and exports for SOEs in Central, and two years of lags for lagged labor costs for private firms in West are used in our estimation.

40% of all industrial firms' employment and 30% of their value added in 2008 (Figure 10-3A), this suggests that, overall, the labor market tightness has not had much impact on labor costs in China. In East China, the affected firms accounted for close to 60% of industrial firms' employment and 45% of their value added (Figure 10-3B).

Table 10-1   Short-term Elasticity of Labor Costs with Respect to Labor Market Tightness across Regions and Firm Ownerships

East China				Central China			
SOE	Foreign	HMT	Private	SOE	Foreign	HMT	Private
−0.035	−0.140	0.162 **	0.234 *	−0.009	−0.135	0.163	−0.413 **
(−0.33)	(−0.83)	(2.21)	(1.61)	(−0.01)	(−0.65)	(1.20)	(−2.20)
West China				Northeast China			
SOE	Foreign	HMT	Private	SOE	Foreign	HMT	Private
0.116	−0.239	0.319	0.336 *	−0.002	0.138	0.713 ***	−0.159
(0.65)	(−0.85)	(1.42)	(1.63)	(−0.01)	(0.31)	(4.05)	(−0.98)

Note: *t*-statistics in the parentheses. * , ** , and *** denote statistical significance at 10% , 5% and 1% confidence levels respectively.

Sources: CASI, CEIC and authors' estimates.

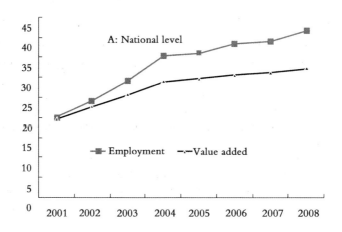

Sources: CASI and authors' estimates.

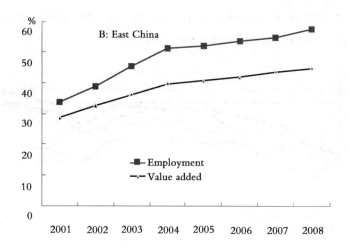

Figure 10-3   Share of the Affected Firms in Terms of Employment and Value Added

Sources: CASI and authors' estimates.

The estimation results reflect an important characteristic of the labor market in China — big differences in labor market tightness across groups of the labor force. As shown in Figure 10-4, the aggregate labor demand-to-supply ratio in cities has been trending upwards since 2001 and exceeded unity in 2010. This appears to indicate that China has labor shortages, as argued by some economists. However, the aggregate demand-to-supply ratio only tells part of the story and it is necessary to look at individual components to get a comprehensive picture of labor market tightness. The demand-to-supply ratios for better-educated workers, namely junior college graduates and university graduates, have been trendless and are still far below unity. In contrast, the demand-to-supply ratios for lower-educated workers, namely junior school or less and regular high-school graduates, have been generally trending upwards and approached unity in 2010.

The reason why the aggregate demand-to-supply ratio exceeded unity in 2010, while the ratios for the four sub-groups were below unity, is that there is a group of job seekers who did not report their education levels at all. As the demand for this group of job seekers has been much larger than supply, the aggregate demand-to-supply ratio has been pushed up to above unity. This group of job seekers have likely been those with little or no schooling at all since there is little obvious reason for well educated people to hide their education background.

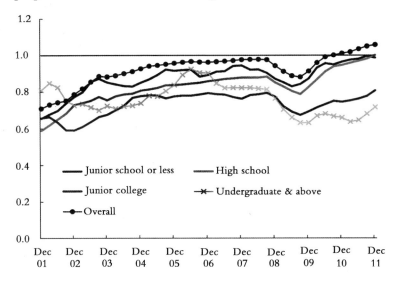

Figure 10-4 Labor Demand-to-Supply Ratios by Education

Sources: CEIC and authors' calculations.

The fact that HMT and private firms have had a relatively larger demand for low-end workers than SOEs and foreign firms, together with the above characteristic of China's labor market, may explain why labor market tightness has had a more significant impact on the labor costs of HMT and private firms than on those of SOEs and foreign enterprises. As shown in Table 10-2, the 2004 data indicates that 64% and 61% of the total staff of private firms and HMT firms had received junior school education or less, while only 49% and 53% of the total staff for SOEs and foreign firms had a similar education background. On the other hand, 4%-5% of the staff of SOEs and foreign firms had university degrees, but less than 2.5% of the staff for HMT and private firms had studied in universities. The long-term elasticity of labor costs with respect to labor market tightness is larger, particularly for private firms. It is 0.64 for HMT firms and 0.99 for private firms in East China (Table 10-3).

Table 10-2　Education Distribution of Employees across Firm Ownerships in 2004

	SOE	Foreign	HMT	Private
Junior school or less	49.4%	52.5%	61.4%	64.1%
High school	36.7%	35.6%	30.7%	28.7%
College	9.9%	7.3%	5.5%	5.2%
University	4.0%	4.6%	2.4%	1.9%

Sources: CASI and authors' estimates.

Table 10-3　Long-term Elasticity of Labor Costs with Respect to Labor Market Tightness in East China

SOE	Foreign	HMT	Private
–	–	0.636 ***	0.987 *
–	–	(2.74)	(1.62)

Note: t – statistics in the parentheses. * and *** denote statistical significance at 10% and 1% confidence level respectively.

Sources: CASI, CEIC and authors' estimates.

Our estimates also show that the impact of minimum wages on labor costs differs across regions and firm ownership. In East China, for instance, the impact has been significant for HMT and private firms and insignificant for SOEs and foreign firms. A 10% rise in minimum wages would push up the labor costs for HMT and private firms by 1.8% and 1.3% respectively in the short run (Table 10-4), and the impact would be larger from a long-term perspective. Our findings are somewhat different from those of Ma et al. (2012) who, using the same data as ours, find that minimum wages have not had a big impact on total wages or employment, with a 10% rise in minimum wages only driving up manufacturing sector wages by 0.4-0.5% and reducing employment by 0.6%. The major reason for the differences between the findings is that we look at the impact at the sectoral level rather than at an aggregate level. As minimum wages have not had a big impact on labor costs of SOEs and foreign firms, it is not surprising that Ma et al. (2012) find limited impact at the aggregate level.

Table 10-4   Impact of 10% Rise in Minimum Wages on Labor Costs in East China

	SOE	Foreign	HMT	Private
Coefficient	0.5%	−0.7%	1.80%	1.28%
T-statistic	1.30	0.56	2.99	1.72

Source: CASI, CEIC and Authors' estimates.

One may argue that the estimation results would be different if the sample period is extended beyond 2008 to more recent years given changes in the labor market in the past 2-3 years. It is likely that the elasticity of labor costs to labor market tightness for HMT and private firms has been larger than our estimates suggest in view of the increasing tightness of the labor market at the low-end, but the main message from our research should not have changed. That is, there have been some structural problems in China's labor market but there should not have emerged an absolute shortage of labor because the demand-to-supply ratios for better-educated workers (junior college and university graduates, for instance) are still far below unity. This suggests that the elasticity of labor costs to labor market tightness for SOEs and foreign firms, whose employees are on average better educated than those of HMT and private firms, should not have changed much even if the sample period for estimation is extended to more recent years.

10.3   HOW BIG HAS THE IMPACT OF LABOR MIGRATION BEEN ON LABOR COSTS IN EAST CHINA?

In recent years, there have been numerous reports of a shortage of migrant workers in East China, although this area remains the major destination for migrant workers[1]. According to the NBS survey, coastal areas have accounted for a declining share of migrant workers in recent years, with the share dropping from about 67% in 2010 to about 65% in 2011. Growth of migrant workers was 2% in coastal areas in

---

[1]   For instance, a report by Xinhua net on 8 April 2010 mentioned that there was a shortage of about one million migrant workers in two delta areas.

2011, compared with 8.1% and 9.6% in central and western areas respectively in the same year. Against this backdrop, this section attempts to explore the extent to which changes in migrant labor forces have affected labor costs and employment in East China. The migrant labor supply is measured as urban labor supply from other cities and from rural areas[1].

Labor migration could affect the labor costs in East China in a dynamic way through both direct and indirect channels. A decline in migrant labor would reduce the supply of labor in East China, and increase pressure on the labor costs in this area accordingly. A rise in the labor costs would weigh on the demand for labor and thus reduce labor market tightness, which would in turn dampen the growth of the labor costs. Such a dynamic process would continue until the demand for and supply of labor reach a new equilibrium. Note that here we not only consider the direct impact of labor migration on the labor costs, but also its indirect impact stemming from labor substitution between firms with different technology and types of ownership. This is because changes in the labor costs would lead to a change in the relative demand for labor between firms, and thus generate some second-round effects on labor costs and employment. As such, the elasticity of labor substitution plays a big role in shaping the impact of labor migration on labor costs. The two key equations in this model are the labor cost equation and the labor demand function. As the labor cost equation is estimated in the previous section, we focus on the labor demand function next.

Following Brucker and Jahn (2010) and Ottaviano and Peri (2012), our analysis is based on a model in which firms maximize profits under a nested constant elasticity-of-substitution (CES) form of labor demand function. The major difference between our model and standard models of labor demand is the structure of labor demand. Specifically, labor demand in East China is split into three parts in terms of firms' location (Bohai gulf, Yangtze delta, and Fujian-Guangdong-Hainan), each location's demand for labor is then divided into four technology levels, and labor

---

[1] Original data on migrant labor are from CEIC. Missing observations for the sub-series of labor demand during 2001-2005 are estimated based on their co-movement with other sub-series for which data are complete for the whole sample period.

demand at each level of technology is further grouped as four classes according to firm ownership. At each level, labor demand is summed up in the form of a CES function. Such a multi-layer structure allows us to estimate the elasticity of substitution for labor across different technology, firm ownership and sources of labor supply, and thus allows us to take into account the second-round impact of labor migration on labor costs in East China. Figure 10-5 shows the labor demand structure in our analysis. The details of the model and the estimation methodology are presented in Appendix 2.

Our estimates show that the labor substitutability across firms with different levels of technology and different ownership is low, other things being equal, but it is easy to substitute labor from different places if other things remain unchanged (the same firm ownership and the same technology). The estimates of elasticity for labor substitution are shown in Table 10-5. Obviously, elasticity of substitution are much lower than unity across ownerships (0. 48) and technologies (0. 54) but much higher than unity across regions (2. 27).

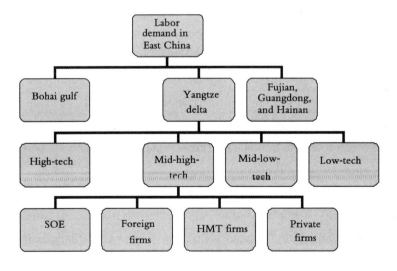

Figure 10-5   Labor Demand Structure

Table 10-5   Elasticity of Substitution for Labor Forces

Ownership	Technology	Region
0. 479 ***	0. 539 ***	2. 271 ***
(4. 23)	(9. 20)	(5. 07)

Note: *t*-statistics in the parentheses. ∗ ∗ ∗ denotes statistical significance at 1% confidence level.
Sources: CASI, CEIC and authors' estimates.

The impact of labor migration on labor costs is negligible for SOEs and foreign firms in East China, but larger for private firms and HMT firms in the same region (Table 10-6). The impact is calculated based on the estimates from our labor cost equation and labor demand equation. A 10% fall in labor migration would raise real labor costs by 0. 9% for private firms and by 0. 3% for HMT firms in the short run. Meanwhile, employment in private firms would fall by 0. 9% , followed by a 0. 6% fall for HMT firms and 0. 5% for SOEs and foreign firms. The impact on labor costs and employment differs little across sub-regions in East China, as shown in Tables in Appendix 3.

Table 10-6   Short-run Effects of a 10% Fall in Labor Migration on Labor Costs and Employment in East China

	SOE	Foreign	HMT	Private
Real Labor costs	0. 0%	0. 0%	0. 3%	0. 9%
Employment	−0. 5%	−0. 5%	−0. 6%	−0. 9%

Sources: CASI, CEIC and authors' estimates.

The long-term effect on labor costs and employment would be noticeably larger for HMT and private firms, with a 10% fall in labor migration leading to a 3. 6% rise in labor costs for private firms and a 0. 9% rise in labor costs for HMT firms (Table 10-7). Meanwhile, the responses of employment to the shock are around 4 times those in the short run. As shown in Tables in Appendix A3, the long-run responses of labor costs and employment across ownership differ slightly across provinces in East China.

Table 10-7 Long-run Effects of a 10% Fall in Labor Migration in East China

	SOE	Foreign	HMT	Private
Real Labor costs	0.0%	0.0%	0.9%	3.6%
Employment	−2.0%	−2.0%	−2.5%	−3.8%

Sources: CASI, CEIC and authors' estimates.

10.4 DISCUSSIONS

The main message from our research is that, despite slower growth in the labor supply, labor market developments have not had significant impact on labor costs in China, suggesting that there is no absolute shortage of labor yet. In fact, the working-age population (15-64 years old) has trended upwards from around 340 million in early 1950s to about 970 million in 2010, while there is evidence that the unemployment rate is relatively high. For instance, according to China Household Finance Survey by Southwest University of Finance and Economics (SWUFE), urban unemployment rate reached 8.0% in 2011 (6.9% in East China, 8.3% in Central China and 14% in West China), much higher than the officially released registered unemployment rate of about 4.0% in the same year. This is different from the arguments by Cai et al. (2007), Cai (2010) and Cai and Wang (2008) that China has passed the Lewis turning point and there is no more surplus labor.

Nevertheless, labor market tightness and labor migration have had some impact on labor costs of HMT and private enterprises, particularly in coastal areas. Our research appears to support the argument of Knight et al. (2010) that the phenomenon of migrant labor scarcity co exists with the fact that there has not yet emerged an absolute shortage of labor. The co-existence of migrant labor scarcity and surplus labor could partly be attributed to institutional factors.

First of all, there is a segmentation of labor markets in rural and urban areas. Despite the progress made in the past few decades in deregulating labor markets in China, there still exist institutional barriers that hinder rural labor forces working in cities, with the Hukou system being a typical hurdle. As discussed in Meng (2012), restrictions on migrant access to social welfare and social services in cities (e.g.

children' schooling) have prevented rural labor forces from working in cities on a permanent basis. Meng (2012) further shows that migrant workers usually go to cities in their late teens, with female migrant workers typically starting to return home to get married and have children at the age of 25 and male migrants starting to return home in their mid30s. On average, migrants work in cities for only seven years. Using a Prohbit model, Knight et al. (2010) find that marriage reduces the probability of migration by 8 to 11 percentage points in 2007, especially for those with children, and the probability of migration declines sharply after age 31. As HMT and private enterprises are major employers of young migrant workers, such institutional factors have likely played a big role in pushing up wages for these firms.

Secondly, there seems to be a mismatch between labor demand and supply. China has played the role of "world-factory" in past decades and experienced a boom in construction with fast development of transportation and real estate in the past decade, with the demand for young skilled workers and low-end labor increasing rapidly accordingly, as pointed out by Wang el al. (2012). The one-child policy, which has partly contributed to negative growth in the supply of young workers since the 1990s, and the segmentation of rural and urban labor markets, have contributed to labor market tightness in some sectors, China's education system also appears to have been a major factor behind a skill-mismatch problem. China has expanded traditional high school and university enrolment at a rapid pace since the mid-1990s, while vocational training has lagged behind (Figure 10-6).

Although higher education supports an economy's growth from a long-term perspective, the rapid expansion in college enrolment in the past 15 years has created some structural problems in the Mainland's labor market in the short run as the level of education attainment has not matched the demand for labor. In other words, low-end industries are still important in the Chinese economy while the development of high-end sectors that demand high-end labor forces has been slow. For instance, China Household Finance Survey shows that among the working population aged 21-25, there is a positive relationship between the unemployment rate and level of education (Figure 10-7). Specifically, the unemployment rate for the group of

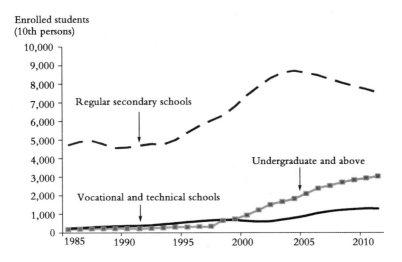

Figure 10-6   Student Enrolment

Sources: CEIC and authors' calculations.

primary school and less was 4. 2% in 2011, while that for college graduates was 16. 4% in the same year.

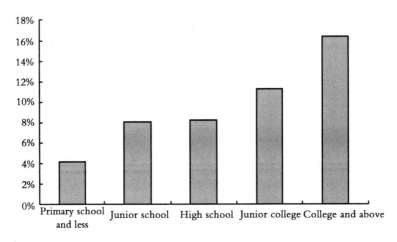

Figure 10-7   Unemployment Rate and Education Aged 21-25 in China (2011)

Source: China Household Finance Survey 2012 by Southwest University of Finance and Economics.

The structural problems, if not well addressed, would continue to add wage pressures for HMT and private enterprises, and weaken the competitiveness of China's exports. It has been reported that some foreign producers have shifted their production base from China to other Asian economies with lower labor costs like Indonesia. According to the World Investment Report 2012 by the United Nations, FDI to Indonesia grew by 26% in 2011, while FDI to China only grew by 8%.

Noticeable wage differentials between East China and inland provinces appear to suggest that HMT and private enterprises could relocate the production to reduce labor costs. Our estimates using the industrial firm-level data suggest that labor costs in East China for HMT and private enterprises were about 20%-25% higher than their counterparts in inland provinces in 2008 (Figure 10-8). As the estimates in the previous section show, the elasticity of substitution for labor forces across regions, given other things unchanged, is pretty high (2. 27) so producers could relocate productions to reduce labor costs in principle. In fact, some HMT firms (Foxconn, for instance) have attempted to shift production from coastal areas to inland provinces in China in recent years.

Nevertheless, labor cost is only one of the factors that determine the location of production. Many other factors, such as the public infrastructure, business climate, distance from the end markets, could be even more important. Despite labor cost differentials, Sun and Peng (2012) find that the scale of industrial transfer has been small, and only nine of the 20 manufacturing industries studied have attempted to move from East China to inland provinces, while the opposite is true for the remaining 11 manufacturing industries. They also find most of the industries that transferred from East China to inland provinces have been capital or resource intensive rather than labor-intensive.

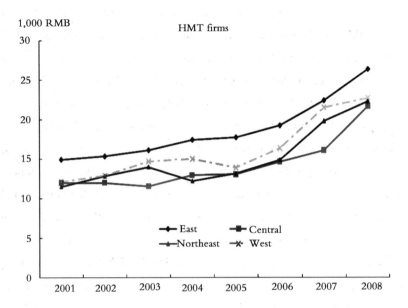

Sources: CASI and authors' estimates.

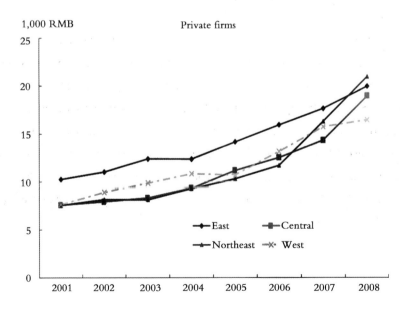

Figure 10-8   Labor Costs of HMT and Private Firms across Regions

Sources: CASI and authors' estimates.

As such, it is necessary to address the fundamental issues of China's labor markets to reduce wage pressures. First of all, removing the restrictions on migration from rural areas to urban areas would be crucial. The initiatives to reform the "Hukou" system stated in the report of the 18th National Congress of the Communist Party of China are a welcome step in this direction. Secondly, it is useful to develop vocational and technical training to increase the supply of young skilled workers. Finally, it is imperative to upgrade production chains to increase demand for high-end labor to reduce the degree of skill mismatch in labor markets. As shown in Table 10-8, in 2004 around 64% of low-tech industrial firms' employees received education of junior school or less, compared with only 40% for high-tech industries. In contrast, about 8% of high-tech industries' employees were undergraduates or above, compared with only 1.7% for low-tech industries.

Table 10-8   Education Background of Employees across Technology Levels

	High-tech	Medium-tech	Medium-low-tech	Low-tech
Junior school and below	39.6%	43.9%	56.4%	63.9%
High school	42.6%	39.1%	33.1%	29.2%
Junior college	10.1%	11.4%	7.6%	5.2%
University	7.6%	5.7%	2.9%	1.7%

Sources: CASI and authors' estimates.

10.5   CONCLUDING REMARKS

Using above scale industrial firm-level data of 2001-2008, this paper studies the impact of labor market development on labor costs in China. The main findings are summarized as follows:

Overall, the impact of labor market tightness on labor costs has been limited, but the effect has been more significant for HMT and private enterprises, particularly in coastal areas. Labor migration has had some impact on labor costs and employment for HMT and private firms in East China, and the impact on other firms in the same region has been small.

Our analysis appears to suggest that China has not yet seen an absolute shortage of labor, but there have been structural problems in the labor market.

For instance, demand for young low-end labor and, in many cases, for young skilled workers has increased at a much faster pace than supply, while the opposite is true for better-educated workers such as young college graduates.

As the majority of the employees of HMT firms and private enterprises are less educated, wage pressures of these firms have increased accordingly.

In order to reduce wage pressures for HMT and private firms, it is necessary to remove the barriers that hinder rural labor forces from working in urban areas, and to develop vocational and technical training. It is also useful to upgrade production chains to reduce the demand for low-end labor and increase that for better-educated labor such as college graduates.

References

[1] Blanchard, Olivier Jean, and Lawrence Katz, 1999. "Wage Dynamics: Reconciling Theory and Evidence." NBER Working paper No. w6924, National Bureau of Economic Research.

[2] Borjas, George J., 2009. "The Analytics of the Wage Effect of Immigration." NBER Working Paper No. w14796, National Bureau of Economic Research.

[3] Bratsiotis, George, and Christopher Martin, 1999. "Stabilization, Policy Targets and Unemployment." The Scandinavian Journal of Economics, 101 (2), 241-56.

[4] Brucker, Herbert, and Elke J. Jahn, 2010. "Migration and Wage-setting: Reassessing the Labor Market effects of Migration." CEPR Final Conference of the Marie Curie Research Training Network on Transnationality of Migrants.

[5] Cai, Fang, 2010. "Demographic Transition, Demographic Dividend, and Lewis Turning Point in China." Economic Research (in Chinese), V4.

[6] Cai, Fang and Wang Meiyun, 2008. "A Counterfactual of Unlimited Surplus Labor in Rural China", China and the World Economy, 16 (1), 51-65.

[7] Cai, Fang, Yang Du and Changbao Zhao, 2007. "Regional Labor Market Integration since China's WTO Entry: Evidence from Household-level Data." in R. Garnaut and Ligang Song (eds), China: Linking Markets for Growth, Canberra: Asia Pacific Press: 133-150.

[8] Coricelli, Fabrizio, Alex Cukierman, and Alberto Dalmazzo, 2006. "Monetary Institutions, Monopolistic Competition, Unionized Labor Markets and Economic Performance." The Scandinavian Journal of Economics, V108 (1), 39-63.

[9] Dustmann, Christian, Albrecht Glitz, and Tommaso Frattini, 2008. "The Labor Market Impact of Immigration." Oxford Review of Economic Policy 24 (3), 477-494.

[10] Falk, Armin, Ernst Fehr, and Christian Zehnder, 2005. "The Behavioral Effects of Minimum Wages." Working Paper Series ISSN 1424-0459, Institute for Empirical Research in Economics, University of Zurich.

[11] Ge, Suqin, and Dennis T. Yang, 2011. "Accounting for Rising Wages in China." Manuscript, Virginia Tech and Chinese University of Hong Kong.

[12] International Monetary Fund, 2012. "Demographics — Has China Reached the Lewis Turning Point?" IMF Country Report No. 12/195.

[13] Meland, Frode, 2006. "A Union Bashing Model of Inflation Targeting." The Scandinavian Journal of Economics, V108(3), 419-432.

[14] Knell, Markus, 2002. "Wage Formation in Open Economies and the Role of Monetary and Wage-setting Institutions." Working Paper No. 63, Oesterreichische Nationalbank.

[15] Knight, John, Deng Quheng and Li Shi, 2010. "The Puzzle of Migrant Labor Shortage and Rural Labor Surplus in China", Department of Economics, University of Oxford, Discussion paper series ISSN 1471-0498.

[16] Kwan Fung, 2009. "Agricultural Labor and the Incidence of Surplus Labor: Experience from China during Reform." Journal of Chinese Economic and Business Studies, 7 (3), 341-361.

[17] Li, Hongbin, Lei Li, Binzhen Wu, and Yanyan Xiong, 2012. "The End of

Cheap Chinese Labor." Journal of Economic Perspectives, 26(4), 57-74.

[18] Manacorda, Marco, Alan Manning, and Jonathan Wadsworth, 2012. "The Impact of Immigration on the Structure of Wages: Theory and Evidence from Britain." Journal of the European Economic Association, V10(1), 120-151.

[19] Ma, Shuang, Jie Zhang, and Xi zhu, 2012. "The Effect of Minimum Wage on Average Wage and Employment." Economic Research (in Chinese), V5.

[20] Meng, Xin, 2012. "Labor Market outcomes and Reforms in China." Journal of Economic Perspectives, 26(4), 75-201.

[21] Nickell, Stephen, and Jumana Saleheen, 2008. "The Impact of Immigration on Occupational Wages: Evidence from Britain." FRB of Boston Working Paper No. 08-6.

[22] OECD, 2011. "OECD Science, Technology and Industry Scoreboard 2011." OECD Publishing.

[23] Ottaviano, Gianmarco I. P., and Giovanni Peri, 2012. "Rethinking the Effect of Immigration on Wages. " Journal of the European Economic Association, V10 (1), 152-197.

[24] Ottaviano, Gianmarco, and Giovanni Peri, 2007. "The Effects of Immigration on US Wages and Rents: A General Equilibrium Approach." Discussion Paper, No. 6551, Center for Economic Policy Research.

[25] Sun, Jiuwen, and Peng Wei, 2012. "A Study on Regional Industrial Transfer under the Background of Rising Earnings." Journal of Renmin Univeristy of China (in Chinese), V4.

[26] Wang, Jing, and Morley Gunderson, 2007. "Minimum Wage Impacts in China: Estimates from a prespecified Research Design, 2000—2007." Contemporary Economic Policy 29 (3), 392-406.

[27] Wang, Tao, and Harrison Hu, 2012. "China's Next Decade II: The Challenge of Aging." UBS Investment Research.

[28] Wang, Xiaobing, Thomas Herzfeld, and Thomas Glauben, 2007. "Labor Allocation in Transition: Evidence from Chinese Rural Households." China Economic Review 18 (3), 287-308.

[29] Yang, Du, 2012. "The Responsiveness of Firms to Labor Market Changes in China: Evidence from Micro Level Data", memo, Institute of Population and Labor Economics, CASS.

Appendix 1　GMM estimates for labor cost equation

Table A1-1　Estimated Results for labor cost equation: East

	SOE	Foreign	HMT	Private
$w-1$	0. 797 ***	0. 943 ***	0. 744 ***	0. 763 ***
	(15. 52)	(13. 89)	(15. 32)	(6. 79)
φ	−0. 034	−0. 140	0. 162 **	0. 234 *
	(−0. 33)	(−0. 83)	(2. 21)	(1. 61)
mw	0. 050	−0. 067	0. 180 ***	0. 128 *
	(1. 30)	(−0. 56)	(2. 99)	(1. 72)
x	0. 013 *	0. 009	0. 012 ***	0. 014 *
	(1. 85)	(1. 29)	(2. 50)	(1. 91)
t	0. 026 ***	0. 030 **	0. 002	0. 007
	(3. 33)	(1. 99)	(0. 25)	(0. 61)
Obs	276	275	276	236
Adj R^2	0. 80	0. 83	0. 84	0. 69
J-statistic	0. 06	1. 76	1. 78	5. 9

Note: *t*-statistics in the parentheses. * , ** and ** * denote statistical significance at 10% , 5% and 1% confidence level respectively.

Sources: CASI, CEIC and authors' estimates.

Table A1-2　Estimated Results for labor cost equation: Central

	SOE	Foreign	HMT	Private
$w-1$	0. 899 ***	0. 762 ***	0. 638 ***	0. 801 ***
	(11. 44)	(17. 10)	(7. 16)	(10. 95)
φ	−0. 009	−0. 135	0. 163	−0. 413 **
	(−0. 01)	(−0. 65)	(1. 20)	(−2. 20)

Continued

	SOE	Foreign	HMT	Private
mw	0. 114	−0. 095	0. 114	−0. 092
	(1. 00)	(−1. 02)	(1. 05)	(−1. 40)
x	−0. 017	0. 051 ***	0. 055 ***	0. 014
	(−0. 86)	(2. 68)	(3. 00)	(1. 48)
t	−0. 002	0. 045 *	0. 114	0. 063 ***
	(−0. 08)	(1. 90)	(1. 05)	(5. 18)
Obs	144	168	168	168
$Adj\ R^2$	0. 70	0. 74	0. 62	0. 83
J-statistic	0. 30	0. 13	1. 29	1. 32

Note: t-statistics in the parentheses. ＊, ＊＊ and ＊ ＊ denote statistical significance at 10% , 5% and 1% confidence level respectively.

Sources: CASI, CEIC and authors' estimates.

Table A1-3　Estimated Results for labor cost equation: Northeast

	SOE	Foreign	HMT	Private
$w−1$	0. 356 ***	0. 765 ***	0. 228 ***	0. 680 ***
	(3. 05)	(9. 02)	(3. 77)	(7. 83)
φ	−0. 002	0. 138	0. 713 ***	−0. 159
	(−0. 01)	(0. 31)	(4. 05)	(−0. 98)
Mw	0. 001	0. 130	0. 737 ***	0. 023
	(0. 01)	(0. 50)	(5. 13)	(0. 34)
X	0. 098 ***	0. 009	0. 025	0. 010
	(4. 10)	(0. 63)	(1. 34)	(0. 99)
t	0. 080 ***	0. 048	−0. 072 **	0. 075 ***
	(5. 53)	(1. 07)	(−2. 31)	(5. 24)
Obs	84	84	83	84
$Adj\ R^2$	0. 79	0. 71	0. 55	0. 86
J-statistic	0. 01	1. 29	0. 67	1. 76

Note: t-statistics in the parentheses. ＊, ＊＊ and ＊ ＊ denote statistical significance at 10% , 5% and 1% confidence level respectively.

Sources: CASI, CEIC and authors' estimates.

Table A1-4 Estimated Results for labor cost equation: West

	SOE	Foreign	HMT	Private
$w-1$	0.495 ***	0.557 ***	0.545 ***	0.927 ***
	(5.53)	(6.41)	(8.70)	(5.27)
φ	0.116	−0.239	0.319	0.336 *
	(0.65)	(−0.85)	(1.42)	(1.63)
Mw	0.122 ***	−0.014	0.536 ***	0.100
	(3.14)	(−0.09)	(3.18)	(1.53)
X	0.046 ***	0.045 ***	0.155 ***	0.015 *
	(3.38)	(2.86)	(6.04)	(1.72)
t	0.051 ***	0.043	−0.059 *	−0.004
	(3.23)	(1.59)	(−1.73)	(−0.19)
Obs	269	251	236	234
$Adj\ R^2$	0.64	0.51	0.64	0.51
$J-statistic$	0.87	0.58	0.05	2.01

Note: t-statistics in the parentheses. $*$, $**$ and $**$ $*$ denote statistical significance at 10%, 5% and 1% confidence level respectively.

Sources: CASI, CEIC and authors' estimates.

Appendix 2　The theoretical framework for labor demand and labor migration

(1) Labor demand

A nested CES labor structure is used to capture the heterogeneity of labor demand. Suppose the aggregate production function is in a standard Cobb-Douglas form

$Y_t = A_t K_t^{1-\alpha} L_t^{\alpha}$, or $y_t = a_t + (1-\alpha) k_t + \alpha l_t$ in logs　　　(A1) where labor is grouped as three layers in terms of firms' locations (denoted as "g"), technology (denoted as "q"), and ownership (denoted as "n"). Accordingly, labor at each layer reads:

$$L_t = [\sum_{g=1}^{3} \theta_g L_{gt}^{(\delta-1)/\delta}]^{\delta/(\delta-1)}, \quad \sum_{g=1}^{3} \theta_g = 1 \qquad (A2)$$

$$L_{gt} = \left[\sum_{q=1}^{4} \theta_{gq} L_{gqt}^{(\rho-1)/\rho} \right]^{\rho/(\rho-1)}, \quad \sum_{q=1}^{4} \theta_{gq} = 1 \tag{A3}$$

$$L_{gqt} = \left[\sum_{n=1}^{4} \theta_{gqn} L_{gqnt}^{(\sigma-1)/\sigma} \right]^{\sigma/(\sigma-1)}, \quad \sum_{n=1}^{4} \theta_{gqn} = 1 \tag{A4}$$

where θ is the weight for each cell, σ, ρ, δ are elasticities of labor substitution between firms at each layer that are of interest, and $g = [$ Bohai gulf, Yangzi delta, Fujian, Guangdong and Hainan $]$;

$q = [$ Hi-tech, Mid-tech, Mid-low-tech, Low-tech $]$; $n = [$ SOE, Foreign, HMT, Private $]$.

Profit maximization with respect to labor composite L_{gt}, L_{gqt}, and L_{gqnt} given real labor costs results in the following labor demand equations:

$$w_{gt} = [\ln(\mu^{-1}\alpha) + y_t - l_{t\delta}^{+1}l_t + \ln\theta_g - \delta^1 l_{gt} \tag{A5}$$

$$wgqt = [\ln(\mu - 1\alpha) + yt - lt + \delta\underline{1}lt + \ln\theta g$$
$$- \left(\frac{1}{\delta} - \rho\underline{1}\right)lgt + \ln\theta gq - \rho\underline{1}lgqt \tag{A6}$$

$$wgqnt = [\ln(\mu - 1\alpha) + yt - lt) + \delta\underline{1}lt + \ln\theta g$$
$$- \left(\frac{1}{\delta} - \rho\underline{1}\right)lgt + \ln\theta gq - \left(\frac{1}{\rho} - \sigma\underline{1}\right)$$
$$lgqt + \ln\theta gqn - \sigma\underline{1}lgqnt \tag{A7}$$

where μ is the mark-up under imperfect goods market, and the labor costs and labor demand are in logs. The labor demand equations are estimated in three steps.

Step 1: Estimating the elasticity of labor substitution between foreign and other firm types based on equation (A7):

$$lgqjt\text{-}lgqst = Dgqj\text{-}\sigma(wgqjt\text{-}wgqst) + \gamma xt + \xi gqjt \tag{A8}$$

where $j = [$ "SOE", "Private", "HMT" $]$; $s = [$ "Foreign" $]$. By definition, $Dgqj = \sigma(\ln\theta gqj\text{-}\ln\theta gqs)$, which implies that

$$\theta_{gqj} = \frac{\exp\left(\frac{D_{gqj}}{\sigma}\right)}{\left[1 + \sum_{j}\exp\left(\frac{D_{gqj}}{\sigma}\right)\right]} \text{ for each ownership } j \tag{A9}$$

and

$$\theta_{gqs} = \frac{1}{\left[1 + \sum_j \exp\left(\frac{D_{gqj}}{\sigma}\right)\right]} \tag{A10}$$

θ_{gqj}^i, θ_{gqs}, and $\sigma\,\hat{}$ are used to construct L_{gqt} according to equation (A4). L_{gqt} constructed is in turn used in Step 2.

Step 2: Estimating elasticity of labor substitution between firms with different technologies based on equation (A6):

$$l_{gqt} = D_t + D_{gt} + D_{gq} - \rho w_{gqt} + \zeta_{gqt} \tag{A11}$$

where D_t controls for $\rho[\ln(\mu^{-1}a) + y_t - l_t)]^+ - \delta^\rho l_t = \rho\ln(\mu^{-1}MPL_t)^+ - \delta^\rho l_t$, D_{gt} controls for $-\rho\left(\frac{1}{\delta} - \rho^1\right)l_{gt} + \rho\ln\theta_g$, and D_{gq} controls for $\rho\ln\theta_{gq}$. The estimates of elasticity parameter ρ and the control variable D_{gq} are used to calculate the weight θ_{gq} as $\theta\hat{}_{gq} = D\hat{}$ for each technology q,

$$\frac{\exp\left(\frac{D_{gqj}}{\sigma}\right)}{\sum^q \exp\left(\frac{gq}{\rho}\right)} \tag{A12}$$

which along with ρ is used to construct labor composite L_{gt} defined in equation (A3). L_{gt} constructed is then used in Step 3.

Step 3: Estimating elasticity of labor substitution between firms at different locations based on equation (A5):

$$l_{gt} = D_t + D_g + \beta_g \tau_{gt} - \delta w_{gqt} + \varsigma_{gqt} \tag{A13}$$

where D_t controls for $\rho[\ln(\mu^{-1}a) + y_t - l_t]^+ - \delta^\rho l_t = \rho\ln(\mu^{-1}MPL_t)^+ - \delta^\rho l_t$, D_g is the the location-specific fixed effect and τ_{gt} the location-specific time trend. The estimates of elasticity parameterδ and the control variableD_g are used to calculate the weight θ_g as

$$\frac{\exp\left(\frac{D_g}{\delta}\right)}{\theta\hat{}_g = D\sum_g \exp\left(\frac{g}{\delta}\right)} \tag{A14}$$

which along with $\hat{\delta}$ is used to construct labor composite L_t defined in equation (A2).

(2) *Impact of labor migration on wages*

Labor migration changes labor supply and hence the labor demand-supply ratio φ, affecting cohorts' bargaining power. On the other hand, changes of labor demand in response to changes in labor costs may alter the capital-labor ratio and hence the marginal product of labor, in turn, causing labor costs to change. Let M denote the migrant labor forces and $L^{\sim}$ the labor supply, the real labor costs in equations (A5)-(A7) can be written as marginal product of labor:

$$W = \mu^{-1}MPL = \mu^{-1}MPL(L,K(L^{\sim}(M))) \qquad (A15)$$

where W, L and K are vectors. The impact of labor migration on labor costs can be expressed as

$$\underline{dW}dM = \partial(\mu - \partial 1 LMPL) \ dM \ \underline{dL} + \partial(\mu - \partial 1 KMPL) \ \underline{\partial\partial KL}^{\sim} \ dM \ \underline{dL}^{\sim} \quad (A16)$$

On the other hand, the labor cost function can be re-written as

$$W = f(\varphi) = f(\varphi(L,L)) \qquad (A17)$$

It follows from equations (A15)-(A17) that

$$V = \mu^{-1}MPL(L,K(L^{\sim}(M))) - f(\varphi(L,L^{\sim})) = 0$$

$$= \left(\frac{\partial(\mu^{-1}MPL)}{\partial L}\right) - \frac{\partial f}{\partial \phi}\frac{\partial \phi}{\partial L}^{-1}\left(\frac{\partial f}{\partial \phi}\frac{\partial \phi}{\partial \tilde{L}}\frac{\tilde{dL}}{dM} - \frac{\partial(\mu^{-1}MPL)}{\partial K}\frac{\partial}{\partial}\right) \qquad (A18)$$

which indicates the response of labor demand to the migration shock reads:

$$dM\underline{{}^{dL}} {}^{-K}L^{\sim} \ dM\underline{{}^{dL}}) \qquad (A19)$$

$dM\underline{{}^{dL}}$ calculated from Equation (A19) is then used to calculate $\frac{dW}{dM}$ in Equation (A16).

Appendix 3: Tables

Table A3-1 Short-run Effects of a 10% Fall in Labor Migration on Labor Costs in East China

	SOE	Foreign	HMT	Private
Bohai gulf			0.3%	0.9%
Yangtze delta Fujian-			0.2%	0.8%
Guangdong-Hainan			0.3%	0.9%

Sources: CASI, CEIC and authors' estimates.

Table A3-2 Short-run Effects of a 10% Fall in Labor Migration on Employment in East China

	SOE	Foreign	HMT	Private
Bohai gulf	−0.5%	−0.5%	−0.6%	−0.9%
Yangtze delta Fujian-	−0.6%	−0.6%	−0.7%	−1.0%
Guangdong-Hainan	−0.5%	−0.5%	−0.6%	−0.9%

Sources: CASI, CEIC and authors' estimates.

Table A3-3 Long-run Effects of a 10% Fall in Labor Migration on Labor Costs in East China

	SOE	Foreign	HMT	Private
Bohai gulf			1.0%	3.7%
Yangtze delta Fujian-			0.7%	3.5%
Guangdong-Hainan			1.1%	3.7%

Sources: CASI, CEIC and authors' estimates.

Table A3-4   Long-run Effects of a 10% Fall in Labor
Migration on Employment in East China

	SOE	Foreign	HMT	Private
Bohai gulf	-1.9%	-1.9%	-2.4%	-3.7%
Yangtze delta Fujian-	-2.3%	-1.3%	-2.7%	-4.0%
Guangdong-Hainan	-1.8%	-1.8%	-2.3%	-3.6%

Sources: CASI, CEIC and authors' estimates.

(Wenlang Zhang and Gaofeng Han, Research Department Hong Kong Monetary Authority, Hong Kong)

CHAPTER 11   Constructing Peace-Oriented Power in Chinese Diplomacy

Wu Xinbo

Power exists in nature as well as in human society. Study on power in nature leads to developments of modern physics, while study on power in human society (strength and power) gives birth to science of international politics. Study of natural power in physics focuses on three elements; that is, the magnitude, direction, and application point of power. The studies of international politics, however, mainly concern with the capacity and features of power (e. g. political power, economic power, military power, or hard and soft power, etc.) with less attention to the direction in which power is applied. Does this mean the application direction of strength or power is not important in international relations? Of course not. While analyzing factors in international politics, we need to take into consideration their capabilities as well as intentions as the latter determines how the actors shall utilize their capabilities; that is, the direction in which strength or power is applied. It also determines whether the actors will bring forth cooperation or cause conflicts, whether they would strengthen stability or weaken it, etc. The "peace-oriented power" we discuss in this article relates to the way strength or power is applied.

11.1 HISTORICAL CONTEXTS FOR THE BUILDING OF PEACE-ORIENTED POWER

It is against the background of China's rise that the construction of China's "peace-oriented power" has been proposed. China, as a country with a long history, vast territory, large population, geopolitical location and socialism with Chinese characteristics, its rise critical would surely produce all-encompassing global impacts and lead to changes in international power structure and established distribution of power. China needs to elaborate on two key questions in order to make the world precisely understand the impacts of its rise: one is how to use its ever-increasing power, and the other is how to establish checks and balances between great powers. Those two questions are closely related to each other.

In the history of mankind hitherto, big countries or great powers have mainly used their power in three ways. First, ancient China emphasized the strength of "civilization" and sought to influence others through the spread its superior culture. Meanwhile, it constructed relations with the outside world in accordance with the latter's identification with and acceptance of the Chinese civilization, thus forming a specific regional order, namely, the so-called Sino-centric system and the tribute-paying system. As China and the world have undergone great changes by now, it is impossible for China to copy such a model today. Second, in modern times, Western nations, after acquiring tremendous material strength through industrialization, began to abuse their "hard power" to engage in military expansion and armed conquest and plunder abroad, carving up colonies in the world and competing for spheres of influence with each other. It gave lise to incessant warfare, particularly the two world wars, which inflicted catastrophes to mankind. As a victim of foreign aggression and expansion in modern history, China firmly rejects such stereotype by sticking to the principle of "do not impose on others what you would not like others to impose on you". Last, after becoming the world's hegemony, the United States has not only given prominence to hard power by maintaining its supreme military power and using armed forces frequently. Meanwhile, it tends to rely on soft power to actively expand the influence of American culture and values. In this way, the United States used the "carrot and stick" simultaneously. Whether using hard power or soft power, or applying the "carrot and stick" tactics, they both aim to serve the U. S. hegemony, which often lead to such negative consequences as impinging on other nations' interests and undermining world peace and justice. As China is opposed to hegemonism, such a model is unacceptable either. Learning a lesson from the Bush administration's abuse of America's hard power, President Obama raised the concept of "smart power", indicating the United States would choose from its diplomatic, economic, military, political, legal and cultural toolkit, as well as appropriate policy tools or even the combination of them according to the situation it faces. As it only means the proper use of both hard and soft power but not a new form of power, the "smart power" concept does not go beyond the traditional domain of hard power and soft power: it just offers a tactic of using power, and hence it is of very limited reference to China.

Under new historical circumstances, China, as an emerging power, has to put forward a new concept of power and propose a new way of applying power in order to go beyond the conventional method adopted by other big powers. Eventnally it will help shape China's figure as a big player with new diplomatic stances. Just as former Japanese ambassador to China Yuji Miyamoto said recently, "In order to become a real leading power in the world, China needs to put forward its own ideal, ideas and value system. "

On the other hand, as the rise of new powers in history often leads to changes in both regional and international orders, people are often concerned about what kind of order the emerging power is seeking and how it plans to construct such an order. At the beginning of the 21st century, China raised the concept of "peaceful rise" and proposed the prospect of building a "harmonious world" as the new world order, which reflected China's prudence in searching for the proper way of its own development and the future of humanity. However, China has not proposed an effective way of applying the idea of peaceful rise to promoting the building of a harmonious world. Against such a background, China should construct and enhance the peace-oriented power in its diplomacy in order to advance human progress through enhancing mutual development, maintaining peace in an active way, settling differences effectively, resolving conflicts peacefully and promoting common interests among nations, thus making it possible to build a harmonious world.

11. 2   THEORETICAL PROP FOR PEACE-ORIENTED POWER

Different from the traditional way of categorizing and defining power, peace-oriented power not only refers to power itself (hard power and soft power) but also includes the directive application of such power, that is, the way of applying power. If a definition is needed, peace-oriented power means the ability of a nation to utilize its comprehensive strength positively to promote "peace", "harmony" and "cooperation" in a global scale based on the ancient Chinese interpretation of "harmony and synergy". Therefore, peace-oriented power is composed of the idea, the composition, and the way of application of power.

The key conceptual element of peace-oriented power is "harmony and synergy", which is not only a philosophical idea but also a value orientation in Chinese culture. Philosophically, the concept of harmony and synergy emphasizes coordination and complementation among things. In sense of values, it refers to "peace", "harmony", "integration" and "cooperation".

The concept of peace-oriented power is not only rooted in the harmonious feature of the traditional Chinese culture, but also is a summarization of China's diplomatic practices in the past 30 years with "peace, development and cooperation" as the purposes. In the meantime, it comes into being on the basis of China's contemplation of the experience and lessons of big powers in their rise and fall (which indicates that China should not take the old road of using force or engaging in aggression and expansion abroad) and derives from China's perception of the real world (i. e., the deepening of globalization and interdependence). In fact, three essential questions at present have given birth to the concept of peace-oriented power, which are: What kind of world we are facing today? How should we pursue our national interests? And how can we address confrontations and differences among states? Contemplation on and answers to the above-mentioned questions constitute the world outlook, view of interests and view of contradiction that support peace-oriented power.

Peace-oriented power is rooted in the following view on the world: economic globalization has become a significant trend that influences international relations and promotes interdependence and integration of interests among nations; global challenges have become the main threats to the world and some common security issues faced by human beings have become increasingly salient, which require the international community to tackle with concerted efforts. Meanwhile, the world is heading toward multipolarization in an accelerated manner and the rise of emerging powers has broken the traditional international patterns of power and governance, and hence the international rules and norms need to be revised and renovated. Against such a background, mankind should promote the construction of a community of common destiny and shared interests with new ideas and in new ways.

Pursuing national interests is the starting point of a country's foreign policy. Different methods in interest seeking, however, have led to different outcomes such as war or peace, confrontation or coordination. The view of interests on which peace-oriented power relies is different from the previous ones regarding national interests. First, it stresses a win-win situation in interest-seeking. In today's world featuring globalization and interdependence among nations, the interests of all countries are intertwined and integrated, and therefore they should not view inter-state relations as a zero-sum game but need to pursue national interests through win-win cooperation. Only in this way could all countries interact in a friendly manner and ensure the sustainable development of each other's own interests. Second, shared interests are emphasized. To promote mutual interests, one should not focus only on the realization of its own interests but should join others to increase the size of shared interests, which is conducive to enlarging one's own interests as well. Third, the principle of seeking balanced interests should be followed. All nations, big or small, strong or weak, rich or poor, have their core interests and legitimate interests. All members of the international community should respect each other's core interests and major concerns while attending to each other's legitimate interests instead of seeking to maximize one's own interest. Only in this way, could states build mutual trust and make cooperation possible.

Confrontation (including divergences, disputes and conflicts, etc.) is the normal state of inter-state relations. How to address confrontation has always been a test of the political wisdom of mankind, which also reflects the level of evolution the human society achieves. The view of confrontation on which peace-oriented power is based calls upon states to address differences and disputes in ways conforming to the 21st century. First of all, it advocates resolving divergences through dialogue, consultation and negotiation rather than confrontation and settling disputes through peaceful means instead of using force. Even in some circumstances where the use of force is inevitable, force must be used in a limited and appropriate way only to promote the eventual political settlement of the disputes. Second, it insists that the settlement of disputes should follow its natural course and, when conditions are not ripe, disputes should be shelved until the right time comes. In addition, it also calls on nations to resolve their divergences in a tolerant manner. The best way to address contradiction is to find the equilibrium of interests for all countries concerned instead of seeking for complete victory over others, which requires both the sense of compromise and tolerance and creative thinking.

11.3 COMPOSITION OF PEACE-ORIENTED POWER AND ITS APPLICATION

Peace-oriented power is constituted by various integrative elements including economy, diplomacy, culture, security and international politics. More importantly, each element of power is closely connected with its specific way of application.

11.3.1 The economic element and its application.

The economic element of peace-oriented power takes the form of economic interaction with the outside world. This interaction conforms to the general trend of globalization and regionalization and serves to advance globalization toward achieving balanced and universal benefits as well as win-win results, promote the establishment of just and reasonable international institutions and rules, and push forward regional economic cooperation in an equal, mutually beneficial and practical manner. External economic exchange should seek mutual benefits and win-win results, rather than pursuing the maximization of one's own interests; and foreign aid should aim at accelerating the economic and social development of the recipient countries, rather than being used as a tool to influence the internal affairs of the recipients and obtain political influence over them.

11.3.2 The diplomatic element and its application.

The diplomatic element of peace-oriented power calls for promoting trust and cultivating goodwill as well as expanding inter-state connection, communication and cooperation with other countries. Interactions between states should be based on sincerity and integrity and avoid playing double game, showing bad faith or sowing dissension and framing evidence. When divergences arise between two countries, diplomacy should function as a means of persuasion and negotiation instead of imposing pressures and making threats. Diplomacy should pursue the principle of non-interference of the internal affairs of other countries and never be used as a tool to exercise political control over other countries. Meanwhile, in an era of globalization and mutually independent interests, diplomacy should play the role of promoting peace and stability for the country beset by internal conflicts and turbulence.

11.3.3 The cultural element and its application.

The cultural element of peace-oriented power refers to cultural exchange. While facilitating the exchange of various cultures, globalization may lead to expansion of the strong cultures and contraction of the weak ones. The external cultural exchange advocated by peace-oriented power is aimed at promoting the communication and understanding between different countries and different cultures, enriching the spiritual world of mankind, and elevating the cultural attainment of various nations through learning from and complementing each other. While pursuing the traits of the times, cultural interaction should also respect the diversity of cultures and acknowledge the fact that diverse and colorful cultures are more helpful to meet the spiritual need of mankind than the single culture. The cultural element of peace-oriented power refrains from exporting values and ideology through cultural exchanges as well as seeking cultural hegemony.

11.3.4 The security element and its application.

Peace-oriented power pursues common security and cooperative security, rather than absolute security and security through alliance. It advocates settling international disputes through peaceful means and opposes using force at will. The essential attitude of peace-oriented power toward military forces is: it does not oppose building a moderate defense force by a country but opposes the practice of seeking excess military advantage; not oppose using military force but advocates that the use of military force should be strictly confined to the maintenance of its core interests (such as state sovereignty and territorial integrity), self-defense (such as fight against invasion, protection of its domestic and overseas legitimate interests from threat), as well as the provision of public goods to the international community such as peace-keeping, disaster relief, maintenance of free navigation and humanitarian intervention, rather than using it to seek geopolitical interests or regime change in other countries.

11.3.5 The international politics element and its application.

The international politics element of peace-oriented power implies that China shall play a leadership role in world affairs in a responsible and constructive manner, which includes putting forward progressive ideas, setting action agendas, providing public goods, and advancing international cooperation. Along with the rise of its comprehensive national strength, China has been playing and will play an even greater leading role in world economic and political affairs. It is the result of globalization as well as the demonstration of China as a responsible big power. But China does not consider itself as the sole leader of the world, and would never seek to monopolize the leadership of world affairs. Instead, China stands for a collective leadership, that is, countries concerned take the responsibilities together and cooperate in dealing with world affairs. In the meantime, China attaches importance to playing the international role in a multilateral approach, with international mechanisms as the platform and international norms as the guiding principle. China will reform the incumbent mechanisms, create new ones and reasonably adjust and modify the rules of game in line with the changing international situation.

11.4 FEATURES OF PEACE-ORIENTED POWER

First, **it is unique and creative.** As a world power that inherits profound and harmonious cultural traditions, persists in taking the road of peaceful development, and advocates the building of a harmonious world, China puts forward the concept of peace-oriented power, which highlights the diplomatic style of China with Chinese characteristic and unique Chinese wisdom. In the meantime, the peace-oriented power concept composed of the idea, power and way of application has transcended the traditional power classification (for example, political, economic and military power, or hard and soft power) and shifted the focus from the magnitude and nature of power alone to the way of its application. This creative thinking has not only renovated the understanding of power and enriched its connotation but also deepened the perception of and contemplation on state actions in international politics.

Second, **it integrates values, policy conception and practice.** As mentioned above, the values advocated by peace-oriented power include peace, concord, harmony, integration and cooperation; its policy conceptions are cherishing peace and cooperation, maintaining harmony in diversity and treating each other as equals, balancing interests, having sense of propriety, and seeking common interests and taking common responsibilities. A review of China's diplomatic practices since reform and opening up shows that the active promotion of "peace and development" in the world in the 1980s and 1990s, the advocacy for "peace, development and cooperation" at the beginning of the 21st century, and the implementation of China's diplomatic goal of "peace, development, cooperation and responsibility" against the backdrop of fast rise of China's comprehensive national strength have exactly fitted with the values and policy conceptions of peace-oriented power, indicating that peace-oriented power has rich contents of practice.

Third, it is inclusive and symbiotic in nature. In the West-led international system since the modern era, the dominating power highlights the balance of power and superiority and pursues uniformity of its values; its application of power (hard and soft power) has been confrontational and exclusive, which often led to confrontations and conflicts. On the contrary, the values and policy conceptions of peace-oriented power advocate peace, concord, harmony in diversity, and balanced interests, etc., embodying the inclusive and symbiotic nature of peace-oriented power.

Fourth, it bears distinct characteristics of the times. The concept of peace-oriented power reflects the need of the international politics in the 21st century. The deepening of interdependence of inter-state interests calls for win-win cooperation; the mounting common challenges confronting mankind demand for joint efforts of various countries; and the evolution of ideas and behavioral norms of the international community further shape "peace", "harmony" and "cooperation" as the mainstream values. Against such background, the concept of peace-oriented power emerges as is required, vividly annotating the characteristics of our times.

Fifth, it is strongly oriented. With the continued increase of China's comprehensive national strength, the world is concerned over how China will use its superior power outside. It is not sufficient for China to dispel the concerns of the outside world if China only repeatedly emphasizes its goodwill that it will not seek hegemony and engage in armed expansion abroad. Only by clearly and systematically expounding how China will use its power abroad and what is the difference between the way China applies its power and that the big powers in the history used to do can China really answer the external concerns.

It is of great realistic significance for China to positively build and advocate peace-oriented power in the diplomatic realm. On the one hand, the concept of peace-oriented power reflects the determination of China, a rapidly rising country, to become a new-type great power, which is conducive to shaping a more positive international image for China. On the other, given the significant changes in balance of power in the world and the prominence of global issues, the progressive concept of peace-oriented power will help push to handle international relations with a new and constructive approach so as to enhance international cooperation and establish new type of great power relations.

It goes without saying that the building of peace-oriented power will confront a number of challenges. Just take two for example. One is whether China will be able to maintain sound economic, social and political development, effectively resolve the various external restraints, and properly handle all sorts of challenges from the outside. The other is whether the international community, especially some big powers, the United States in particular, will be able to respond positively to the progressive concepts raised by China and willing to push for the transformation of the international system and international politics.

(Wu Xinbo, Institute of International Studies, Fudan University, Shanghai, China)

CHAPTER 12　Optimal Path for Controlling CO_2 Emissions in China: A Centralized DEA Approach

P. Zhou, Z. R. Sun, D. Q. Zhou

Abstract: This paper proposes several centralized data envelopment analysis (DEA) models for determining the optimal allocation of CO_2 emissions under spatial, temporal and spatial-temporal allocation strategies, respectively. The centralized DEA models have been applied to study the optimal path for controlling CO_2 emissions in China. A sensitivity analysis of optimal emission path on the change in emission control coefficient under spatial-temporal allocation strategy is further carried out. Our empirical results suggest that earlier emission reduction strategy is more appropriate for economically developed regions in China. Of the three strategies, spatial-temporal allocation strategy seems to be the most promising for achieving the optimal control of CO_2 emissions at national level since it is more encompassing by considering both time and space dimensions. It is also found that there exist an inverted U-shape relationship between aggregate optimal GDP and emission control coefficient, which indicates that modest emission reduction policies could be more appropriate for China in order to achieve the joint goals of economic growth and CO_2 emission reduction.

Keywords: CO_2 emissions; Allocation; Data envelopment analysis; Undesirable outputs

12. 1　INTRODUCTION

As one of the most populous developing countries, China has gained rapid economic growth supported by huge energy consumption for the past several decades. Accordingly, the amount of CO_2 emissions in China has also kept increasing over time although its per capita CO_2 emission is still relatively low. To control the increase in CO_2 emissions and promote low-carbon development, China central government has set the target of reducing its unit GDP CO_2 emissions (i. e. CO_2 emission intensity) by 17% by the end of 2015 with 2010 as the reference year in its "Twelfth Five-Year Plan". A series of energy conservation and emission reduction strategies have also been formulated and implemented, which signals China's domestic intent to control and even reduce CO_2 emission. For instance, China central government has decomposed the national target into provincial ones by considering many factors including economic development level, industrial structure, energy conservation potential, environmental capacity and national economic planning. Due to the complexity of reaching a compromise between different provinces in China, the current decomposition method may not be optimal in economic sense. It is meaningful to further look into the optimal control of CO_2 emissions in China.

Many earlier studies have developed models for examining the optimal control of CO_2 and other greenhouse gases (GHGs) emissions by linking world economy and its interactions with climate. For instance, Nordhaus (1992) proposed the DICE model for estimating the optimal path of reducing GHGs. Tol (1997) developed the FUND model to study the optimal emission control strategies under corporation and non-corporation scenarios. Ha-Duong et al. (1997) used a compact intertemporal optimization model to examine CO_2 emission abatement paths under the constraints of long-term CO_2 concentrations. The study by Tol (1999) applied the FUND model to examine the implications of various discount rates on the optimal emission control. Tol (2002) further employed the FUND model to systematically investigate the sensitivity of the optimal control of CO_2 emissions to the specification of the social welfare function. Although these studies have substantially examined the issue of optimal emission control, Nordhaus (2007) pointed that how much and how fast GHGs emissions should be reduced remain an open question.

On the other hand, differing from the above studies based on integrated assessment models, some researchers have recently applied data envelopment analysis (DEA) to investigate the timing of GHG emission reduction and the reallocation of emission permits[1]. Kuosmanen et al. (2009) developed a DEA approach to performing efficiency analysis of alternative timing strategies in GHGs abatement. Lozano et al. (2009) presented a DEA approach to address the centralized reallocation of emission permits by considering three alternative objectives. Färe et al. (2010) proposed a general DEA framework for determining the optimal intertemporal resource allocation, which was further used by Färe et al. (2012) to study the timing reductions of CO_2 emissions in 28 OECD countries over time. Wei et al. (2012) used a slacks-based DEA model to study the regional allocation of CO_2 reduction burden in China.

In line with previous work on DEA-based CO_2 emission allocation, this paper attempts to use DEA to model the optimal control of CO_2 emissions in China from an efficiency analysis point of view. While earlier studies mainly focused on temporal or spatial allocation, in this study we attempt to investigate both spatial and temporal allocation of CO_2 emissions simultaneously in order to determine the optimal path for controlling CO_2 emissions. Methodologically, this paper extends Färe et al. (2012) by developing a DEA model for spatial-temporal allocation of CO_2 emissions. In empirical study, we not only derive the optimal emission path at province level under three alternative emission allocation strategies but also investigate the sensitivity of optimal emission path on emission control coefficient.

---

[1] DEA, a well-established nonparametric efficiency evaluation methodology, has attracted great attention in energy and environmental studies (Barros, 2008; Barros and Peypoch, 2008; Zhou et al., 2008). It has also been used to study the problem of efficient resource allocation. Examples of such studies include Lozano and Villa (2004), Korhonen and Syrjanen (2004), Asmild et al. (2009), Chen and Zhu (2011), and Wu et al. (in press). The fact that emissions permit is also a kind of resource in the era of climate change demonstrate the appropriateness of DEA in CO_2 emission allocation.

The remainder of this paper is organized as follows. Section 2 introduces several centralized DEA models for spatial, temporal and spatial-temporal allocation of CO_2 emissions. In Section 3, we apply the centralized DEA approach to modeling the optimal control of CO_2 emissions in China and present the results obtained. Section 4 concludes this paper with the main findings as we as the limitations of this study.

12.2　METHODOLOGY

12.2.1　Environmental DEA technology

Consider a production process that converts M inputs to single desirable output (y) and CO_2 emissions (c) as one undesirable output. Let $x = (x_1, x_2, \cdots, x_M)$ denote the vector of inputs. Then the environmental production technology can be conceptually described as (Färe et al., 2005) :

$$T = \{ (x, y, c) : x \text{ can produce } (y, c) \} \qquad (1)$$

In production economics, T is often assumed to be a closed and bounded set, which implies that finite inputs can only generate finite outputs. In addition, inputs and desirable output are assumed to be strongly or freely disposable, while undesirable output is supposed to be weakly disposable[1]. The weak disposability of CO_2 emissions implies that reducing CO_2 emissions is not free while it is possible to reduce desirable output and CO_2 emissions proportionally. The nulljointness condition of desirable and undesirable outputs is also imposed, which implies that CO_2

[1] Modeling weak disposability in DEA has received much attention in the literature (Kuosmanen, 2005; Zhou et al. 2008b). Several recent studies such as Forsund (2009) and Murty et al. (2012) have discussed the weakness of weak disposability in modeling the generation of bad outputs. More recently, Sueyoshi and Goto (2012a) revisited the concepts concerning disposability and proposed the concepts of "natural disposability" and "managerial disposability" from the viewpoint of corporate strategy for adapting regulation change on undesirable outputs. This novel classification of disposability represents an important theoretical development in modeling undesirable outputs which laid an alternative theoretical foundation for future studies. Under the conceptual framework of natural/managerial disposability, Sueyoshi and Goto have also carried out a number of theoretical and empirical studies on DEA for environmental assessment. See, for example, Sueyoshi and goto (2012b,c,d).

emissions are unavoidable in order to produce certain amount of desirable output in the production process. Mathematically, the weak disposability and nulljointness assumptions can be respectively represented by

(i) If $(x,y,c) \in T$ and $0 < \theta \leqslant 1$, then $(x,\theta y,\theta c) \in T$.

(ii) If $(x,y,c) \in T$ and $c = 0$, then $y = 0$.

The environmental production technology for modeling the joint production of y and c has so far been conceptually defined, which requires further characterization to be used in practical studies. A common practice is to formulate the environmental production technology by using the piecewise linear combinations of the observed data. Assume there are $k = 1,2,\cdots,K$ decision making units (DMUs) and the vectors of inputs for DMUk is $x_k = (x_{1k},x_{2k},\cdots,x_{Mk})$. Further assume that the amounts of desirable output and CO_2 emissions by DMUk are respectively y_k and c_k. Then the piecewise linear environmental production technology exhibiting constant returns to scale can be formulated as

$$T = (x,y,c): \sum_{k=1}^{K} z_k x_{mk} \leqslant x_m, m = 1,2,\cdots,M$$

$$\sum_{k=1}^{K} z_k y_k \geqslant y$$

$$\sum_{k=1}^{K} z_k c_k = c \tag{2}$$

$$z_k \geqslant 0, k = 1,2,\cdots,K$$

T and its extensions have been widely used in energy and environmental studies (Managi and Jena, 2008; Oh, 2010; Zhou et al, 2010, 2012; Barros et al., 2012; Jaraite and Di Maria, 2012; Mekaroonreung and Johnson, 2012; Kim and Kim, 2012). As T is formulated in a nonparametric DEA framework, it can also be referred to as an environmental DEA technology.

12.2.2　DEA model for spatial CO_2 allocation

The basic idea for using centralized DEA to allocate CO_2 emissions is to allow the adjustments for CO_2 emissions between different DMUs or different periods of time for the purpose of maximizing aggregate desirable output. We first model the reallocation of total CO_2 emissions permit among different DMUs at a certain period of time (e. g. t). Suppose that all the variables at period t are attached with a subscript t. Further assume that regulators have set an emission control coefficient δ for the period t, which implies that the total emissions permit is equal to δ multiplying by the aggregate baseline emissions for all the DMUs. Then the centralized DEA model for spatial reallocation of CO_2 emissions can be formulated as

$$\max \sum_{k=1}^{K} \bar{y}_k^t$$

$$s.t. \quad \sum_{k=1}^{K} z_{kl}^t x_{mk}^t \leqslant x_{ml}^t, \quad m = 1, \cdots, M; l = 1, \cdots, K$$

$$\sum_{k=1}^{K} z_{kl}^t y_k^t \geqslant \bar{y}_l^t, \quad l = 1, \cdots, K$$

$$\sum_{k=1}^{K} z_{kl}^t c_k^t = \bar{c}_l^t, \quad l = 1, \cdots, K \tag{3}$$

$$\sum_{k=1}^{K} \bar{c}_k^t = \delta \cdot \sum_{k=1}^{K} c_k^t$$

$$z_{kl}^t \geqslant 0, \quad k, l = 1, \cdots, K$$

Models (3) attempts to maximize the aggregate desirable output for all the DMUs through reallocating the total CO_2 emissions permit to different DMUs. Meanwhile, the virtual input-output pairs are required to fall within the space of environmental DEA technology. The total CO_2 emissions permit is equal to $\delta \cdot \sum_{k=1}^{K} c_k^t$, which indicates that the aggregate CO_2 emissions need to be reduced by $100(1 - \delta)$ percent compared to the aggregate baseline emissions.

Figure 12-1 provides a simple graphical illustration of model (3). Assume that three DMUs, i. e. A, B and C, employ the same inputs to produce different output combinations as shown in Figure 12-1. Then the environmental DEA technology constructed by A, B and C can be represented by the area OABCD. Compared to B, C is technically inefficient as it produces more undesirable output with the same desirable output. Spatial allocation allows regulators to reallocate CO_2 emissions permit between A, B and C in order to maximize their aggregate desirable output. If $\delta = 1$, the optimal solution to model (3) is $\overline{y}_A^* = \overline{y}_B^* = \overline{y}_C^* = 3.67$ and $\overline{c}_A^* = \overline{c}_B^* = \overline{c}_C^* = 2.67$, which is corresponding to point E in Figure 12-1. It indicates that A, B and C all become technically efficient after the spatial CO_2 reallocation. Meanwhile, their aggregate desirable output increases by 10%, which should be attributed to the elimination of technical inefficiency. If regulators expect to decrease the amount of aggregate CO_2 emissions to 7, we can set δ as 87.5% and solve model (3). The optimal solution then becomes $\overline{y}_A^* = \overline{y}_B^* = \overline{y}_C^* = 3.33$ and $\overline{c}_A^* = \overline{c}_B^* = \overline{c}_C^* = 2.33$, which is corresponding to point F in Figure 12-1. It shows that the same aggregate desirable output can be achieved with less aggregate CO_2 emissions through spatial reallocation of CO_2 emissions.

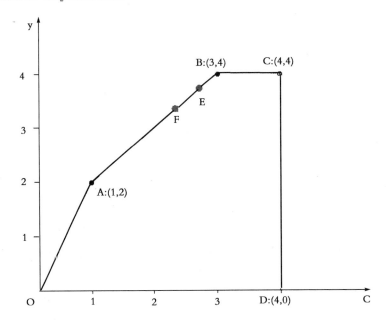

Figure 12-1   An illustration of the DEA model for spatial CO_2 allocation

12.2.3 DEA model for temporal CO_2 allocation

Temporal CO_2 emission allocation allows the timing substitution of CO_2 emissions for each DMU in order to maximize its aggregate desirable output over time. The studies by Färe et al. (2010, 2012) have provided DEA models for timing substitution of CO_2 emissions. Under the temporal allocation strategy, regulators control the CO_2 emissions permit for each DMU within a certain period of time. Each DMU seeks to maximize its aggregate desirable output through reallocating its CO_2 emissions to each period of time. Here we still assume that the total emission permit for each DMU from period of time 1 to T is equal to δ multiplying by its aggregate baseline CO_2 emissions over the same period of time. Following Färe et al. (2012), we formulate the following centralized DEA model for temporal CO_2 allocation for DMU1:

$$\max \sum_{t=1}^{T} \bar{y}_l^t$$

$$\text{s. t.} \quad \sum_{k=1}^{K} z_{kl}^t x_{mk}^t \leq x_{ml}^t, \quad m = 1, \cdots, M; t = 1, \cdots, T$$

$$\sum_{k=1}^{K} z_{kl}^t y_k^t \geq \bar{y}_l^t, \quad t = 1, \cdots, T$$

$$\sum_{k=1}^{K} z_{kl}^t c_k^t = \bar{c}_l^t, \quad t = 1, \cdots, T \tag{4}$$

$$\sum_{t=1}^{T} \bar{c}_l^t = \delta \cdot \sum_{t=1}^{T} c_l^t$$

$$z_{kl}^t \geq 0, \quad k = 1, \cdots, K$$

12.2.4 DEA model for spatial-temporal CO_2 allocation

Spatial-temporal CO_2 allocation, which is an integration of spatial and temporal allocation strategies, refers to the allocation of emissions permit between DMUs over time. Under the spatial-temporal allocation strategy, regulators control the CO_2 emissions permit for all the DMUs from period 1 to T. The purpose is to maximize the aggregate desirable output for all the DMUs during the period by allowing both DMU and timing substitutions of CO_2 emissions. The resulting centralized DEA model is formulated as

$$\max \sum_{t=1}^{T} \sum_{k=1}^{K} \overline{y}_k^t$$

$$s.t. \quad \sum_{k=1}^{K} z_{kl}^t x_{mk}^t \leqslant x_{ml}^t, \quad m = 1, \cdots, M; t = 1, \cdots, T; l = 1, \cdots, K$$

$$\sum_{k=1}^{K} z_{kl}^t y_k^t \geqslant \overline{y}_l^t, \quad t = 1, \cdots, T; l = 1, \cdots, K$$

$$\sum_{k=1}^{K} z_{kl}^t c_k^t = \overline{c}_l^t, \quad t = 1, \cdots, T; l = 1, \cdots, K \qquad (5)$$

$$\sum_{t=1}^{T} \sum_{k=1}^{K} \overline{c}_k^t = \delta \cdot \sum_{t=1}^{T} \sum_{k=1}^{K} c_k^t$$

$$z_{kl}^t \geqslant 0, \quad k, l = 1, \cdots, K; t = 1, \cdots, T$$

Clearly, model (5) is more encompassing than models (3) and (4) since it is based on the panel data and considers both spatial and temporal dimensions. By solving model (5), we may determine the optimal path for controlling CO_2 emissions at DMU level under the spatial-temporal allocation strategy. Model (3) may be regarded as a special case of model (5) when only one period of time is considered. It is required to be solved by T times in order to find the optimal paths for controlling CO_2 emissions for all the DMUs. Model (4) is a simplification of model (5) when only one DMU is considered, which needs to be solved by K times in order to find the optimal control paths of CO_2 emissions for all the DMUs. With regarding to their modeling results, the aggregate optimum desirable output under spatial-temporal CO_2 allocation strategy is not less than the sum of the time-dependent aggregate optimum desirable outputs under spatial CO_2 allocation strategy or the sum of DMU-dependent aggregate optimum desirable output under temporal CO_2 allocation strategy.

12. 3　EMPIRICAL STUDY

12.3.1　Data

We apply the centralized DEA approach described in Section 2 to investigate how the aggregate CO_2 emissions are efficiently allocated to different provinces in China during 1995-2010. In addition to take CO_2 emissions as the single undesirable output, we choose capital stock (K), labor force (L) and energy consumption (E) as inputs and regional gross domestic product (GDP) in 2000 constant prices as the single desirable output. This input-output setting is essentially consistent with many earlier studies such as Zhou et al. (2010), Guo et al. (2011) and Wang et al. (2012).

The data on provincial capital stock are estimated by using the perpetual inventory approach with 1952 as the starting year. In estimating capital stock, gross fixed capital formation was employed as the annual investment data, which is converted to 2000 constant prices by using the investment price index developed by Zhang (2008). The data on labor force, GDP and energy consumption are collected from various issues of China Statistical Yearbook released by the National Bureau of Statistics of China. With regards to provincial CO_2 emissions, there are no officially released data in China. In this study, we use the data on final energy consumption breakdown by energy type and the IPCC emission factors to estimate the provincial CO_2 emissions.

To investigate the optimal emission path at regional level, we divide 30 provinces into four areas, i. e. east, central, west and northeast areas. The four areas are further divided into eight economic regions by following the report "Strategy and Policy for Regional Harmonious Development" released by China State Council Development Research Center. Table 12-1 shows the compositions of four areas and eight economic regions.

Table 12-1 Compositions of four areas and eight economic regions in China

Area	Economic Region	Provinces
East	Northern Coastal	Beijing, Tianjin, Hebei, Shandong
	Eastern Coastal	Shanghai, Jiangsu, Zhejiang
	Southern Coastal	Fujian, Guangdong, Hainan
Central	Middle Yellow River	Shanxi, Inner Mongolia, Henan, Shaanxi
	Middle Yangtze River	Anhui, Jiangxi, Hubei, Hunan
West	Southwest	Guangxi, Chongqing, Sichuan, Guizhou, Yunan
	Northwest	Gansu, Qinghai, Ningxia, Xinjiang, Tibet
Northeast	Northeast	Liaoning, Jilin, Heilongjiang

Figure 12-2 shows the trends in GDP and CO_2 emissions for the four areas over time. Clearly, there was an increasing trend in the regional GDP and CO_2 emissions, and east area registered for the largest growth rate in CO_2 emissions. The variation in the regional CO_2 emissions across different areas has become larger, which could be explained by the increasing discrepancy in their economic outputs. It can also be seen from Figure 12-2 that since 2005 east area has cutting down its growth in CO_2 emissions while kept relatively faster economic growth. However, central and west areas have shown a higher growth rate for CO_2 emissions than that for GDP, which might be attributed to the domestic transfer of energy-intensive industries from east area to central and west areas.

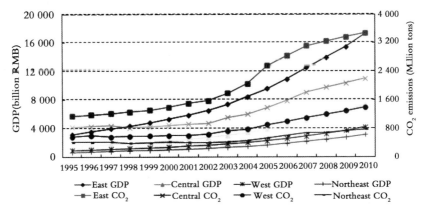

Figure 12-2 Trend in GRP and CO_2 emissions in four areas in China, 1995-2010

12.3.2 Estimation results

We first use the three centralized DEA models with emission control coefficient $\delta = 1$ to study the optimal allocation of CO_2 emissions between different provinces in 1995-2010 under spatial, temporal and spatial-temporal allocation strategies, respectively. In this analysis, the baseline aggregate CO_2 emissions are assumed to be the same as the actual aggregate CO_2 emissions. For spatial allocation, $\delta = 1$ implies that for each year the total emissions permit is equal to the sum of the provincial CO_2 emissions. For temporal allocation, $\delta = 1$ implies that for each province the total emissions permit from 1995 to 2010 is equal to the sum of its actual CO_2 emissions during the period. For spatial-temporal allocation, $\delta = 1$ implies that the total emissions permit for all the provinces in 1995-2010 is equal to China's cumulative CO_2 emissions during the period.

Figure 12-3 shows the optimal emission paths for the provinces in the east area under the three allocation strategies. Their actual CO_2 emission paths are also provided for comparison purpose. It can be seen from Figure 12-3 that for most of the provinces in east area their CO_2 emissions after reallocation are quite close to their actual emissions. It indicates that these provinces can reach the production frontier through minor adjustments for CO_2 emissions due to their relatively advanced level of production technology. Under the three allocation strategies, the optimal emissions for all the provinces but Hainan in east area are smaller than their actual emissions after 2005, while before 2005 an opposite phenomenon is observed. It implies that the strategy of "first increasing, later reducing" might be more appropriate for the provinces in east area to control their CO_2 emissions. One possible explanation is that the technology gap between east area and other areas has become enlarged since 2005, which provides possibility for east area to allocate its 'redundant' CO_2 emissions to earlier stage under temporal and spatial-temporal allocation strategies. As a result, reducing CO_2 emissions at a later stage for east area would possibly benefit the provinces in other areas to catch up with the production frontier. On the other hand, under spatial allocation strategy, the 'redundant' CO_2 emissions are often allocated to the provinces in central and west areas with lower technology levels in order to maximize the aggregate desirable output. As a result, the emissions permit allocated to the provinces in east area are generally lower than their actual emissions.

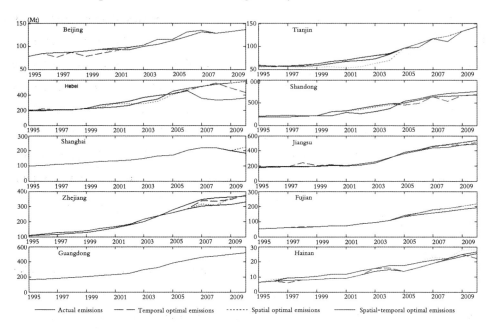

Figure 12-3   Optimal emissions paths for the provinces in east area

Figure 12-4 shows the optimal emission paths for the provinces in central area under three allocation strategies together with their actual emissions. It can be found that under the spatial allocation strategy, the optimal emission allowances for central provinces are generally lower than their actual emissions before 2005. Under the spatial-temporal allocation strategy, most of the provinces in central area have exhibited "later reducing" characteristic although it is not as obvious as eastern area. For instance, the optimal emission allowances for Shanxi provinces are obviously lower than its actual emissions since 2007, which indicates that this province should reduce more emissions at a later stage.

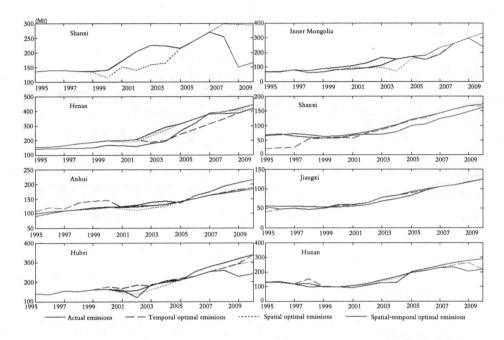

Figure 12-4   Optimal emission paths for the provinces in central area

Figure 12-5 shows the optimal CO_2 emission paths for the provinces in west area under three allocation strategies together with their actual emissions. It can seem that the optimal emission allowances for western provinces are generally higher than their actual emissions, which implies that western area should be given more CO_2 emission allowances in order to maximize the aggregate GDP. Under spatial-temporal allocation strategy, the optimal emission allowances for provinces like Sichuan are obviously greater than their actual emissions.

Figure 12-6 shows the optimal emission paths for the three provinces in northeast area under three allocation strategies. Under temporal allocation strategy the optimal emission allowances for Heilongjiang are lower than its actual emissions after 2005. It indicates that Heilongjiang needs to reduce more emissions at a later stage in order to maximize its cumulative GDP over time. Of the three provinces, Liaoning and Heilongjiang will be given more emission allowances under spatial-temporal allocation strategy than under temporal allocation strategy.

223

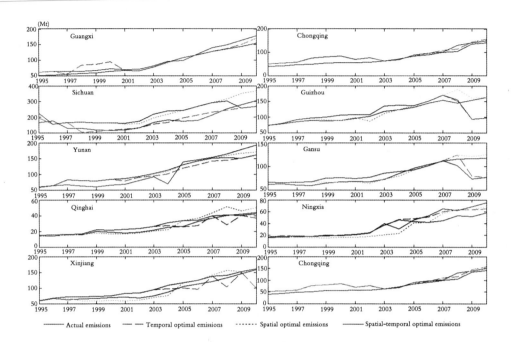

Figure 12-5　Optimal emission paths for the provinces in west area

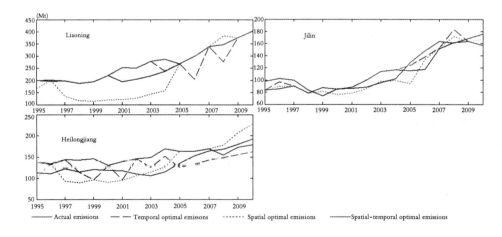

Figure 12-6　Optimal emission paths for the provinces in northeast area

Figure 12-7 shows the optimal emission paths under three allocation strategies for eight economic regions. It can be seen from Figure 12-7 that the optimal emission path for northeast region is most while that for southern coastal region is least sensitive to the choice of emission allocation strategy. The turning point after which the optimal emission allowances become lower than the actual emissions varies across different regions. Under the spatial-temporal allocation strategy, the turning points for the northern coastal, eastern coastal and southern coastal areas appear in 2005. The turning points for northeast and middle Yangtze River regions arises in 2006, while those for northwest and middle Yellow River regions arise in 2007 and that for southwest region occurs in 2008. These results suggest that the turning point appear earlier for more developed regions than for less developed regions. It implies that less developed regions should implement emission reduction later than more developed regions from the point of view of efficiency analysis.

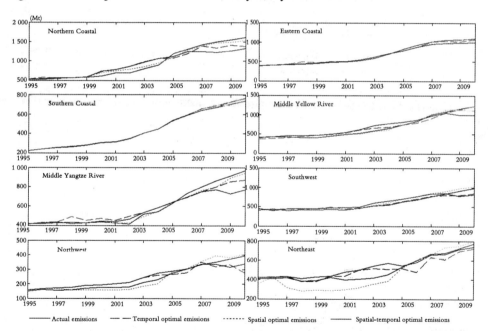

Figure 12-7 Optimal emission paths for eight regions in China, 1995-2010

Table 12-2 shows the aggregate optimal GDP and CO_2 emissions for eight regions after the emission reallocation under three allocation strategies during the period 1995-2010. No matter which allocation strategy is taken, the regional aggregate optimal GDP are all greater than their actual GDP which could be attributed to the elimination of inefficiency. On the other hand, some regions increase while others decrease their CO_2 emissions after reallocation. At state level, spatial-temporal allocation strategy would achieve higher aggregate desirable output through removing inefficiency, which may be explained by the fact that spatial-temporal strategy adjust CO_2 emissions in two dimensions and have more relaxed constraints. At regional level, under spatial-temporal allocation strategy four regions including Northern Coastal, Eastern Coastal, Southern Coastal and Middle Yangtze River would achieve the joint goals of increasing GDP and reducing CO_2 emissions.

Table 12-2   Regional aggregate optimal GDP and emission allowance
under three allocation strategies, 1995-2010

Region	GDP (unit: 100 million RMB)				CO_2 emissions (unit: Mt)			
	Actual	Spatial allocation	Temporal allocation	Spatial-temporal allocation	Actual	Spatial allocation	Temporal allocation	Spatial-temporal allocation
Northern Coastal	457373	555294	564504	578480	15030	15101	15030	14629
Eastern Coastal	490420	548978	545195	558979	10876	10774	10876	10578
Southern Coastal	378557	382040	379440$^\triangle$	385506 *	7049	7051	7049	6974
Middle Yellow River	263398	371434	370566	381445	10831	11091	10831	11098
Middle Yangtze River	287028	369832	363295	383744	9366	9182	9366	8936
Southwest	254951	392631	402087	408560	9261	9917	9261	9637
Northwest	69127	118456	122448	121631	3781	3785	3781	3888
Northeast	236898	276167	271815	265329	8073	7364	8073	8526
Total	2437751	3014832	3019350	3083674	74266	74266	74266	74266

12.3.3 Sensitivity analysis

The results presented in Section 3.2 are based on the assumption of emission control coefficient equal to unity, which implies that the total emissions permit is the same as the baseline emissions. Although the empirical study is based on historical data, it would still be meaningful to examine how the change in total emissions permit affects the aggregate optimal desirable output and the optimal emission path under three allocation strategies. In this section, we gradually change the emission control coefficient δ from 1.0 to 0.5 and resolve models (3) to (5), which means that the total emissions permit changes from 100% to 50% of the baseline emissions. Figure 12-8 shows how the aggregate optimal GDP varies with different δ under alternative allocation strategies.

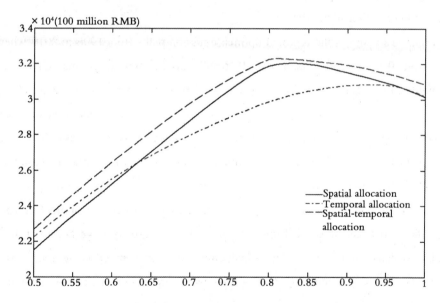

Figure 12-8　Aggregate optimal GDP with different δ

It can be seen from Figure 12-8 that there is an inverted U relationship between optimal GDP and δ under the three allocation strategies. It implies that controlling CO_2 emissions to a certain degree will not affect the optimal desirable output with inefficiency being eliminated. However, too strict emission reduction policy may negatively affect optimal desirable output. Under the spatial-temporal allocation strategy, the aggregate optimal GDP is the same as the actual GDP level when $\delta = 0.55$. It suggests that it would be possible to reduce 45% of CO_2 emissions while producing the same desirable output through eliminating inefficiency. When δ is equal to 0.93, 0.83 and 0.81, temporal, spatial and spatial-temporal strategies would still respectively achieve their optimal GDP levels. Figure 12-8 also shows that the optimal GDP under spatial-temporal allocation strategy is always above that under spatial or temporal allocation strategy no matter how the emission control coefficient varies. It is an indication that spatial-temporal allocation strategy has the largest potential in producing more desirable output without increasing CO_2 emissions. Therefore, it is meaningful to further investigate the optimal emission path at regional level under the spatial-temporal allocation strategy.

Figure 12-9 shows the regional optimal emission paths from 1995 to 2010 when δ varies from 0.5 to 1.0. As $\delta = 0.81$ results in the highest optimal GDP, it is reasonable to take the regional optimal emission path with $\delta = 0.8$ as the benchmark emission path. As shown in Figure 12-9, for southern coastal and eastern coastal regions the optimal emission paths with $\delta = 0.8$ are consistent with their actual emission paths. It indicates that the emission allowances for southern coastal and eastern coastal regions would not be affected if the total emissions permit is reduced by 20%. Figure 12-9 also shows that the derivations between the optimal emission path with $\delta = 0.8$ and those with other δ values were relatively large before 2007. A possible explanation is that the marginal emission abatement costs at a later stage become larger so that reducing CO_2 emissions at an earlier stage would be more beneficial.

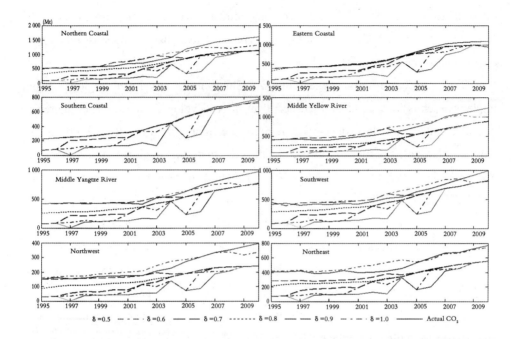

Figure 12-9　Regional optimal emission path under spatial-temporal allocation strategy

12.4　CONCLUSION

Investigating the optimal path for controlling CO_2 emissions would provide analytical foundation for the design of efficient emission reduction policies. Many earlier studies have developed integrated assessment models for determining the optimal path for controlling CO_2 emissions at global level. Besides, DEA, a well-established efficiency evaluation and resource allocation tool, has also been used to study the optimal allocation of emission allowance at different levels. In this paper, we propose several centralized DEA models for the spatial, temporal and spatial-temporal allocation of CO_2 emissions from the point of view of maximizing desirable output. The models have been applied to study the optimal allocation of CO_2 emissions between different provinces in China from 1995 to 2010, based on which the optimal paths for controlling CO_2 emissions at regional and provincial levels under three different allocation strategies are determined. We have also investigated the sensitivity of optimal GDP and CO_2 emissions on the change in emission control coefficient at regional level.

Our empirical results suggest that in China more developed regions should implement emissions reduction earlier than less developed areas. The aggregate desirable output for less developed regions are more sensitive to the change of emission control coefficient, which indicates that the regional discrepancy in economic development level needs to be considered in designing emission reduction policies in China. Comparing the three alternative allocation strategies, spatial-temporal allocation strategy seems to be the most promising for achieving the optimal control of CO_2 emissions at nation level since the strategy is more encompassing by considering both time and space dimensions. We also find that there exist an inverted U-shape relationship between aggregate optimal GDP and emission control coefficient, which indicates that modest emission reduction policies could be more appropriate for China to achieve the joint goals of economic growth and CO_2 emission reduction.

Despite the contributions of this work, it has inevitably some limitations. First, the centralized DEA approach allocates CO_2 emissions in an efficient way and the fairness criterion is not considered in the models. It is meaningful to extend the centralized DEA approach proposed in this paper by incorporating the criterion of fairness in appropriate ways. Second, our empirical study is only based on China's historical data, while a study based on future data may provide more useful results for the design of efficient emission reduction policies in China. Third, our proposed approach is built upon the traditional environmental DEA technology exhibiting constant returns to scale. Since many scholars have developed alternative environmental production technologies as well as new disposability concepts on modeling the generation of undesirable outputs, it would also be worthwhile extending the centralized DEA models for CO_2 emission allocation based on the new developments. Finally, although our empirical study is based on the provincial data in China, given data availability, the approach can be applied to lower-level (e. g.

plant level) cases to explore the optimal path for controlling and reducing CO_2 emissions in one specific sector.

References

[1] Asmild, M., Paradi, J. C., Pastor, J. T., 2009. Centralized resource allocation BCC models. Omega 37, 40-49.

[2] Barros, C. P., 2008. Efficiency analysis of hydroelectric generating power plants: A case study for Portugal. Energy Economics 30, 59-75.

[3] Barros, C. P., Managi, S., Matousek, R., 2012. The technical efficiency of the Japanese banks: Non-radial directional performance measurement with undesirable output. Omega 40, 1-8.

[4] Barros, C. P., Peypoch, N., 2008. Technical efficiency of thermoelectric power plants. Energy Economics 30, 3118-3127.

[5] Chen, C. M., Zhu, J., 2011. Efficient resource allocation via efficiency bootstraps: An application to R&D project budgeting. Operations Research 59, 729-741.

[6] Färe, R., Grosskopf, S., Margaritis, D., 2010. Time substitution with application to data envelopment analysis. European Journal of Operational Research 206, 686-690.

[7] Färe, R., Grosskopf, S., Noh, D. W., Weber, W., 2005. Characteristics of a polluting technology: theory and practice. Journal of Econometrics 126, 469-492.

[8] Färe, R., Grosskopf, S., Margaritis, D., Weber, W. L., 2012. Technological change and timing reductions in greenhouse gas emissions. Journal of Productivity Analysis 37, 205-216.

[9] Forsund, R., 2009. Good modeling of bad outputs: Pollution and multiple-output production. International Review of Environmental and Resource Economics 3, 1-38.

[10] Guo, X. D., Zhu, L., Fan, Y., Xie, B. C., 2011. Evaluation of potential

reductions in carbon emissions in Chinese provinces based on environmental DEA. Energy Policy 39, 2352-2360.

[11] Ha-Duong, M., Grubb, M. J., Hourcade, J. C., 1997. Influence of socioeconomic inertia and uncertainty on optimal CO_2-emission abatement. Nature 390, 270-273.

[12] Jaraite, J., Di Maria, C., 2012. Efficiency, productivity and environmental policy: A case study of power generation in the EU. Energy Economics 34, 1557-1568.

[13] Kim, K., Kim, Y., 2012. International comparison of industrial CO_2 emission trends and the energy efficiency paradox utilizing production-based decomposition. Energy Economics 34, 1724-1741.

[14] Korhonen, P., Syrjanen, M., 2004. Resource allocation based on efficiency analysis. Management Science 50, 1134-1144.

[15] Kuosmanen, T., 2005. Weak disposability in nonparametric production analysis with undesirable outputs. American Journal of Agricultural Economics 87, 1077-1082.

[16] Kuosmanen, T., Bijsterbosch, N., Dellink, R., 2009. Environmental cost-benefit analysis of alternative strategies in greenhouse gas abatement: A data envelopment analysis approach. Ecological Economics 68, 1633-1642.

[17] Lozano, S., Villa, G., Brannlund, R., 2009. Centralised reallocation of emission permits using DEA. European Journal of Operational Research 193, 752-760.

[18] Lozano, S., Villa, G., 2004. Centralized resource allocation using data envelopment analysis. Journal of Productivity Analysis 22, 143-161.

[19] Managi, S., Jena, P. R., 2008. Environmental productivity and Kuznets curve in India. Ecological Economics 65, 432-440.

[20] Mekaroonreung, M., Johnson, A. L., 2012. Estimating the shadow prices of SO_2 and NOx for U. S. coal plants: A convex nonparametric least squares approach. Energy Economics 34, 723-732.

[21] Murty, S., Russell, R. R., Levkoff, S. B., 2012. On modeling pollution-

generating technologies. Journal of Environmental Economics and Management 64, 117-135.

[22] Nordhaus, W. D., 1992. An optimal transition path for controlling greenhouse gases. Science 258, 1315-1319.

[23] Nordhaus, W. D., 2007. Critical assumptions in stern review on climate change. Science 317, 201-202.

[24] Oh, D. H., 2010. A meta-frontier approach for measuring an environmentally sensitive productivity growth index. Energy Economics 32, 146-157.

[25] Sueyoshi, T., Goto, M., 2012a. Environmental assessment by DEA radial measurement: U. S. coal-fired plants in ISO (Independent System Operator) and RTO (Regional Transmission Organization). Energy Economics 34, 663-676.

[26] Sueyoshi, T., Goto, M., 2012b. DEA radial and non-radial models for unified efficiency under natural and managerial disposability: Theoretical extension by strong complementary slackness conditions. Energy Economics 34, 700-713.

[27] Sueyoshi, T., Goto, M., 2012c. DEA environmental assessment of coal fired power plants: Methodological comparison between radial and non-radial models. Energy Economics 34, 1854-1863.

[28] Sueyoshi, T., Goto, M., 2012d. Returns to scale and damages to scale on U. S. fossil fuel power plants: Radial and non-radial approaches for DEA environmental assessment. Energy Economics 34, 2240-2259.

[29] Tol, R. S. J., 1997. On the optimal control of carbon dioxide emissions: An application of FUND. Environmental Modeling and Assessment 2, 151-163.

[30] Tol, R. S. J., 1999. Time discounting and optimal emission reduction: An application of FUND. Climate Change 41, 351-362.

[31] Tol, R. S. J., 2002. Welfare specifications and optimal control of climate change: An application of fund. Energy Economics 24, 367-376.

[32] Wang, K., Wei, Y. M., Zhang, X., 2012. A comparative analysis of China's regional energy and emission performance: Which is the better way to deal with undesirable outputs? Energy Policy 46, 574-584.

[33] Wei, C., Ni, J., Du, L., 2012. Regional allocation of carbon dioxide abatement in China. China Economic Review 23, 552-565.

[34] Wu, J., An, Q., Ali, S., Liang, L., in press. DEA based resource allocation considering environmental factors. Mathematical and Computer Modeling, doi: 10. 1016/j. mcm. 2011. 11. 030.

[35] Zhang, J., 2008. Estimation of China's provincial capital stock (1952-2004) with applications. Journal of Chinese Economic and Business Studies 2, 177-196.

[36] Zhou, P., Ang, B. W., Poh, K. L., 2008a. A survey of data envelopment analysis in energy and environmental studies. European Journal of Operational Research 189, 1-18.

[37] Zhou, P., Ang, B. W., Poh, K. L., 2008b. Measuring environmental performance under different environmental DEA technologies. Energy Economics 30, 1-14.

[38] Zhou, P., Ang, B. W., Han, J. Y., 2010. Total-factor carbon emission performance: A Malmquist index analysis. Energy Economics 32, 194-201.

[39] Zhou, P., Ang, B. W., Wang, H., 2012. Energy and CO_2 emission performance in electricity generation: A non-radial directional distance function approach. European Journal of Operational Research 221, 625-635.

(P. Zhou, Z. R. Sun, D. Q. Zhou, College of Economics and Management, Research Centre for Soft Energy Science, Nanjing University of Aeronautics and Astronautics, Nanjing, China)

CHAPTER 13   Pakistan-India Issues: New Thinking and Approach

Riaz Mohammad Khan

13.1   INTRODUCTION

History of distrust, tensions and conflict between Pakistan and India can be traced to the circumstances of partition and freedom from the British colonial rule and tragic experiences of communal violence and large scale migrations at that time. Immediately following independence, hostilities broke out between the two countries over the disputed State of Jammu and Kashmir which persists as the root cause of conflict and a bitter legacy of the colonial era. Over the decades, the two countries have fought three wars and have had several large scale skirmishes. At times, they also engaged in serious efforts to resolve their differences, both in multi-lateral and bilateral context, with sporadic but in some cases significant success such as the Indus Water Treaty that has survived five decades of difficult relations. None of the disputes and problems that bedevil relations between the two countries are ideological or inherently intractable; they are essentially political and, thereby, resolvable.

The problems between Pakistan and India are multiple, but these can be broadly categorized into three areas. Historical disputes which include first and foremost Jammu and Kashmir, a somewhat linked issue of the Siachen Glacier, and the boundary dispute in Pakistan's south known as the Sir Creek issue. Secondly, issues relating to normalization of bilateral relations such as streamlining of trade, consular and cultural matters. Lastly, are the new issues that relate to water and combating terrorism and extremist violence.

Before a discussion of these disputes and issues, a clarification is necessary at the outset about an argument that Pakistan and India would be better advised to place the difficult Kashmir dispute on the back burner and proceed by addressing less complicated issues which could help progress towards normalization and create an environment of better trust in which ways may open up to resolve even the Kashmir dispute. The argument has a flaw and secondly efforts have been made in the past to agree on CBMs and to address other issues but success remained tentative and fragile prone to accidents causing return to regression and even hostility in bilateral relation. The flaw is that Kashmir is not simply a border or a territorial dispute such as the Kurile Islands or the Sino-Indian border dispute. It involves people in much the same way as the Palestinian issue. A territorial or a border dispute can be shelved and momentarily set aside, but the same does not apply to issues that involve basic rights of a people who cannot wait for more propitious circumstances to emerge.

This paper does not attempt detailed history and background of the various issues and only makes brief references where necessary to give the context to their present status and what could be the way forward.

13.2 THE JAMMU AND KASHMIR DISPUTE

The Jammu and Kashmir dispute is arguably the oldest issue existing on the agenda of the United Nations Security Council (UNSC) since 1948 when it was brought to the Council by India following a controversial claim that the Hindu Maharaja had acceded to India while the princely state was being invaded by Pakistan based tribes. Pakistan had expected Kashmir to its part as the population was overwhelmingly Muslim. The UNSC Resolution 47 (1948) called for a ceasefire and UN supervised plebiscite. It asked for the vacation of the Pakistani tribal elements from the State but not of the Indian troops that had been introduced ostensibly to thwart the tribal fighters. A follow-up Resolution 98 (1952) allowed both Pakistan and India to keep up to 6,000 and 18,000 troops respectively while reiterating call for plebiscite. India gradually demurred on the demand for plebiscite citing change of circumstances as Pakistan had joined the U. S. sponsored military pacts. Pakistan had done so motivated by its security concerns vis-a-vis India.

The decade-long UN efforts including [space] 11 proposals for synchronized withdrawal of troops and plebiscite as well as the Owen-Dixon plan for regional plebiscite failed mainly because of Indian opposition. India had little interest in changing the status quo as it occupied two-thirds of the Kashmir territory, including the valley. Since late 1950s, India started claiming Kashmir to be its integral part, even though Article 370 of the Indian Constitution accorded the territory a special status separate from those of the states/provinces constituting the Indian Union. There have been attempts to diplomatically resolve the dispute, in particular the foreign minister level talks in 1963 before the two countries went to war over the dispute in 1965. The next important reference to Kashmir was made in a bilateral context in the 1972 Simla Agreement concluded by the two countries in the wake of the 1971 war. The Simla agreement committed the two countries to seek a peaceful resolution of the problems and "pending (their) final settlement" agreed not to "unilaterally change the situation." With some modifications, the ceasefire line was turned into the new Line of Control (LoC) and the two sides agreed to "respect" the line "without prejudice to the positions of the two sides on the dispute."

Since the Simla Agreement, India insists on a bilateral format for resolving the dispute and rejects any UN or international intercession. The last UN reference urging both countries to settle the dispute was included in resolution 1172 adopted following nuclear tests by India and the Pakistan in 1998.

Over the past three decades, there have been a number of Kashmir related skirmishes and ingresses around the LoC, the most serious being the Siachen conflict sparked off by Indian military occupation of the Glacier in 1984. The conflict continues to this day. The other was the 1999 Kargil conflict that lasted a few months and was the result of Pakistani advance and occupation of Kargil heights overlooking the strategic Srinagar-Drass road that was the main supply line for the Indian troops positioned in the Siachen area.

While Siachen issue would be discussed separately, the reference to Kargil is important as it foreshadowed an important new approach to addressing Kashmir. Before throwing light on that approach, it is important to have a brief overview of developments within Kashmir. A disputed election in the Indian-held-Kashmir resulted in wide spread protests that by early 1990s turned into a simmering insurgency. By mid 1990s, as the insurgency intensified it was joined by elements from Azad Kashmir (Pakistan-administered-Kashmir) and Pakistan who had already been galvanized by the success of Afghan Mujahedin against the Soviet military intervention. These elements and the Kashmiri struggle received backing from official circles within Pakistan where Kashmir remains a deeply emotive issue. The Kargil operation was also justified by its proponents on the basis that it had raised the profile of the Kashmir issue and the Kashmiri struggle internationally.

The Kashmiri insurgency subsided subsequent to the Kargil crisis and the military stand-off in 2002-2003 following a terrorist attack on the Indian Parliament which the Indian government blamed on Pakistan based elements. The two countries came to the verge of another armed conflict when in May 2003, President Musharraf offered ceasefire along the Line of Control, and thus commenced a new phase of almost five years of serious efforts to reduce tensions, address unresolved issues, including Kashmir. This period saw a modicum of progress towards normalcy in bilateral relations. During the next five years period that coincided with the tenure of the newly elected democratic government in Pakistan, relations came under severe stress because of the Mumbai terrorist attacks in July 2008. Meanwhile, the Indian-held-Kashmir saw a succession of spontaneous uprisings in late 2009 and mid-2010 triggered by local incidents once again underscoring the need to heal this festering wound.

The most serious and sustained effort to address the Kashmir dispute has been made in 2005-2006 under President Musharraf and Prime Minister Manmohan Singh through the modality of what came to be known as "back channel" diplomacy. The process suffered a setback on account of the internal political crisis in Pakistan in early 2007 that eventually led to the exit of President Musharraf. It then came to a standstill after the Mumbai incident in 2008. Unlike the earlier efforts which had not gone beyond discussions and looking for possible common ground, this effort articulated clear concepts and evolved a specific structure for an agreement. In that sense the progress achieved was substantive and importantly, it still survives in a document however inconclusive.

The elements of this framework agreement that could be described as an interim settlement have been identified in various public statements by President Musharraf and include a regional division of both sides of the Line of Control, maximum self-governance for each region and facilitation of intra-regional trade and travel, softening of the LoC, thinning out of military presence and its removal from population centers, and a joint mechanism that could serve as a safeguard for protection of vital interests of both Pakistan and India as relevant to the region. In a broader sense, the concept was based on limited sovereignty of the three sides, namely, Pakistan, India and the Kashmiri people but optimum self-governance for the latter so that they become fully autonomous in managing their affairs. This has been a novel approach and it could only be possible in the post-Cold War environment when the precept of state sovereignty has softened and many of its Westphalian connotations have lost their rigor. While the process was on, the participants recognized that pushing for such a solution, even if interim, would require political measures and preparations in addition to political will and determination on the part of the political leadership in both countries.

Barring a military solution which can be ruled out as both states are declared nuclear weapon states, any political solution will have to be based more or less on similar elements, the key being maximum self-governance for the Kashmiri people and removal of the conflict-related barriers and impediments that have constricted their centuries old mutual interaction. A partial step towards that end had been taken in the shape of Kashmir related CBMs agreed between the two countries to facilitate visits across the LoC by members of divided families, and limited trade in local produce. The Srinagar-Muzaffarabad bus service was a beginning. While these tentative steps have survived they suffered set back first on account of the 2005 earthquake that had damaged roads and bridges in the area, and then because of the downturn in Pakistan-India relations since 2008. These measures need to be expanded and made robust as the two sides wait for more conducive circumstances to revive efforts for a political settlement.

A no-war or non-aggression pact has come up for discussions between the two countries and is inextricably linked to the Kashmir dispute, notwithstanding the fact that the Simla Agreement commits the two countries to peaceful settlement of disputes. Pakistan sees little sense in such an agreement while Kashmir remains unresolved and a continuing source of tension. On the other hand, India sees Pakistani support to Kashmiri insurgent elements as a form of covert war. Thus, a no-war or non-aggression pact is unlikely to precede progress on Kashmir but it could supplement a settlement agreement, if and when achieved, as an additional confidence building measure.

Subsisting agitation and the intermittent uprisings in the Indian-held-Kashmir are rooted in Kashmiri disaffection and rejection of their current political predicament. Deployment of over half million security forces and imposition of coercive special laws by India have failed to pacify the Kashmiris to accept the status quo. These factors by themselves may not combine to bring about a change, but they make a case and are a constant reminder for addressing the longstanding Kashmir dispute in the interest of peace and normalcy in South Asia. Another sinister aspect of the persistence of disputes such as Kashmir in South Asia and Palestine in the Middle East is that it feeds the narrative of extremist elements who justify armed struggle and violence to rectify the continuing denial of justice.

13.3   THE SIACHEN GLACIER CONFLICT

The Siachen Glacier is part of the erstwhile state of Jammu and Kashmir and therefore the conflict is an extension of the Kashmir dispute; but it can be resolved independently. Efforts to address it on its own had preceded the Composite Dialogue initiated between Pakistan and India in 1997 where Siachen figured as a separate agenda point. The conflict had resulted from Indian military ingress into the uninhabited glacier area, taking advantage of the absence of demarcation of the LoC beyond point NJ9842, which in Pakistani view should have extended to the Karakoram Pass, the last point of the delineated provisional boundary between Pakistan and China agreed in 1963. More importantly, Pakistan regarded the Indian ingress as a clear violation of the 1972 Simla Agreement that committed the two sides not to change the ground situation unilaterally. The three decade long conflict on this highest battle field in the world has inflicted a large number of casualties on both sides mainly resulting from extreme weather conditions.

The earliest thinking about redeployment/disengagement of forces is attributed to meetings between Prime Minister Benazir Bhutto and Prime Minister Rajiv Gandhi on the margin of the December 1988 SAARC Summit in Islamabad. In July 1989, the two Prime Ministers endorsed an understanding reached at defense secretaries level talks earlier in June for redeployment of forces, avoidance of use of force and determination of future positions on the ground. In 1992, the two sides were close to signing an agreement for redeployment to positions at the time of the Simla Agreement, when the Indian side raised the question of authentication of the line of actual control on the Glacier. Pakistan refused as it apprehended that such authentication could be tantamount to recognition of the Indian ingression. Subsequent efforts to overcome the problem of authentication failed.

The idea of disengagement was once again picked up when Prime Minister Manmohan Singh made a public statement towards end 2004 that "(Siachen Glacier) should be turned into a mountain of peace." During the third round of Composite Dialogue in 2005, Pakistan suggested creation of a zone of disengagement with provisions of joint monitoring and management and maps attached showing schedule of disengagement which by definition would show the current line of actual control. While India has not rejected the idea of such a zone, there have been indications of

Indian Army's objection to withdrawal from the Glacier. Following initial doubts expressed through press articles that Pakistan could take advantage of the disengagement process, something that could be easily addressed, the tone changed to simple assertion of the claim that Indian troops were present in their own territory. In the wake of the Gayari avalanche in April 2012 in which 140 Pakistanis, mostly soldiers, lost their lives, Pakistani Army Chief's offer for early resolution of the issue did not elicit any response, suggesting Indian reluctance to address the issue at least on stand-alone basis.

Incidentally, a track-II exercise that involved senior civil and army retired officers of both countries extensively discussed the issue and made detailed recommendations for the creation of a zone of disengagement.

The Siachen conflict has an important environmental dimension beyond political and military consideration, and needs to be factored in to underscore the urgency to end this senseless conflict and jointly and thoughtfully manage the Glacier. This should be the basis of the new approach to the issue.

The Karakoram-Himalayan glacier systems form one the most fragile eco-systems in the world. They are also critically important to the survival of hundreds of millions of people living in Pakistan and northern India where agriculture depends on glacier fed river systems. The presence of large number of troops with logistical activity and burning of energy, including heated igloos on its surface are damaging the Siachen Glacier, besides the pollution caused by the use of equipment and ammunition that eventually washes downstream. If this activity accelerates melting of this large glacier, the impact on the surrounding eco-system will be disastrous and thereby on the livelihood of hundreds of millions of those dependent on this vital source of fresh water. It is in the interest of both Pakistan and India that they should give up myopic considerations and join hands to save this fragile eco-environment. Indeed they should also cooperate with China and other regional countries in this endeavor. Establishment of a zone replacing military activity with cooperation for the protection of the Glacier will be one step to secure not just peace but future of coming generations in the area.

13.4 SIR CREEK

The Sir Creek problem is a quintessential boundary issue. Pakistan claim that the boundary should run along the eastern bank of the creek is based on a 1914 map prepared when the Sind province was separated from Bombay Presidency during the colonial period. India invokes the Talweg principle. Today the issue has become further complicated because since the early maps were drawn nearly one century ago, the configuration of this semi-marsh land has changed. While there are three distinct segments to the boundary dispute, the two main segments relate to the Sir Creek and the maritime boundary for the exclusive economic zone. The Sir Creek surface area is close to 70 sq. Km. whereas the sea-surface area in dispute on the basis of maximalist claims of the two sides is over 1,000 Sq. Km. One related irritant is the frequent arrest by both sides of fishermen who stray into the disputed waters.

In late 1990s, the two sides agreed to survey the Sir Creek to ascertain depths. That could help quantify the problem. However, the survey could not be undertaken until February 2007 because of differences on the location of the mouth of the creek. This technical difficulty was circumvented in 2005 by agreeing to enlarge the area of survey within selected coordinates without prejudice to the positions of the two sides. In May 2007, maps were exchanged showing the depths and topography of the creek and surrounding area as well as the common maritime boundary of exclusive economic zone to the extent it can be agreed. Now the challenge is to reach an agreement which would require compromise on the basis of give and take as part of a stand-alone settlement or as part of a package involving other issues such as Siachen. Again this decision would require political will.

In its technical aspects, Sir Creek issue lends itself to innovative approaches, which are not necessarily contingent upon an agreed solid boundary. For example, in areas where a compromise proves to be difficult zone(s) under common management can be envisaged for mutual exploitation of sea-bed resources under agreed formulas and sanctuaries can be created for marine life. Such arrangement(s) can also serve as an important confidence building measure. Undoubtedly, however, an agreement on a solid boundary, if achieved, will be a neat solution.

13.5 TRADE AND ECONOMIC COOPERATION

Trade and economic cooperation between Pakistan and India is a fraction of its potential because the political relations remain afflicted with tension and conflict. This situation has also constricted cooperation within the South Asian Association for Regional Cooperation (SAARC). The issues relevant to trade can be considered in three aspects: bilateral, transit to landlocked Afghanistan and overland transit trade facility to India through the territory of Pakistan.

Over the years, Pakistan linked bilateral trade with normalcy in relation and progress towards resolution of political disputes, while India had generally emphasized opening of trade without such linkage. The two countries traded with each other on the basis of a positive list of limited tariff lines which was expanded from time to time from a figure of mere 04 in early 1970s to 1965 in 2011. The positive list was abolished in March 2012 and replaced with a negative list of tariff lines/items. Because of the expansion in the positive list, there has been corresponding increase in official trade between the two countries from a figure of 319 million Dollars in 1999 to 1578 million in 2007. Much of the trade between the two countries is, however, known to be routed through Dubai and Singapore, and this indirect trade is estimated to be close to 6 billion.

The two countries had obtained exemption from according Most Favored Nation (MFN) treatment to each other under the WTO rules. However, the issue came up when under the SAARC a free trade arrangement was being negotiated in 2005 leading to the adoption of South Asia Free Trade Agreement (SAFTA) one year later. In principle, thus, Pakistan agreed to delink its trade with India from progress on bilateral political issues, even though in a psychological sense subsisting tensions underpin over all behavior including trade. In the context of the implementation of SAFTA, India saw the denial of MFN status as a non-tariff barrier, Pakistan saw the

Indian tariff structures (a system of composite tariffs) and various other trade related conditions as impediments in Pakistani export to India even though these were not Pakistan specific. Indian system of composite tariffs effectively blocks Pakistani textile exports and phytosanitary requirements make overland export of fruits and other agricultural produce impossible. The Pakistani argument has been that MFN and replacement of the positive (restrictive) list by a negative list must lead to advantage to both sides. Pakistani exports should be able to access and fairly compete in the Indian market. To be sustainable, freer trade must benefit both countries.

In 2007, both sides had agreed to set up technical level committees to look into the issue of non-tariff barriers and two-way trade facilitation. Progress was slow as following the Mumbai incident in 2008, the composite dialogue which provided umbrella for the talks was suspended only to be resumed two years later. In September 2012, the Committee worked out three frame work agreements, namely, Redressal of Trade Grievance Agreement, Mutual Recognition Agreement and Customs Cooperation Agreement. These are aimed at harmonizing tariff lines, facilitation of banking arrangements for expeditious opening of letter for credit and payments and visa facilitation for businessmen. The Pakistan government also took a decision to formally accord MFN treatment to India but it has to go through Parliamentary approval. There is debate in the country how such a step would affect domestic industries and what would need to be protected through the mechanism of the negative list and whether the three framework agreements would help Pakistani exports access the Indian market. The signing of the three agreements and introduction of a negative list are expected to give a boost to direct bilateral trade.

Pakistan allows transit trade to landlocked Afghanistan through Karachi port. This facility can be availed by India as well. Overland transit to India, which is a much shorter route, is allowed for Afghan exports, mainly fresh fruit, but the route cannot be used to carry Indian goods. Pakistan has made exceptions on case to case basis mainly for the transit of humanitarian assistance. Over the years, Pakistan has also improved facilitation for Afghan trucks to carry goods to Wagah border with India and transshipment arrangements. Overland transit of Indian exports to

Afghanistan is linked to the larger issue of overland transit facility to India and subject to negotiating a bilateral agreement which is not on the cards. The only overland transit facility Pakistan has agreed to in the case of India has been with respect to gas pipelines from Iran and from Turkmenistan through Afghanistan. While the latter can become feasible only after the conflict in Afghanistan subsides, India dropped out of the Iran gas pipeline project after showing initial interest, ostensibly on account of its concerns over the security of the pipeline, but in reality perhaps in view of its civilian nuclear deal with the United States and the open U. S. opposition to the Iran gas pipeline project.

13.6 WATER ISSUES

The landmark Indus Water Basin Treaty of 1960 negotiated between the two countries under the auspices of the World Bank has survived tensions and wars, but of late has come under stress for a variety of reasons which range from demographic pressures on water resources to climate change and to issues and controversy over permissible use of water under the treaty for power generation in areas under Indian control. According to the treaty, India gained exclusive rights to utilize waters of the three eastern rivers of the basin and Pakistan was allocated the three western rivers. The World Bank helped build a vast system of reservoirs and canals for diversion of water from the three western rivers to feed into areas in Pakistan deprived of the waters of the three eastern rivers. The treaty however allowed construction of run of the river hydro-electric projects on the upper reaches of the western rivers in the Indian controlled areas. This provision has since created numerous issues of water storage (pondage), capacity to manipulate water flows especially during crop-sowing season, diversion of water for hydropower projects from tributaries affecting their flow into Pakistan and host of issues linked to timely communication of information in particular on planned projects.

The problems have assumed seriousness as the region is receiving on average less precipitation apparently on account of climate change and because of the many fold increase in population dependent on the waters of the Indus river basin. According to estimates, availability of water per capita has reduced from 5600 cubic meters in 1947, to merely 1000 cubic meters per person today, making Pakistan one of the water scarce regions of the world.

On the technical side relating to permissible projects in the upper riparian zone of the three western rivers, two examples would be illustrative of the problems: Bagliar project and the Kishan Ganga project, both of which were taken to arbitration under the treaty provisions. Bagliar dam is run of the river hydropower project with a new design providing for low level gates for silt removal. Pakistan took it to neutral expert as provided under the treaty in 2006 who accommodated Pakistan's concerns over pondage and height of the main spillway gates, but allowed the low gates as new and effective method against silting. Pakistan still remains concerned over this aspect as it gives India a capacity to drain the water and then stop the flow at a time when needed downstream especially during the sowing season. The Kishan Ganga project is based on a diversion canal that brings water to the main river but cuts flow to the tributary flowing into Pakistan on which Pakistan is constructing a 900 megawatt Neelum-Jehlum project. Reduction of flow into this tributary would affect this downstream project. The matter is being adjudicated by a court of arbitration which has yet to pronounce itself on the technicalities of assured flow for operating Neelum-Jehlum project. The broader issue remains that construction of a large number of even run-of-the-river projects, especially on numerous tributaries, would affect flows and at the same time increase India's capacity to manipulate these flows.

In addition to disputes about the design features of projects, there have been recurrent Pakistani complaints by Pakistan Indus Water Commission that its Indian counterpart does not provide timely information in particular about new planned projects and that information is received only after construction is in hand and the projects become a virtual fait accompli. Water is a sensitive issue and it is dangerous to play politics with it. Both sides affirm the value of the treaty and it is imperative to implement it in letter and spirit. Pakistan must receive information and data about plans as well as cooperation such as for on-the-spot and timely inspections to which it is entitled to under the treaty. There ought to be better system of telemetry to measure flows as well as transparency and coordination about draining and filling of reservoirs, and expeditious resort to dispute resolution before projects enter implementation stage. The system should work regardless of the political vicissitudes of the bilateral relationship. Any major crop failure that is seen to be the result of manipulation of flow of water on the Indian side could have disastrous consequences.

The new factors entering the equation such as climate change and long dry spells coupled with rising demand on water for an expanding population, pose a more difficult challenge. While there is consensus that the treaty must be preserved, it is also felt that the new circumstances may require adjustments and additional measures or clarity. This can be accomplished by negotiating an addendum/protocol to the treaty with the active involvement of the World Bank and necessary international expertise. It will be important to clearly identify issues that require remedial measure not anticipated in the treaty. In addition, in both countries there is need to adopt best practices, new methods and modern techniques for better usage of water, particularly in the agricultural sector. Recently, a good deal of useful work has been done in track II discussions under the auspices of South Asia Center of Washington-based Atlantic Council.

13.7 TERRORISM

Terrorism, extremism and violence by non-state actors have not been a new phenomenon but internationally these acquired new meaning as a strategic threat following 9/11. Efforts to define terrorism at the United Nations had failed because many of the freedom movements and well respected personalities were labeled as terrorist in the past and it proved difficult to develop consensus segregating armed struggles against alien occupation from acts of terrorism. India often described violence in Kashmir related uprisings as terrorism and accused Pakistan of instigation and abetment.

9/11 has changed the narrative on terrorism. The argument that among the root causes of "acts of terrorism," the phrase which was often used by Western media to describe suicide bombings in Palestine, was a sense of desperation and humiliation over injustice of occupation and failure of the international community to resolve longstanding issues such as Palestine and Kashmir was drowned out by a new post-9/11 narrative highlighting a civilizational argument. This argument, popularized in the West, emphasized that war against terrorism was a clash between systems; between those who espoused freedom and democracy and those attached to an authoritarian way of life. Regardless of the merit of these contradictory arguments and the fact that there are local motivations and causes behind acts of terrorism such as have been committed in the United States and Europe by individuals influenced by indigenous extremist ideologies, a worldwide sentiment and international cooperation grew against random violence by non-state actors. Following 9/11, Pakistan cooperated with the U. S. and other countries in dismantling Al Qaeda. Pakistan also cooperated with China in countering ETIM elements that had escaped Afghanistan into the tribal areas of Pakistan.

India blamed the December 2001 attack on the Indian Parliament building on elements of Pakistan based Lashkar e Tayaba formed in early 1990s in support of the uprising in the Indian-held-Kashmir. The incident escalated tension between the two nuclear-armed neighbors to the verge of conflict, and for over one year the two armies remained in a state of "eye-ball-to-eye-ball" confrontation. By 2003, with Pakistan's offer of ceasefire, relations started to improve. Against the backdrop of 9/11, Pakistan had already banned Lashkar e Tayaba and another Kashmir related militant group Jaish e Muhammad. In January 2004, on the margins of the Islamabad SAARC summit which was held after considerable delay, the two countries adopted a declaration which called for efforts to resolve Kashmir and also committed Pakistan not to allow territory under its control to be used for "acts of terrorism" against India. In September 2006, following bomb blast on a commuter train in Mumbai, the two countries agreed on an Anti-Terrorism Mechanism (ATM) for exchange of information and cooperation in investigation. The ATM, however, became a forum of mutual recrimination instead of a vehicle for cooperation; while India accused

Pakistani intelligence of complicity with militant elements, Pakistan brought its set of complaints about Indian support for separatist elements in Baluchistan. Pakistan also suspected Indian intelligence of carrying out covert funding and supplies to anti-state militant elements in its tribal areas adjoining Afghanistan, including militants who had fled Swat and continued to operate from Kunar in Afghanistan.

The 2008 Mumbai terrorist attack derailed bilateral relations. The Indian print and electronic media went into hype and started demanding action against Pakistan. India froze dialogue process with Pakistan which was revived two years later. Bilateral relations have yet to come out of the shadow of the Mumbai incident, an act by non-state actors which Pakistan had strongly condemned and offered India cooperation in investigation. Pakistan arrested several individuals belonging to the banned Lashkar e Tayaba group and suspected of planning the attack. However, court proceedings are slow as they place the burden of proof on the prosecution in a case where all perpetrators of the act are dead. The head of the banned group was also arrested but acquitted by courts for lack of evidence. The case demonstrates the accident prone nature of Pakistan-India relations and raises the question whether these relations should remain hostage to such sporadic acts of militancy and extremist violence.

Extremism and terrorism have a history and varied motivations in the region and are not likely to disappear any time soon. Indian media and official circles are always quick to point finger at Pakistan, even though a number of terror incidents resulting in scores of casualties, it turned out after years of investigation, were perpetrated by home grown extremist group. Samjhauta Express train blasts in 2007 and 2002 Godhra train burning incident which led to large scale anti-Muslim riots in Gujerat state were carried out by Hindu extremist elements. The local mafia and Islamist militants were found to be responsible for 2006 Mumbai commuter train blasts. Furthermore, Pakistan can be expected to offer cooperation in investigation but cannot guarantee against recurrence of terrorist incidents in India. Indeed, April 2005 summit level communiqué had anticipated the occurrence of such incidents and had, therefore, affirmed that "acts of terrorism will not be allowed to impede the peace process" between the two countries and that this process was "irreversible. "

The issue has yet another ominous dimension. A significant segment of India media and nationalist circles continue to argue for military action against Pakistan in the event of another terrorist incident. More disturbingly, this sentiment is echoed in the Indian Cold Start Doctrine predicated on permanent forward deployments close to Pakistani border and quick action. To deter such a possibility, in view of its obvious disadvantage in conventional capacity, Pakistan is considering the development of tactical nuclear weapons. All this portends serious escalation in the region.

What is the way forward? First and foremost the wisdom of the 2005 Joint Communiqué must not be overlooked. The two countries must keep the dialogue and diplomatic communications open. History has shown that Pakistan has little to gain from acts of terrorism inside India, and that it is fighting its own battle against militancy and extremism. Pakistan maintains counter-terrorism cooperation with many countries in the world and there is no reason why it cannot have similar cooperation with India on the basis of mutually acceptable parameters. On a broader level, improved relations between the two countries, in particular, progress towards resolution of issues would discourage those elements who think that they stand to gain from tension and conflict between the two countries. Also, greater confidence building is needed though exchanges and contacts at military and intelligence level in addition to more expanded political and diplomatic exchanges.

13.8   CONCLUSIONS

As the above discussion of the major issues between Pakistan and India shows, none of the issues are of an ideological character and therefore resolvable, given political will, flexibility and courage to take difficult decisions based on, where necessary, out-of-the-box-thinking. It is also clear that while trade, CBMs measure for cultural and travel facilitation are important, they have failed to consolidate relationship to the extent that it can withstand terrorist incidents. The ability of the two countries to resolve outstanding disputes can provide a more enduring basis for maintaining normal relations.

Efforts to develop agreement on prioritizing issues or to have synchronized progress have proved to be counterproductive. The approach of dealing with whatever is possible is a pragmatic course of action, but it is not an alternative to addressing in earnest the outstanding disputes, namely, Kashmir, Siachen and Sir Creek. These issues lend themselves to innovative approaches and new thinking for solutions based on loose or partial sovereignty and where possible joint management such as associated with a zone of disengagement covering the Siachen Glacier. Such solutions have become possible in the transformed post-Cold War global environment.

Lastly, the Pakistan-India tensions have been costly not just for the two countries but the entire South Asian region. This vast region has not been able to develop its full potential for cooperation in the interest of progress and well being of its people who represent one quarter of the entire humanity.

(Riaz Mohammad Khan, Former Foreign Secretary of Pakistan)

CHAPTER 14   DCFR and Revise of the *Civil Code Korea*

— Preface to "Interpretation and Comments of DCFR"

Young June Lee

14.1   INTRODUCTION

This book explains the drafting background, structure and application scope of the Draft Common Frame of Reference ("DCFR"), and the relationships with other model laws and guidance principles, and then mentions a revision of the *Civil Code of Korea*. Section 17.2 of this book is intended to fully introduce the full edition[1] and the outline edition[2] of the DCFR. This is because they are drafted under the names of Christian von Bar, Eric Clive and Hans Schulte-Nölke, editors of the DCFR, and therefore, they are clearly shown why and how the DCFR was prepared and what the guidance principles of the DCFR are. In addition to these, views and opinions I have

---

[1]   Principles, Definitions and Model Rules of European Private Law, Draft Common Frame of Reference, Full Edition, Prepared by the Study Group on a European Civil Code and the Research Group on EC Private Law (Acquis Group), Based in part on a revised version of the Principles of European Contract Law, Edited by Christian von Bar and Eric Clive (2009), pp.131.

[2]   Outline Edition, Christian von Bar, Eric Clive and Hans Schulte-Nölke, (2009), pp.1-46.

shared with Pf. Christian von Bar[1] are greatly helpful to prepare this introduction.

I have participated in revising the *Civil Code of Korea*, and therefore have a great interest in this field. The purpose of this project is not to revise the Korean Civil Code itself but to translate the DCFR into the Korean language and to add comments and explanations. For this reason, I will confine to mentioning the view that I have had with respect to a revision of the law of Korea pertaining to the non-performance of contracts in light of related rules of the DCFR and the *Principles of Asian Contract Law*[2].

The DCFR may be referred to as the treasury of global private law assets besides the European private law. I would like to positively assert that the DCFR is the latest edition and the epitome of the most abundant and ample academic theories since the enactment of the French civil law. Therefore, the DCFR provides lots of implications for a revision of the *Korean Civil Code*.

Despite some deficiencies resulted from time constraints, the publication of this book regarding the comments and translation of DCFR is highly meaningful in that

[1] Sonderkolloquium mit Prof. Dr. Christian von Bar über die Vereinheitlichung Europäischen Privatrechts und die Aufgabe unserer Zivilrechtswissenschaft p. 3 (published by Korea Civil Law Association, February 23, 2011). In this publication, Pr. von Bar fully answered tricky questions asked by Pf. Young-Bok Park. This material is also found on the homepage of the Research Institute for Asia Private Law (http://www. kcjlaw. co. kr.).

[2] *The Principles of Asia Contract Law* ("PACL") consist of five Chapters of general provisions, formation, effect, performance and non-performance of contracts. PACL was deliberated and passed after the three-year long discussions carried out by the PACL Study Group organized by representatives from Korea, China, Japan, Cambodia, Singapore, Vietnam, Thailand and etc.. For the draft background of PACL, please refer to Japan NBL, No. 977 (written by Young-June Lee, May 15, 2012), p. 74. Detailed materials can be found on the homepage of the Research Institute for Asia Private Law (http://www. kcjlaw. co. kr.). The part regarding nonperformance of obligations of PACL consists of five sections (i. e., general provisions, enforcement of performance, request for the reduction of the amount and request for substitution, termination, damages, *force majeure*, and change of circumstances) and 30 provisions. The provisions, comments, questionnaires and national reports regarding non-performance are contained in *Asia Private Law Review* No. 4 Special, Draft Article Non-Performance of Contract for Principles of Asian Contract Law, Dec. 2010. Research Institute for Asia Private Law (pp. 1446).

this is the first attempt made in Asia①. I would also like to mention that this work would be impossible without dedicated efforts made by the senior researcher and lawyer Tae-Yong Ahn and his team.

14.2   OUTLINE OF THE DCFR AND PRINCIPLES

14.2.1   Formation, Application Scope and Relationships with Other Model Rules

A.   The purposes of the DCFR

The DCFR, as described below, might have several purposes, but one of the most important purposes thereof is to help enact a more systematic European contract law. To put it more specifically, the European Union ("EU") announced the Action Plan on a More Coherent European Contract Law in February 2003. The Action Plan includes the first call for drafting the Common Frame of Reference ("CFR"), and one of the purposes of the DCFR is to serve as a draft for drawing up the CFR.

The DCFR is the text having the form analogous to legal provisions and the result of a "twenty-five year" long research and mutual discussions among scholars specialized in private law, the comparative law and the EU laws. In 1998, the Study Group was organized. In 2002, the Acquis Group was formed. From 2005, the Study Group, the Acquis Group and the Insurance Contract Group formed the so-called "drafting teams" of the CoPECL network. The DCFR is referred to as the result of the work of the Study Group, the Acquis Group and the Insurance Contract Group. The Coordinating Group also participated in the work. When I briefly reckon the number of professors and young scholars mentioned to participate in the work, more than 200 professors and scholars seem to participate in the work. The DCFR is

---

① According to Pf. kunihiro Nakata of Ryukoku University, who participated in the international seminar titled "Protection of Consumers' Interests and Rights from the Perspective of Civil Law" hosted by the Legal Science Research Center of the Renmin University of China on August 18, 2012 as the Second East Asia Civil Law Academic Seminar, Japan is now translating the DCFR and expects to published a Japanese version in early next year. The chief professor Yang Lixin of the Legal Science Research Center of the Renmin University of China informed that some Chinese scholars are translating the DCFR.

distinctive from a "political" CFR, which would be drafted with intention to prepare a uniform European law, in that the DCFR is an "academic" text that can "stand on its own. " At the same time, the DCFR identifies similarity, association and common characteristics with the private laws of the member states of the EU. By doing so, the DCFR provides a new foundation for the concept of private law in Europe and contributes to furnishing the notion of a harmonious European private law in an informal way. I wish to expect that all or at least significant part of the DCFR to be part of the CFR at a certain appropriate time in accordance with a political decision of the EU by taking the foregoing process.

The DCFR of 2008 was published as the Interim Outline Edition. About one year later, the Full Edition was published by supplementing comments and notes to the Outline Edition. It is known that the Outline Edition was published on the basis of judgment that the announcement of the DCFR would help promote discussions on the text.

The Outline Edition has three major revisions compared to the Interim Outline Edition: (i) it covers some matters of movable property law, namely the acquisition and loss of ownership, proprietary security and trust law (in Books VIII, IX and X) as well as lease loan contracts and donation (in Book IV); (ii) some part of the Outline Edition was revised by considering public discussions on the Interim Outline Edition; and (iii) the principles were categorized into four principles from 15 ones of the Interim Outline Edition.

B. Formation of the DCFR

The DCFR consists of principles, definitions and model rules.

a) Principles

The term, "principles" has multiple meanings in the DCFR. First, they are used to mean rules that do not have legal effect as used in the Principles of European Contract Law ("PECL") or the Unidroit Principles of International Commercial Contracts. For example, I. -1:101(1) of the DCFR defines matters applicable and I. -1:101(2) states matters excluded from application. In that sense, these rules constitute "principles." Second, "principles" sometimes refer to rules of more general nature such as the freedom of contract or good faith. Third, the principles also mean underlying principles of interpretation as guidance principles indicating fundamental and abstract basic principles like social justice. In the DCFR, the principles of the foregoing nature are often described as fundamental principles. I will further elaborate this matter in Section 17.2.2 below.

b) Definitions

The definitions have a greatly significant function in the field of law. In the DCFR, the definitions particularly have a function of proposal for the unification of legal terms in Europe. Specifically important concepts are defined in Book I. The other terms not referred to in Book I are defined in Annex, which is part of the DCFR (I. -1:108).

c) Model rules

Most of the DCFR consist of "model rules." In other words, the provisions of the DCFR are not put forward as having any normative force but are soft law rules of the kind contained in the PECL.

d) Comments and notes

The model rules are supplemented by comments and notes. The comments elucidate each rule. For example, they illustrate the application of each rule and outline the critical policy consideration. The notes reflect the national legal systems of EU states and the current EU law.

International instruments such as the UN Convention on Contracts for the International Sale of Goods (CISG) and the Unidroit Principles of International Commercial Contracts 2004 are also mentioned.

C. Application Scope of the DCFR

The DCFR covers the outline of rights and the particulars thereof in terms of the notion of the Korean applicable law.

a) The DCFR expands the scope of the existing PECL while maintaining it.

The DCFR has a broad scope applicable to rights including the rules pertaining to contracts such as the formation, effect and interpretation of contracts, plural parties, the transfer of rights, set-off and prescription. Even though the DCFR contains most of the provisions of the PECL, it provides new definitions of each kind of contracts (see Book IV) and define general provisions in a more detailed manner (see Books I through IV). Besides the contracts aforementioned and general provisions, the DCFR further covers non-contractual obligations, which are not covered by the PECL, such as those arising as the result of unjustified enrichment, illegal acts (i. e., rights and obligations arising out of damage inflicted to a third party), and management of affairs (i. e., rights and obligations arising as the result of benevolent intervention in another's affairs). The DCFR also deals with some matters of movable property law such as the acquisition and loss of ownership, proprietary security and trust law (see Books VIII through X).

b) **The DCFR explicitly mentions matters excluded.**

These are in particular: the status or legal capacity of natural persons, wills and succession, family relationships, negotiable instruments, employment relationships, immovable property law, company law, and the law of civil procedure and enforcement of claims.

The coverage of the DCFR is thus considerably broader than what the European Commission ("EC") seems to have in mind for the coverage of the CFR. The editors of the DCFR explained the reason from the fact that the DCFR that is the "academic" frame of reference is not subject to the constraints of the CFR that is the "political" frame of reference. They also mentioned that there was no choice but to govern contractual obligations and non-contractual obligations together because the correct dividing line between contract law (in this wide sense) and some other areas of law is in any event difficult to determine precisely and the DCFR approached the whole of the law of obligations as an organic entity or unit. They further explained that some areas of property law with regard to movable property were dealt with because some aspects of property law were of great relevance to the good functioning of the internal market.

D. **Structure and Language of the DCFR Model Rules**

a) **Structure**

The whole text of the model rules is divided into Books and that each Book is subdivided into Chapters, Sections, Sub-sections (where appropriate) and Articles. In addition, the Book on specific contracts and the rights and obligations arising from them is divided, because of its size, into Parts, each dealing with a particular type of contract (e. g. Book IV. A: Sale)

The mode of numbering the model rules corresponds in its basic approach to the technique used in many of the newer European codifications. This too was chosen in order to enable necessary changes to be made later without more than minor editorial labor. Books and Parts are numbered by capitalized Roman numerals, capital letters, respectively. Chapters, sections (and also sub-sections) and Articles are numbered using Arabic numerals. For example, III. — 3:509 (Effect on obligations under the contract) is the ninth Article in section 5 (Termination) of the third chapter (Remedies for non-performance) of the third book (Obligations and corresponding rights).

The DCFR consists of ten Books. Book I defines the applicable scope, interpretation and development of the DCFR and contains the definitions of major terms. Book II deals with contracts and other juridical acts, namely the formation, interpretation, contents and effects of contracts. Book III covers matters commonly applicable to contractual and non-contractual obligations while clearly indicating certain provisions applicable to contractual obligations only. For example, III. -1:101 provides, "This Book applies, except as otherwise provided, to all obligations within the scope of these rules, whether they are contractual or not, and to corresponding rights to performance. " In addition, the provisions pertaining to termination are applicable to contractual rights only (see III. -3:501). Book IV covers types of contracts and the rights and obligations arising in relation to the contracts. Book V deals with the rights and obligations arising as the result of benevolent intervention of another's affairs. Books VI through X cover non-contractual liability arising out of damage caused to another (illegal acts), unjustified enrichment, the acquisition and loss of ownership of goods, proprietary security in movable assets and trusts, respectively.

b) Language

The DCFR was published in English. The researcher teams are intent on publishing the model rules of the DCFR in as many languages as is possible. The DCFR has been already translated into several languages, but the only reliable version of the DCFR is the English version. The DCFR tried to avoid legalese and technicalities drawn from any one legal system to ensure that the terminology should be as suitable as possible for use across a large number of translations. It is for this reason that words like "rescission," "tort" and "delict" have been avoided in the DCFR.

E. Relations with the PECL, the PEL, the ACQP and the CFR

a) The relation of the DCFR with the PECL

In Books II and III, the DCFR contains many rules derived from the PECL. These rules are adopted with the express agreement of the Commission on European Contract Law with the drafting teams, and the Study Group which is one of the drafting teams is the successor to the Commission on European Contract Law. Notwithstanding this, however, it was unavoidable for the DCFR to partly revise the PECL and to broaden its scope by adding new provisions to the DCFR due to the different purpose, structure and coverage of the DCFR and in part because the scope of the PECL needed to be broadened so as to embrace matters of consumer protection. Unlike the PECL, the DCFR more clearly draws distinction between a contract and the relationship to which it gives rise. For example, under the DCFR a "contract is not performed," but the "contract is concluded," and "obligations are performed." The rules on representation, pre-contractual statements forming part of a contract, variation by a court of contractual rights and obligations on a change of circumstances and so-called "implied terms" of a contract are also changed in several significant respects on the basis of the input from stakeholders to the workshops held by the EC on selected topics.

b) The relation of the DCFR with the PEL series

The Study Group began its work in 1998 and published the result in a separate series, the Principles of European Law ("PEL"). They cover sales, leases, services, commercial agency, franchise and distribution, personal security contracts, and benevolent interventions in another's affairs.

c) The relation with the Acquis Principles

The Research Group on the Existing EC Private Law, commonly called the Acquis Group, is also publishing its findings in a separate series. Its output contributes to the task of ensuring that the existing EC law is appropriately reflected. The ACQP is one of the sources from which the Compilation and Redaction Team has drawn.

d) The relation with the CFR

The EC's "Action Plan on A More Coherent European Contract Law" of January 2003 called for comments on three proposed measures: increasing the coherence of the acquis communautaire, the promotion of the elaboration of EU-wide standard contract terms, and further examination of whether there is a need for an "optional instrument." Its principal proposal for improvement was to develop a Common Frame of Reference (CFR) which could then be used by the EC in reviewing the existing acquis and drafting new legislation. In October 2004, the EC published a further paper, "European Contract Law and the revision of the acquis: the way forward." This proposed that the CFR should provide "fundamental principles, definitions and model rules" ' which could assist in the improvement of the existing acquis communautaire, and which might form the basis of an optional instrument if it were decided to create one. The DCFR and the draft horizontal directive propose general rules on pre-contractual information duties or withdrawal rights and a model set of sanctions for breach of information duties.

The research preparing the DCFR aims to identify best solutions, taking into account national contract laws (both case law and established practice), the EC acquis and relevant international instruments, particularly the UN Convention on Contracts for the International Sale of Goods of 1980.

14.2.2 Principles

A. Development and Basis

The discussions on the guidance principles of the DCFR have gone through an intriguing development process. The Interim Outline Edition lists fifteen items of principles: justice; freedom; protection of human rights; economic welfare; solidarity and social responsibility; establishing an area of freedom, security and justice; promotion of the internal market; protection of consumers and others in need of protection; preservation of cultural and linguistic plurality; rationality; legal certainty; predictability; efficiency; protection of reasonable reliance; and the proper allocation of responsibility for the creation of risks.

The Association Henri Capitant and the Société de législation comparée published their Principes directeurs du droit européen du contrat ("Principes directeur") in early 2008. The Principes directeur identifies three main principles — contractual freedom; contractual security; and contractual loyalty — each with sub-principles. The Principes directeur uses the PECL and the national systems of mainly the Dutch, English, French, German, Italian and Spanish. The UN Convention on Contracts for the International Sale of Goods, the Unidroit Principles on International Commercial Contracts (2004) and the draft European Code of Contract produced by the Academy of European Private Law based in Pavia are also used to draw up the principles.

The Outline Edition points out that the Pinciples directeurs are not sufficient to deal with non-contractual obligations and property law as well as the contract law and proposes, in light of the broad purposes of the DCFR, to categorize the underlying principles of the DCFR into freedom, security, justice and efficiency. It is known that the DCFR does not incorporate contractual "loyalty" into one of the principles because the editors of the DCFR determined that the principle of loyalty would be governed by the principle of justice or transaction security. It is somewhat strange for me that the DCFR identified efficiency as a separate principle having the same footing as freedom, security and justice. The editors of the DCFR explained that although efficiency was often an aspect of freedom, in particular, freedom from unnecessary impediments and costs, it could not always be accommodated under the other principles.

While the Interim Outline Edition of the DCFR states the Pinciples directeurs — protection of human rights; solidarity and social responsibility; preservation of cultural and linguistic plurality; the protection and promotion of welfare and the promotion of the internal market, the Outline Edition does not mention neither of the foregoing principles. The editors of the Outline Edition explained that they were said to be "overriding principles" of a high political nature but could be accommodated by the principles of freedom, security, justice and efficiency in practice.

The principle of the protection of human rights appears in several rules of the DCFR: the model rules are to be read in the light of any applicable instruments guaranteeing human rights and fundamental freedoms (I. -1:102(2)); the rules on non-discrimination (II. 2:101 through II. -2:105 and III. -1:105); and the rules on non-contractual liability arising out of damage caused to another (VI. -2:201, VI. - 2:203, and VI. -2:206). The promotion of solidarity and social responsibility is generally regarded as primarily the function of public law (using, for example, criminal law, tax law and social welfare law) rather than private law. In the contractual context, it is referred to that the word "solidarity" means loyalty or security and that the rules on the management of another's affairs, donation and non-contractual liability (see VI. -2:209, VI. -3:202; VI. -3:206 and VI. -5:103) can be sufficiently governed by the principle of "security."

Explaining the reason why the DCFR Outline Edition does not state the protection and promotion of welfare as the underlying principle unlike the Interim Outline Edition, it states that they embrace all or almost all the other principles, and therefore, it is not useful to state them as separate principle. With regard to the principle of the promotion of the internal market, the Outline Edition states that it is not part of the underlying principles because it is a matter of a political decision.

By going through the process above, freedom, security, justice and efficiency have been settled as the underlying principles of the DCFR. The editors of the DCFR also emphasized that they did not mean that all the four principles had the same value or the order of priority as stated in the order of statement in the DCFR.

They added that "people have fought and died for" freedom, security and justice because they were ends in themselves but "efficiency is less dramatic." In addition, the principles would conflict with each other. For example, as happens under the rules of prescription, on occasion, justice in a particular may have to make way for legal security or efficiency. Freedom from discrimination restricts another's freedom to discriminate, and equality of treatment may conflict with the protection of the weak.

B. Freedom

There are at least two aspects to freedom as an underlying principle in private law. First, freedom does not impose mandatory rules and restrictions of a formal or procedural nature on people's transactions. In this aspect, party autonomy is stressed. The second aspect is related to enhancing capabilities by utilizing default rules, which makes it easier and less costly for people to enter into legal relationships.

The freedom of contract starts from being free to decide whether or not to contract, with whom to contract on what terms and when the contractual relationship terminates. II. -1:102 (1) provides the parties' freedom to conclude a contract or other juridical acts subject to applicable mandatory rules, and II. -1:103(3) provides the freedom of modification and waive of such contract or other juridical acts.

A contract is, in principle, not related to a third party other than the parties to the contract. The Principles directeurs stated above expresses the same intention in Article 0:101 as mentioned in the preceding sentence. The DCFR also fully reflects such legal theory. In other words, the DCFR premises that the parties to a contract may conclude the contract only for themselves and the contract regulates the rights and obligations of the parties entering into the contract unless otherwise stipulated. The DCFR merely spells out the exceptions, principally the rules on representation (II. -6) and the rules on stipulations in favor of a third party (II. -9:301 through II. -9:303, III. -5 and III. -5:401).

A contract harmful to society is prohibited. To put it more specifically, an illegal contract and a contract contrary to public policy is deemed void and null. The DCFR does not spell out when a contract is illegal or contrary to public policy because that is a matter for law outside the scope of the DCFR — the law of competition or the criminal law of EU member states.

When consent is defective, the freedom of contract is also restricted. The DCFR premises that a contract concluded as the result of mistake or fraud or which was the result of duress or unfair exploitation can be canceled by the aggrieved party. The DCFR provides that in cases of fraud and duress, the remedies given by the DCFR cannot be excluded or restricted but in cases of mistake which do not involve deliberate wrongdoing, the remedies may be excluded or restricted (II. -7:215).

The DCFR guarantees freedom to choose a contracting party. However, it does not accept discrimination on the grounds of gender, race or ethnic origin and provides appropriate remedies (II. -2:101 through II. -2:105 and III. -1:105).

The DCFR restricts freedom to withhold information at pre-contractual stage. It recognizes pre-contractual liability even outside the classic cases of procedural unfairness such as mistake, fraud, duress and the exploitation of a party's circumstances to obtain an excessive advantage. In particular, the DCFR concerns a case where a party was not fully informed and as a result the party concluded a contract that the party would have not concluded had the party been fully informed. The foregoing case is particularly applied to a consumer contract but is applicable to a contract between businesses.

Freedom of contract is also restricted in the case of the lack of information on the terms of the contract. In particular, this notion has been evolved with the development of longer-term contracts or the use of standard terms. Existing EC law addresses this problem and gives protection to consumers when the term in question is in a consumer contract and was not individually negotiated (see Directive on Unfair Terms in Consumer Contracts). The DCFR goes a step further to restrict the freedom to contract in cases where a party to a contract is a small business or where the relevant term is contained in a standard form contract document prepared by the other party.

Restriction on the freedom of contract is imposed to correct inequality of bargaining power. When one party takes advantage of the other party's urgent needs and lack of choice to extort an unfairly high price for goods or services, bargaining power between the two parties become unequal. Such problems are most common when a consumer is dealing with a business, but can also occur in contract between businesses, particularly when one party is a small business. It is known that the DCFR takes a balanced view regarding the removal of inequality of bargaining power, suggesting an extension beyond the existing laws of the EU member states.

The drafters of the DCFR emphasize that the restrictions on the freedom of contract should be limited to minimum intervention. The method of intervention is also tried to be limited minimum in the DCFR. For example, in a case where a party to a contract is not provided with information before the conclusion of the contract, rather than making the contract invalid or allowing to claim damages regard should be paid whether a right to withdraw the contract should be recognized or not.

C. Security

Security means to ensure that a person's rights and interests or the status quo are not interfered by unlawful invasions or unwanted disturbance. The Principles directeurs indicates the following five items as the main ingredients of security: (1) a contract shall be complied with unless circumstances are unexpectedly changed; (2) the party to the contract shall cooperate in performing the contract in good faith and the party shall not conduct an act incompatible with the previous acts in breach of reliance; (3) the parties to the contract shall have a right to enforce the performance of contractual obligations; (4) a third party must respect the situation created by the contract; and (5) the parties to the contract shall maintain the effect to the contract in question relating to interpretation, invalidity or performance of the contract pursuant to the approach of "favoring the contract (faveur pour le contract)."

The DCFR adds a further ingredient of contractual security: the availability of adequate remedies for non-performance of the contractual obligations; and the protection of reasonable reliance and expectations.

With regard to the expansion of the effect of a contract to a third party (e. g., a tenant's visitor claims damages from the landlord as the tenant could do under the contract, because the visitor falls down the stairs as a result of a broken handrail, the landlord was obliged to repair under the contract), Germany has relevant provisions in favor of the visitor, but the DCFR regulates the relevant issue in the subject of noncontractual liability (illegal acts).

The DCFR contains rules to ensure security. Examples are the objective rules on interpretation (II. -8:101) and the restriction of avoidance for mistake to cases in which the non-mistaken party contributed to the mistake (II. -7:201), and the rule that imposes on a business which has failed to comply with a pre-contractual information duty (II. -3:107(3)).

The editors of the DCFR refer to the binding force of contracts and a change of circumstances. The Principles directeurs states in Article 0-201, "A contract which lawfully concluded has binding force between the parties." Article 0-103 of the Principles directeurs mentions, "By their mutual agreement, the parties are free, at any moment, to terminate the contract or to modify it. Unilateral revocation is only effective in respect of contracts for an indefinite period." The foregoing provision is succeeded by the DCFR (see II. -1:103 along with III. -1:108 and III. -1:109). The DCFR further provides rules that the party wishing to terminate must give a reasonable period of notice (see III. -1:109), that contracts negotiated away from business premises (e. g., at the doorstep or at a distance) may be withdrawn (see II. -5:201), and that a cooling off period shall be furnished for complex contracts (e. g., timeshare contracts) (see II. -5:202).

The DCFR contains a more detailed rule pertaining to the exceptional change of circumstances than the provision stipulated in Article 0-201(3) of the Principles directeurs as follows: if the circumstances in which the obligations were assumed were completely different to those in which they fall to be enforced, it may be unjust to enforce the performance of contractual obligations according to the original contract terms. In particular, the DCFR recognizes that the parties' freedom to exclude any possibility of adjustment without the consent of the other party (see II. -1:102 and III. 1:110(3)(c)).

As a tool to enhance contractual security, the DCFR also contains rules that use open terms such as "reasonable" or "fair dealing." In this respect, the DCFR have special provisions on the giving of warnings of impending changes known to one party in service contracts, and on variation of the contract (IV. C. -2:102, IV. C. -2:103, IV. C. 2:107, IV. C. -2:108, IV. C. -2:109 and IV. C. -2:110). The DCFR points out rigid rules (e. g. "within 5 days" instead of "within a reasonable time") would be liable to increase insecurity in circumstances.

The DCFR views that applying the principle of good faith and fair dealing would harm security but this is a matter of justice beyond the provision of contractual security.

It is referred to that security can be promoted by imposing an obligation to cooperate (III. -1:104) and prohibiting inconsistent behaviors.

Enforcement of performance is the most powerful means to secure security. Therefore, the DCFR, irrespective of monetary obligations, non-monetary obligations, or obligations to do or transfer something else, provides a right to enforce performance. The DCFR, however, recognizes various exceptional cases, stating that the forgoing principle should not apply in cases where literal performance is impossible or would be inappropriate (III. -3:301 and III. -3:302).

In addition to the right to enforce, the DCFR contains other remedies: withholding of performance, termination, reduction of price and damages. The creditor faced with a non-performance may exercise any of these remedies, and may use more than one remedy provided that the remedies sought are compatible (III. -3: 102). In the case where the performance of an obligation is excused due to inability, the creditor may not enforce performance or damages but may exercise other remedies (III. -3:101). As termination often leaves the debtor with a loss (for example, wasted costs incurred in preparing to perform or loss caused by a change in the market), the DCFR points out that the creditor should not be entitled to use termination as a remedy in the case of minor non-performance or a non-performance that can readily be put right.

The DCFR recognizes faveur pour le contrat, which is succeeded from Article 0:204 of the Principles directeurs. For example, the DCFR contains provisions on the preference of the interpretation of the terms of contracts (II. -8:106) , on a debtor's right to cure a non-conforming performance (II. -3:202 through II. -3:204) and on determination of the price and other terms where the price is not specified sufficiently enough to perform the relevant contract (II. -9:104 through II. -9:108).

D. Justice

Justice is referred to as an all-pervading principle within the DCFR. The DCFR takes a pluralistic approach to justice. Within the DCFR, justice is referred to having aspects: (1) ensuring that like are treated alike; (2) not allowing people to rely on their own unlawful, dishonest or unreasonable conduct; (3) not allowing people to take undue advantage of the weakness, misfortune or kindness of others; (4) not making grossly excessive demands; (5) holding people responsible for the consequences of their own actions or their own creation of risks; and (6) protecting those in a weak or vulnerable position.

The aspect mentioned in (1) above is the most obviously manifested in the rules against discrimination (II. -2:101 through II. -2:105 and III. -1:105) , but the big exception to the rule of equal treatment is situations where businesses and consumers are not treated alike. Examples of the principle of mutuality are the rule on the order of performance of reciprocal obligations where one party need not perform before the other (III. -2:104) and the rules on withholding performance until the other party performs (III. -3:401).

The aspect of justice referred to in (2) above is embodied by good faith and fair dealing. III. -1:103 provides, "A person has a duty to act in accordance with good faith and fair dealing in performing an obligation, in exercising a right to performance, in pursuing or defending a remedy for non-performance, or in exercising a right to terminate an obligation or contractual relationship. " A breach of this duty does not itself give rise to a liability to pay damages but may prevent a party from exercising or relying on a right, remedy or defense. The examples of this aspect are the rules that the debtor is not liable for loss suffered by the creditor to the extent that the creditor could have reduced the loss by taking reasonable steps (II. -3:705) , and that prevents the other party from gaining an advantage from conduct such as fraud, coercion or threats (II. -7:206).

The example of the aspect mentioned in (3) above is the provision aforementioned which allows a party, in carefully specified circumstances, to avoid a contract on the ground of unfair exploitation if the party was dependent on or had a relationship of trust with the other party, was in economic distress or had urgent needs, or was improvident, ignorant, inexperienced or lacking in bargaining skill. In this case, to avoid the contract, it is necessary that the other party knew or could reasonably be expected to have known of the vulnerability and exploited the first party's situation (II. -7:207).

The typical example of the aspect referred to in (4) above is the rules on the excuse of obligations. In other words, it is recognized in the rule which regards non-performance of an obligation as excused so that performance cannot be enforced and damages cannot be recovered if the non-performance is due to an impediment beyond the debtor's control and if the debtor could not reasonably be expected to have avoided or overcome the impediment or its consequences (III. -3:104). The other examples in the DCFR are: III. -1:110 that allows contractual obligations to be varied or terminated by a court if they have become so onerous as a result of an exceptional change of circumstances that it would be "manifestly unjust to hold the debtor to the obligation;" III. -3:302 providing that performance of an obligation cannot be specifically enforced if it would be unreasonably burdensome or expensive; and III. -3:712 providing that stipulated payment for non-performance can be reduced to a reasonable amount where it is "grossly excessive" in the circumstances.

The aspect mentioned in (5) above is most prominent in Book VI. One of the examples is the rule that a person cannot resort to a remedy for non-performance of an obligation to the extent that that person has caused the non-performance (III. -3:101 (3)).

The examples of the aspect mentioned in (6) above are the rules pertaining to the restrictions of the freedom to contract as described above, the special protection afforded to consumers (for example, marketing and pre-contractual duties in Book I, Chapter 3, the right of withdrawal in Book II, Chapter 5, unfair contract terms in

Book II, Chapter 4,

Section 4, and Book IV dealing with sale, the lease of goods and personal security).

This aspect also appears in the rules on the special protection afforded to patients (IV. C. 8:103, IV. C. -8:104, IV. C. -8:106, IV. C. -8:108, IV. C. -8:109(5) and IV. C. -8: 111), on the protections afforded to the debtor when a right to performance is assigned (III. -5: 119), on the protections afforded to non-professional providers of personal security (IV. G. 4:101 through IV. G. -4:107), and on the protections afforded to people presented with standard terms prepared by the other party (II. -9:103, II. -9:405, II. -9:406 and II. 8:103).

The DCFR defines the "consumer" as "any natural person who is acting primarily for purposes which are not related to his or her trade, business or profession (I. -1:105(1))." However, the DCFR also raises a question and has doubt about the definition. In particular, the DCFR regards the argument that small businesses or "non repeat players" may be in need of protection as a question to be answered in future.

E. The principle of efficiency

The DCFR states efficiency in two aspects of efficiency for the purposes of the parties and efficiency for wider public purposes.

The DCFR contains examples of minimal formal and procedural restrictions as follows: neither writing nor any other formality is generally required for a contract or other juridical acts (II. -1: 106) with exceptions of personal security provided by consumers (IV. G. -4:204) and donation (IV. H. -2:101); unnecessary procedural steps are kept to minimum and voidable contracts can be avoided by simple notice without any need for court procedures (II. -7:209); a right to performance can be assigned without the need for notification to the debtor (III. -5: 104 (2)); the ownership of goods can be transferred without delivery (III. -5: 104 (2)); non-possessory proprietary security can be readily created and to be effective against third parties registration will be necessary but the formalities are kept to a minimum (Book IX); the rules on set-off (II. -6:102); and set-off can be effected by simple notice without court proceedings (III. -6:105).

As examples of minimal substantive restrictions, the DCFR contains the rules on the absence of any need for consideration or cause for the conclusion of an effective contract (II. -4:101), the recognition that there can be binding unilateral undertaking (II. 1:103(2)), and the recognition that contracts can confer rights on third parties (II. -9:301 through II. -9:303).

With regard to an aspect of efficiency for wider public purposes, the DCFR states that the rules in it generally intended to be such as will promote economic welfare and this is a criterion against which any legislative intervention should be checked. The important task is to reflect the efficiency of the market in the DCFR, and the typical examples are the rules of II. -3:101 through II. 3-107 pertaining to information duties. Interferences with freedom of contract may promote economic welfare. Consumer protection rules, for example, can be seen not only as protective for the benefit of typically weaker parties but also as favorable to general welfare because they may lead to more competition and thus to a better functioning of markets. The other example is the provision of information which allows an "informed decision," and thus promoting the efficiency of markets.

The rule in the DCFR on stipulated payments for non-performance can be said to promote the efficiency of markets (III. 3-712). The rule on the reduction of stipulated payments should be viewed from the perspective of justice (III. -3:712 (2)). The allowance of damages for pure economic loss contributes to promoting the efficiency of markets.

The DCFR contains the other rules envisaged to promote the efficiency of markets: on prescription (Book I, Chapter 7); on withholding performance and terminating the contractual relationship in cases of anticipated non-performance (III. -3:301 and III. 3:504); on discouraging the providing of unwanted performance (III. -3:301 (2), IV. C. 2:111 and IV. D. -6:101); on denying effect to contractual prohibition on the alienation of assets (III. -5:108 and VIII. -1:301); on acquisition in good faith or by continuous possession (VIII. -3:101 and VIII. -4:101); and on proprietary security in movable assets (Book IX).

14.3 REVISION OF *THE CIVIL CODE OF KOREA*

14.3.1 From a small-scale revision to a grand revision

The Civil Code of Korea (the "Civil Code") has been already revised several times. In addition, there have been diverse attempts to revise the Civil Law. Among other things, the Draft Bill of the Amendment to the Civil Code (Draft Bill No. 611, the "Bill"), which had been pending several years after submitted to the National Assembly of Korea on October 2004 but was automatically abolished due to the shuffle of the National Assembly, was proceeded aggressively. In 2009, again, the Civil Code Revision Committee was organized under the Ministry of Justice of Korea. The Committee has been working on the revision of the Civil Code on the basis of the Bill above.

I insisted that the Civil Code should be revised in a "small-scale" at the time of drafting the Bill. However, I have changed my thought and believed that it has become time for Korea to revise the Civil Code in a "grand-scale." In particular, Korea will encounter the ten-year anniversary of signing the United Nations Convention on Contracts for the International Sale of Goods ("CISG") sooner or later. The CISG has the same effect as local law. However, there are little precedents regarding the CISG in Korea. In particular, Germany that has dealt with disputes relating to the CISG has accumulated lots of CISG related precedents. In addition, many other countries including Germany have already revised or are in the process of revising the law on non-performance of contracts in a "grand-scale," while getting away from the legal theory of invalidity of a contract on the ground of initial impossibility. This development has made me think of many things with regard to the revision of the Civil Code in Korea. In this regard, it is my view that Korea should also devise a plan to bring the Civil Code into line with the DCFR that contains rules specifically embodying and expanding international model laws including without limitation the CISG. Given that Korea has executed free trade agreements with many foreign countries and has maintained an export-oriented economy, it would be inefficient in terms of legal and economic aspects to govern cases relating to export and import activities by the legislation system totally separated from that applied to local cases.

14.3.2 An attempt to approach the current the legal system regarding the nonperformance of contracts from the perspective of international model laws

While I studied comparative law of defects liability about 50 years ago in Germany, I envisaged revising the law on defects liability to a single liability system for the nonperformance of contracts from the dualistic liability system where defects liability was parallel with the non-performance of contracts[1]. During the study, I became assured that the legal system of the German civil law had three pillars: (1) the principle where the cases that are set forth in the relevant provisions only will be subject to enforcement; (2) the principle of fault-based liability; and (3) the invalidity of a contract on the ground of initial impossibility, In addition, I was convinced that Korea and Japan had succeeded such legal system and that the three pillars should be significantly retouched or be substituted with other pillars. Through the revision of the law of obligations in 2002, Germany significantly amended the three pillars above: it adopted an all-inclusive concept and allowed to recognize the valid effect to a contact on the ground of initial impossibility. Japan and Korea, however, have not pursued such change yet. I have assurance that the Korean Civil Code should significantly change the legal system of the non-performance of contracts or should adopt strict liability and a new legal principle regarding inability/impossibility.

A. Exit from the tripartite approach

Exit from the tripartite approach to the non-performance of obligations Article

---

[1] DAS JAPANISCHE UND KOREANISCHE GEWÄHRLEISTUNGSRECHT IN SEIER GESETZLICHEN ENTWICKLUNG UND IN DEN FORMULARBEDINGUNGEN DER PRAXIS UNDER DEM EINFLUSS DES DEUTSCHEN RECHTS, Inaugual-Dissertation zur Erlangung des Doktorgrades der Rechtswissenschaftlichen Fakultät der Johann Wolfgang goethe-Universität zu Frankfurt am Main, vorgelegt von Young June Lee aus Seoul/Korea, 1968.

390 of the Civil Code, which adopts the general definition and all-inclusive notion contrary to the German civil law, provides, "in the case where the performance of an obligation is not compatible with the terms of the obligation. " The starting point of a question is why the relevant academic theories and precedents take a tripartite approach consisting of the inability to perform, the delay of performance and incomplete performance notwithstanding the foregoing provision. The types of non-performance of obligations and the remedies for such non-performance should be integrated each other with a flexible approach. In addition to this, broader incidental obligations should be imposed on the debtors and the non-performance of such incidental obligations should be part of grounds for the non-performance of obligations. Meanwhile, the creditors should be subject to an obligation to cooperate in performing obligations. By doing so, it should be attempted to regulate any non-performance of obligations resulted from the delay of performance of obligations by the creditor as non-performance of obligations due to the creditor's non-performance.

III. -1:101 of the DCFR starts from the abstract and all-inclusive concept of non-performance just like Article 390 of the Civil Code and allows to concurrently exercise more than one remedy for non-performance (e. g., mandatory enforcement of performance, termination of a contract, damages, reduction of the price and withdrawal of performance) so long as such remedies are compatible. Article 1 of the *Principles of Asia Contract Law* ("PACL") provides that the nonperformance of an obligation refers to any and all the non-performance of an obligation incompatible with the terms of the relevant obligation including all the types of performance where such performance is not consistent with the prescribed time, is defective, or is incompatible with the terms of the obligation. The Article further provides that the non-performance of an obligation includes cases where any incidental obligation has not performed.

B. Exit from the principle of fault-based liability

Korea needs to try to switch from fault-based liability to strict liability. Strict liability is compatible with the substance of the non-performance of an obligation, namely a "promise" or the "guarantee" of performance. The DCFR perfectly adopts the principle of strict liability, and therefore, does not require willful act or negligence for the constitution of the non-performance of an obligation. For example, the DCFR contains the rule that regards the non-performance of an obligation as excused if the nonperformance is due to an impediment beyond the debtor's control and if the debtor could not reasonably be expected to avoid or overcome the impediment or its consequences. Even in this case, however, the creditor may claim for termination, withdrawal of performance and the reduction of price except for the compensation for damages and the enforcement of performance. In addition, in the case where the excusing impediment is permanent the obligation is extinguished (III. -3:104 of the DCFR). Article 29 of the PACL maintains the same stance as the DCFR. It is surprising that neither Korea, Japan and China of the Study Group of the PACL nor South Eastern Asian countries have challenged the idea of adopting strict liability in the PACL.

A proviso of Article 392 of the Civil Code that provides "[T]his shall not apply to cases where the damage is inevitable even if the debtor performed at the time when the time of performance became due" could be interpreted to the effect that the provision does not stipulate a subjective requirement for non-performance but simply stipulates a requirement for the excuse of the performance of obligations. If the provision is interpreted as proposed in the preceding sentence, it can be viewed that the provision stipulates "strict liability similar to that provided under the English-American law" that deems any absence of performance, irrespective of the existence of willful act or negligence, as non-performance and excuses liability for non-performance in the case of the absence of willful act or negligence. Even though there has been a possibility of such interpretation, the principle of fault-based liability has taken up a firm position with precedents. Although such interpretation conflicts with Articles 397, 401, 537, 538 and 546 of the Civil Code, the conversion to strict liability does not require a separate demanding amendment work except for a revision of the foregoing conflicting provisions. The principle of fault-based liability is no longer part of defects liability and defects liability is regarded as arising out of the effect resulted from the non-performance of an obligation. Indeed, the principle of fault-based liability has become close to strict liability depending on the operation of the burden of proof. The PACL also adopts the principle of liability without fault, and at the same time, contains a rule on excuse (see Article 29 of the PACL).

C. Exit from the principle of invalidity of a contract on the ground of initial impossibility

I am extremely skeptical about the existence of a logical ground or actual need for any juridical act with the purpose of initial impossibility to be invalid. I wonder, for example, why a sale and purchase agreement that is executed with regard to the goods that is supposed to be produced in the future and that is not exist at the time of concluding the agreement is regarded as being valid, but a sale and purchase agreement regarding the goods that has been lost after concluding the agreement is deemed to be invalid. It is my opinion that it will be reasonable to deal with the relevant issue from the perspective of the assumption of a risk or the non-performance of an obligation by treating it the same as subsequent impossibility. Article 535 of the Civil Code is a provision stipulated on the assumption of the invalidity of a contract on the ground of initial impossibility, but it is my view that, rather than narrowly interpreting the provision as one pertaining to the compensation of damages for one type of contractual liability, an aggressive measure needs to be taken as done by Germany.

D. Rationalization of remedies

It will more appropriately regulate the interests of the parties to generally allow the creditor to be entitled to the reduction of price and the creditor/debtor to be entitled to the additional enforcement of obligations than to accept only the enforcement of obligations, damages and termination as the remedies for the non-performance of an obligation. On the foregoing basis, it will be reasonable to allow firstly the reduction of price, the additional enforcement of an obligation, and damages, secondly the claim for damages, and thirdly termination rather than leaving the choice of the remedies on the hands of the creditor. In particular, termination should be allowed not only in the case of defects liability but also in the case where the purpose of a contract may not be achieved due to the non-performance of an obligation (see Articles 380 and 575. 1 of the Civil Code).

In the DCFR, a right to enforce performance is deemed as a primary remedy for nonperformance, but there are many exceptions. The DCFR contains the rule that specific performance cannot be enforced where performance would be unlawful or impossible, performance would be unreasonably burdensome or expensive or performance would be of such a personal character that it would be unreasonable to enforce it (III. 3:302(3) of the DCFR). The PACL has the same stance in Articles 6, 7 and 13. The DCFR states that a creditor may terminate if the debtor's non-performance of a contractual obligation is fundamental (III. -3:502 (1) of the DCFR). In this rule, a non-performance of a contractual obligation is fundamental if it substantially deprives the creditor of what the creditor was entitled to expect under the contract unless at the time of conclusion of the contract the debtor did not foresee and could not reasonably be expected to have foreseen that result or if it is intentional or reckless and gives the creditor reason to believe that the debtor's future performance cannot be relied on. In the foregoing rule, the term "reckless" is stronger than the term, "strongly negligent" (mentioned in III. -3:703 of the DCFR). Article 16 of the PACL has the same intention.

E. The principle of a change in circumstances needs to be stipulated as an exceptional principle.

We should follow the fundamental proposition that the notion, "a contract must be complied with" is compatible with contractual justice only when the contract is complied with on the assumption that the fundamentals of the contract will not essentially change. At the same time, it should be emphasized that there are exceptions and the related requirements should be reinforced. On the basis of the principle of party autonomy, the adjustment and expiration of the contracts rather than the modification of the contracts should be substance.

14. 4 CONCLUSION

First of all, I wish to close this introduction by mentioning the outline of my proposal to amend the law of the non-performance of obligations in a "grand scale." Some of my proposal is to throw away the principle of fault-based liability, to move toward the application of strict liability and to achieve equality by stipulating grounds for excuse. I also suggest adopting a single system where the invalidity of a contract on the ground of initial impossibility, defects liability, liability for the breach of incidental obligations and the creditors' liability for delay are treated as non-performance in line with the general definition and all-inclusive notion. The interest relationship between the creditor and the debtor should be balanced in a more reasonable and practical way by rationalizing the remedies for non-performance. I do not mean to take a standardized approach but to explore specific appropriate solutions. For this reason, I also propose to demand jurists to promote the realization of contractual justice. These suggestions appear to be exceptionally unprecedented at a first glance, but as I stated above they are not difficult to achieve in fact. Of course, the discussions and work to draw up a draft should be proceeded with by taking account of consensus of the academic and the business practice fields of Korea.

The work to revise the law of obligations underway in Japan seems to be less determined than the work done by Germany in 2002. Among Japan, Korea and China, Japan was the last country ratifying the CISG. China early ratified the CISG, and accordingly launched a massive project to reform the contract law (equivalent to the law of obligations of other countries) in 1999. By doing so, China has emerged to be the largest trading country in the world. China has been very progressive, boldly adopting the principle of a change in circumstances, which had not been stipulated under the contract law, as part of the Interpretation of Private Law (which is equivalent to legislation enacted by the Ministry of Justice of China). It is my view that it becomes time for Korea to resolutely revise the Civil Code on a "grand scale" apart from any effect of other countries. The launch of the work to revise the Civil Code should be as quickly as possible, and the conduct of the work should be perfect.

(Young June Lee, President, Research Institute for Asia Private Law, Korea)

CHAPTER 15 Long-term Relationship between the Temporal and Spatial Distribution of Yellow Sea Herring (Clupea Pallasi) and Climate Variability Since the 15th Century

Li Yushang, Chen Liang, & Che Qun

Abstract: This research explores long-term relationship between the temporal and spatial distribution of Yellow Sea herring and climate variability since the 15th century. Based on Chinese and Korean historical resources which contain a large amount of information not only on the variation of Yellow Sea herring abundance roughly, but also an extensive temporal and spatial distribution since the 15th century, we have found that there were four major high abundant periods of herrings during the past 600 years and draw ten geographical distribution range maps from 1417 to 1883. By comparing the Chinese climate variety and fluctuations of eastern coast of Korean Peninsula and Europe herring abundance with Yellow Sea herring, we found that the abundance and distribution ranges of the Yellow Sea herring were mainly impacted by the variation of climate rather than salinity. Finally, according to the relations of distribution ranges and sea surface temperature based on modern data of sea surface temperature and herring catches, the temperature trend line in Shidao March temperature of 600 years was plot also. As a special local population which distributed in the southernmost sea area in the Northern Hemisphere, the Yellow Sea is a perfect case which directly manifests the change of climate and its effect.

15.1　INTRODUCTION

Herring (*Clupea*) is widely distributed in the shallow, temperate waters of the North Pacific and the North Atlantic oceans, including the Baltic Sea. They are forage fish moving in vast schools and usually highly abundant, coming in spring to the shores of Europe, America and the East Asia, where they are caught. It is well known that the herring fishery was one of the most important fisheries in the past centuries, being crucial for many economies of European countries[1]. Besides the herring catching was one of the important commercial fishery in the coast of Korean Peninsula and Shandong Peninsula, China during the past six centuries.

The stocks of the Pacific herring are separated geographically into ten groups. Many of these groups could be further sub-divided into local stocks with isolated spawning grounds but it appears that the mixing may be common throughout the life history between neighboring local stocks, even between neighboring groups. However, it is believed that the northernmost and southernmost stocks, Korfo-Karaginsk and Yellow Sea stocks, have been almost completely isolated from the other stocks due to the geographical conditions there[2].

---

① 　E. E. Rich and C. H. Wilson. *The Cambridge Economic History of Europe Volume V : The Economic Organization of Early Mordern Europe.* London : Cambridge University Press, 1967, 142-155 ; James D. Tracy, Herring wars : The Habsburg Netherlands and the Struggle for Control of the North Sea, ca. 1520-1560. *The Sixteenth Century Journal*, 24 (2) : 249-272.

② 　S. Chikuni, *The Fish Resources of the Northwest Pacific ; FAO Fisheries Technical Paper 266*, Rome : Food and Agriculture Organization of the United Nations, 1985, 59.

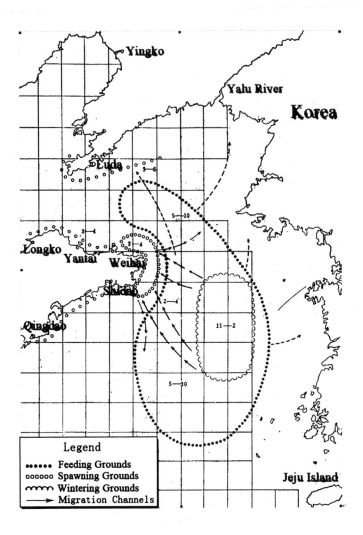

Figure 15.1 Distribution map of Yellow Sea herring in 1972

Data resources: Institute of Oceanology and Marine Fisheries in Shandong Province, *Fishery Manual*, Beijing: Agriculture Press, 1978, 22. Tang Qi-sheng, The Yellow Sea herring, in: Deng Jingyao (Eds), *Biology of Marine Fishery*, Beijing: Agriculture Press, 1991, 297.

The Yellow Sea herring is a local species of Pacific herring (*Clupea pallasii*) only found in the Yellow Sea, which is located between mainland China and the Korean Peninsula. Each year in March, herrings usually swim to the shallow waters along the coast of Rongcheng for their spawning activities[1]. The data of Yellow Sea herring catches had shown severe fluctuations during the past 40 years, which in 1970s was around 200,000 ton per year, whereas in 1980s, the amount fell to 20,000 tons per year, one-tenth of a decade ago[2]. Only few herrings could be caught now and we might say it has disappeared there.

Based on the fishing statistic resources, Tang predicted that the natural environment factors could be regarded as the main cause of the sharply generation fluctuation of the Yellow Sea herring. He indicated that long-term population dynamics of the Yellow Sea herring was correlated with the 36-years cycle of wetness oscillation in the east China. Besides, Tang also thought that the varieties of herring abundance might relate to the parental stock density, although it seemed not very important. What's more, he also mentioned it was unlikely that catching factor could become one of the main factors which had impacted the long-term quantity varieties of herring population in historical periods[3].

The herring fishery both fluctuated dramatically along the coast of some European countries and East Asian countries, not only in modern time but also in the pre-industrial era. It is possible to develop the chronology of climate variations and human impact on marine populations by analyzing some useful historical resources

---

① Tang Qi-sheng, The Yellow Sea herring, in: Deng Jingyao (Eds), *Biology of Marine Fishery*, Beijing: Agriculture Press, 1991, 296-356.

② Chang Cheng Ye, The herring (Clupea harengus pallasi) and its fisheries in the Yellow Sea. *FAO Fisheries Report No.291*, *Volume 2*. Rome: Food and Agriculture Organization of the United Nations, 1983.

③ Tang Qi-sheng, A preliminary study on the cause of generation fluctuation of the Yellow Sea herring (Clupea Harengus Pallasi). *Transactions of Oceanology and Limnology* 3 (02) 37-45; Tang Qi-sheng, The Yellow Sea herring, in: Deng Jingyao (Eds), *Biology of Marine Fishery*, Beijing: Agriculture Press, 1991, 340-344.

such as royal fisheries landings, tax records and trade accounts which were abundant and unique in ancient European countries[1]. A reconstruction of time series of the historical herring fisheries in the Limfjord, Denmark[2], Baltic Sea[3] and the White Sea has been finished[4]. Although such resources were not available in East Asia countries, some major fluctuations of herring fisheries in the Yellow Sea had been revealed by analyzing related Chinese and Korean historical resources which contained a large amount of information not only on the variation of herring abundance roughly, but also an extensive temporal and spatial distribution since the 15th century[5].

More and more studies have indicated that the fluctuations on the abundance of marine fish populations and the changes of distributional ranges of them are

---

① Poul Holm, History of marine animal populations: a global research program of the Census of marine life, *Oceanologica Acta* 25 (2003) 207-211.

② Holm, P.; Bager, M., The Danish fisheries, c. 1450-1800: medieval and early modern sources and their potential for marine environmental history, in: Holm, P. et al. (Ed.). The exploited seas: new directions for marine environmental history. Census of Marine Life, 2001, 97-122.

③ Brain R. MacKenzie, et al. Baltic Sea fisheries in previous centuries: Development of catch data series and preliminary interpretations of causes of fluctuations. *ICES C. M. 2002/L:02*; Julia Lajus, Henn Ojaveer, Erik Tammiksaar, Fisheries at the Estonian Baltic Sea coast in the first half of the 19th century: What can be learned from the archives of Karl Ernst Baer? *Fisheries Research* 87(2-3) 126-136; Henn Objaveer, et al. Swedish Baltic Sea fisheries during 1868-1913: spatio-temporal dynamics of catch and fishing effort, *Fisheries Research* 87(2-3) 137-145.

④ Dmitry L. Lajus, Yaroslava I. Alekseeva, Julia A. Lajus, Herring fisheries in the White Sea in the 18th-beginning of the 20th Centuties: Spatial and temporal patterns and factors affecting the catch fluctuations. *Fisheries Research* 87(2-3) 255-259.

⑤ Li Yushang and Chen Liang, Quantitative Change of herring (Clupea Pallasi) Resources in the Bo Sea and Yellow Sea during the Qing Dynasty — The relations between climatic change and marine fishery, *Agricultural History of China*, 2007 (01) 24-32; Li Yushang and Chen Liang, Fluctuation and its causes of Clupea Pallasi resources in the Bo Sea, Yellow Sea and east coast of Korea Peninsula during the Ming Dynasty, *Agricultural History of China*, 2009 (02) 9-22; Li Yushang, The prosperity of Clupea Pallasi since 1600 and its ecological effects, *Agricultural History of China*, 2010 (02) 10-21; Li Yushang, The Fluctuations of Yellow Sea herring and abrupt climate change since 1816: The impact of Tambora volcano's eruption, *Academics in China*, 2009(5) 42-55.

synchronous with the large-scale climate models[1]. However, these studies almost focused on the variations of marine fish abundance in the time scale of years, ten years or decades. It is necessary to do more case studies in the hundreds years' long-term scale. According to Tang's prediction of the 36 years, cycle based on just one hundred years scale, so far the prosperous herring fishery did not reappear in the Yellow Sea after the last golden time in 1972. And it is believed that the fluctuations of the Yellow Sea herring fishery is not related to the variations of drought, flood and atmospheric circulation.

15.2　MATERIALS DIFFER FROM EUROPE

15.2.1　Annals of the Choson Dynasty

The Annals of the Choson Dynasty, which is the last and longest-lived imperial dynasty (1392-1910) of Korea, comprise 1,893 books covering 472 years (1392-1863) of the history of the Choson Dynasty. It is also regarded as the highly reliable records based on actual historical facts. The contents of these annals are encyclopedic. They include not only general affair of the state but also politics, social

　① 　Richard James Beamish, *Climate Change and Northern Fish Populations*, *Ottawa*: National Research Council,1995; Thomas Brunel & Jean Boucher, Long-term trends in fish recruitment in the north-east Atlantic related to climate change, *Fisheries Oceanography*, 16(4) 336-349; Rose Kenneth A., et al., Climate regime effects on Pacific herring growth using coupled nutrient-phytoplankton-zooplankton and bioenergetics models, *Transactions of the American Fisheries Society*, 137(1) 278-297; Thomas Brunel & Mark Dickey-Collas, Effects of temperature and population density on von Bertalanffy growth parameters in Atlantic herring: a macro-ecological analysis, Marine Ecology Progress Series, 405(15-28); Binet, D., Climate and pelagic fisheries in the Canary and Guinea currents 1964-1993: the role of trade winds and the southern oscillation, *Oceanologica acta*, 20(1) 177-190; Schwartzlose, R. A., et al., Worldwide large-scale fluctuations of sardine and anchovy populations, *South African Journal of Marine Science*, 21(1) 289-347; Yongjun Tian, Hideaki Kidokoro & Tatsuro Watanabe, Long-term changes in the fish community structure from the Tsushima warm current region of the Japan/East Sea with an emphasis on the impacts of fishing and climate regime shift over the last four decades, *Progress In Oceanography*, 68 (2-4) 217-237; JaapJan Zeeberg, et al., Climate modulates the effects of *Sardinella aurita* fisheries off Northwest Africa, Fisheries Research, 89(1) 65-75; Athanassios C. Tsikliras, Climate-related geographic shift and sudden population increase of a small pelagic fish (*Sardinella aurita*) in the eastern Mediterranean Sea, *Marine Biology Research*, 4(6) 477-481.

system, economy, geography, science, etc. For the reason of taxation, the fluctuations of herring fisheries were recorded in the annals from the 15th century to the 17th century.

15.2.2 Geographical document of the Choson Dynasty

As one of the most important historical resources of ancient Korea in the 15th century, *the Augmented Survey of the Geography of Korea*, which was compiled by the high officials, had documented the administrative divisions, mountains, rivers and natural resources, etc at that time. The natural resources of different places such as wild animal, plant were always came from the practical survey of local officials and their assistants. And the distribution range of herring could be easily got from the surveys of different districts.

15.2.3 Chinese local gazetteers

The local gazetteers, sometimes also called the local chorographic books, have existed in China since ancient times[1]. Over 8,000 local gazetteers survived today, most of which dated from the Ming (1368-1644) and Qing (1644-1911) dynasty. As the encyclopedias of regions and places, they always contain invaluable materials on geographic features and changes, administration, economies, natural resources, products, and other regional and local information. Generally speaking, they are usually subdivided into provincial gazetteers, prefectural gazetteers, and county gazetteers. The provincial gazetteers were usually compiled by summarizing the information in the prefectural gazetteers and individual county gazetteers. Usually they were compiled by the local officials and their assistants and all the gazetteers would be augmented in 60 years. And the continuous records of herring could be found in the different county gazetteers or prefectural gazetteers which covered all the administrative areas along the western coast of the Yellow Sea.

---

[1] James M. Hargett, Song Dynasty Local Gazetteers and Their Place in the History of Difangzhi Writing, Harvard Journal of Asiatic Studies, 56 (2) 405-442.

15.2.4　Personal literary works

As the series of unofficial historical documents, abundant volumes of Chinese essays, poems and other literary works which had been written by the native elite or officials in Ming and Qing dynasty were available. Moreover, many of the literary works were based on the writers' own observation. And some descriptions related to the herring fishery in different time or places also provided us another way to understand it in an unofficial background.

15.2.5　Oral History Materials

The folklores about the relations between catching herrings and emigration are popular in the western coast of Yellow Sea and these also attracted the interests of folklorist[1]. For better understanding of the flourishing fisheries in the 1970s, ichthyologists ever made some investigations in the villages around Rong cheng county (N 37°10′, E 122°25) which closes to the spawning ground of Yellow Sea herring in 1980s. By interviewing the native old fishermen, plentiful materials of the herring fisheries in the beginning of the 20th century were recorded[2].

Besides, we had finished our oral history program in some fishing village located in Rongcheng county and Changdao county (N 37°53′30″-38°23′58″, E 120°35′38″-120°56′36″) in 2009. And more details of the spawning ground and the history of the herring fishery had been recorded. The memories of the native fisherman helped us to get more information about the herring fishery during the past century.

15.2.6　Herring Temple

When herring was prosperous, in order to pray god of fish(whale) for catching more herring, many herring temples were built by villagers along the Weihai county

---

①　Shan Pi-gen. The traditional producing conventions of marine fishery in Shandong province, in: Qu Jinliang (Eds), *The study of marine culture*, Beijing: Ocean press, 2000, 167-173.

②　Yan Shu-zhen, Textual research on herring resources in north Yellow Sea I: Textual research on herring resources, *Marine Sciences* 30(1) 88-92.

coast during 1820-1850, which was also the most important spawning grounds of Yellow Sea herring. However, we cannot find these temples today because these fishing villages have become one part of the modern city since 1898.

15.2.7 Modern data of sea surface temperature (SST) and herring catches

It is possible to get the statistical data of herring along the western coast of Yellow Sea after the People's Republic of China was established in 1949. The herring fishery was dominated by several state-owned marine fishery enterprises since that time. As an appendix of the investigation on the fishery natural resources, the annual statistics of each enterprise were collected to be a compilation of data. And the catch data of herring during the past 60 years were kept in this book. More importantly, the shooting frequency was recorded in this book as well, by which the variable CPUE (Catch Per Unit Effort) can be calculated, which may be more precise than CPUE using operation time, fishing power per boat or fishing boat as unit effort in the former Atlantic fishery studies.

The data of monthly SST could be got from the books of *Observed Materials of Oceanic observing station* (*1966-1972*) published by State Oceanic Administration of China. The SOA carries out oceanographic and marine meteorological observations through its branch observing stations, in which five oceanic observing stations nearby herring distribution areas were included.

15.3 SHARPLY FLUCTUATION OF YELLOW SEA HERRING ABUNDANCE DURING THE PAST 600 YEARS

For the reasons of special use of sacrifices and taxation, the historical records of the Yellow Sea herring were kept well in the Annals of the Choson Dynasty. By analyzing these records, we found that Hwanghae-do, Chungcheong-do, Jeolla-do located in the west coast of Korean Peninsula and Gyeongsang-do located in the southeastern coast of Korean Peninsula should be regarded as the main producing regions of herring from 1417 to 1454(More details of the distribution regions could be seen from Figure 15-2). However this situation had changed since 1505. As the herring disappeared, many fishermen at Buan county, Jeolla-do went bankrupt after that year. But for the taxation on herring had not been exempted until 1511 when a county magistrate from Jeolla-do ever mentioned in his memorial to the throne to ask the exemption of herring taxation there. And this suggestion was accepted by the King soon[1].

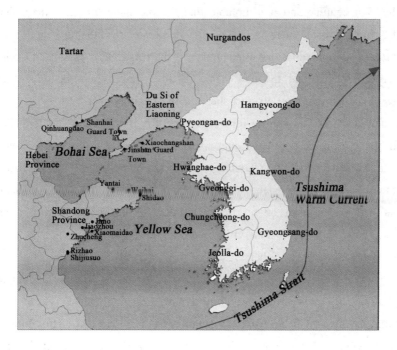

Figure 15-2　Administrative regions around Yellow Sea from 15th century to the mid-17th century

The disappearing herring came back to the west coast of Korean Peninsula after almost 100 years. A finance official wrote a report to the King to ask the permits of re-levying the herring taxes for the flourishing herring fishery in Gyeongsang-do and Jeolla-do in 1603. The herring tax was very benefit to the financial recession caused by the war against Japan in the end of 16th century and the King approved it

---

① *Annals of the Choson Dynasty-Jungjong*, Vol. 13, 4th May, 1511.

certainly[1]. The documents also indicated that the herring came back to the coast of Gangryeong, Hwanghae-do in 1629 and the local magistrate presented it to the King in 1629 and 1630[2].

In Rongcheng county, China, there is an old village located in the coast of Ai-Lian gulf which is the core spawning ground of Yellow Sea herring. This village was called "Ma-Liu" (there were *Pterocarya stenoptera C. DC* all around the village) before the 17th century and it is notable that the old name of this village had been replaced by a new word "herring beach" for the prosperous herring fishery there from 1603 to 1620. At that time, a large number of herrings were caught and pile up on the village's beach[3]. And the new name of this village could be one of the best memories of the prosperous herring fishery in the beginning of 17th century. What's more, a new wave of "migration for herring" to the islands of Shangdong Peninsula appeared at the turn of the Ming and Qing Dynasties. As we know, residing in islands was banned in the Ming Dynasty. After the late Ming Dynasty, fish men in group caught herring in the islands of Shangdong Peninsula and at the same time the governors had no time to attend to this matter. Because of herring's persistent prosperity, they simply built their villages there[4].

Although the records of herrings became fewer in the Annals of the Choson Dynasty, more details of these records could be found in the Chinese documents after the middle of 17th century when the Qing dynasty was established. These documents showed that the herring fishery was prosperous from the mid of 17th century to the mid of 18th century. For example, the gazetteer of Weihai-Wei compiled in 1742 had mentioned that herring was so prosperous that it became the most important fishery economies at that time[5]. What's more one gazetteer compiled in 1734 had recorded

---

①   *Annals of the Choson Dynasty-Seonjo*, Vol. 164, 20th July, 1603.

②   *Annals of the Choson Dynasty-Injo*, Vol. 20, 5th March, 1629.

③   Li Yushang, Environmental change and Pacific herrings' transferring of spawning sites within the Ailian Bay, *Ludong University Journal* 27(5)85-88.

④   Shan Pi-gen. The traditional producing conventions of marine fishery in Shandong province, in: Qu Jinliang (Eds), *The study of marine culture*, Beijing: Ocean press, 2000, 167-173.

⑤   The gazetteer of Weihai-Wei, Vol. 7, 1742.

that many whales were attracted to the northern coast of Yellow Sea by the abundant herrings[1].

Herrings were regarded as one kind of an ill-boding fish among the Chinese people. And the high yields of herrings were always related to the crop failure and the unstable situation in politics. However this folk experience seemed to be confirmed during the period of "Daoguang Depression" (1820-1850) in Qing dynasty. The high yields of herrings not only appeared along the coast of Shandong and Liaodong peninsula where belongs to the traditional spawning ground of herrings, but also appeared along the coast of Bohai Sea. For example, Linyu county, which is situated on the Bohai Sea and near Qinghuandao, *the gazetteer of Linyu county* compiled in 1878 had mentioned that the high yields of this fishery had made herrings became one of the cheapest fishes since Jiaqing Dynasty. When ship carried them to other places, it was slightly more expensive. But even so, a fish was only worth a copper coin[2].

However, the yields of herrings along the coast of Bohai Sea and Yellow Sea began to decrease from 1850 to 1883 and the distribution range of them also shrank at same time. Leting county, not far from Qinghuandao and Linyu county, *The gazetteer of Leting county* compiled in 1877 had recorded such words: "it was the early Daoguang Dynasty that herring abundance was at the height and every net could catch tens of thousands of fishes at that time. However it is rare now and we heard that it is still rich in Korea "[3] The Yellow Sea herring disappeared from the coast of China in 1884 and although a few herrings came back in 1930s, the real high yields of this fishery just appeared around 1970s.

15.4 VARIATION OF DISTRIBUTIONAL RANGES IN DIFFERENT PERIODS

By analyzing the historical materials kept in the China and Choson Dynasty, we

---

[1] The gazetteer of Sehngjing province, Vol. 107, 1734.

[2] The gazetteer of Linyu county, Vol. 8, 1878.

[3] *The gazetteer of Leting county*, Vol. 1, 1877.

have found that there were four major high abundant periods of herrings in the coast of Yellow Sea and the east coast of the Korean Peninsula during the past 600 years.

What's more, at least eight major changes of distributional ranges of the Yellow Sea herring had been revealed in the Figure 15-3-15-12 during the past six centuries. In each figure, we can see the distributional range of herring school around the coast of Shandong and Liaodong Peninsula of China and the Korean Peninsula in different periods since the early 15th century. And the active ranges of the herring school ever changed continually and clearly during the centuries by analyzing the geographical distribution ranges showing in the following ten figures.

Figure 15-3 1417-1450	Figure 15-4 1451-1504

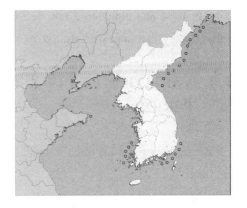

Figure 15-5 1505-1602	Figure 15-6 1603-1620

Figure 15-7   1629

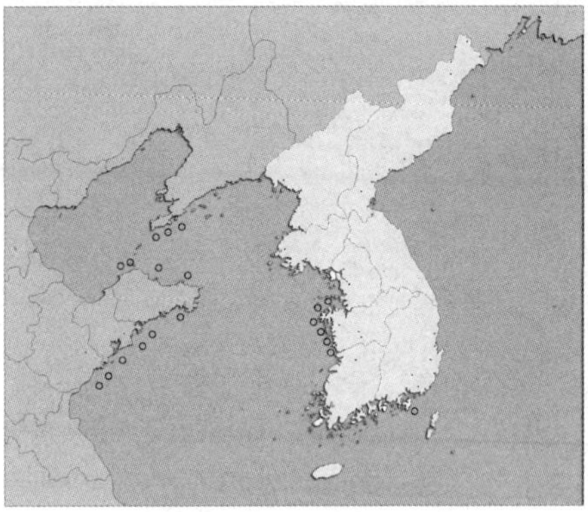

Figure 15-8   1662-1722

Figure 15-9   1736-1795

Figure 15-10   1821-1850

Figure 15-3 and Figure 15-4 were drawn according to the records kept in the *Annals of the Choson Dynasty-geography records* (1418-1450) and *the Augmented Survey of the Geography of Korea* (*finished in 1481, augmented in 1530*). The administrative regions (county) which was famous for the herring fisheries were recorded in these books (see Table 15-1).

 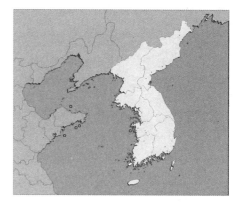

Figure 15-11   1851-1870   **Figure 15-12   1871-1883**

Resource: Figure 15-3-16-12 have shown us the distribution ranges of the Yellow Sea herring respectively in the periods of 1417-1450, 1451-1504, 1505-1602, 1603-1620, 1629, 1662-1722, 1736-1795, 1821-1850, 1851-1870, 1871-1883. And these distributional maps are drew according to our former research articles①.

Table 15-1   Distribution regions of herring recorded by the Annals of the Choson Dynasty-geography records and the Augmented Survey of the Geography of Korea

	Annals of the Choson Dynasty-geography records			Augmented Survey of the Geography of Korea	
Dao (Province)	Fu/Ju/Mu (Prefecture)	County	Dao (Province)	Zhen/Duhu-Fu (Prefecture)	Gun/County
Hwanghae	Haeju	Yongkang Ongin Gangryeong Jangyeon	Hwanghae	Haeju Zhen	Haeju Pungcheon Ongin Gangryeong Jangyeon

① Li Yushang and Chen Liang, Quantitative Change of herring (Clupea Pallasi) Resources in the Bo Sea and Yellow Sea during the Qing Dynasty — The relations between climatic change and marine fishery, *Agricultural History of China*, 2007 (01) 24-32; Li Yushang and Chen Liang, Fluctuation and its causes of Clupea Pallasi resources in the Bo Sea, Yellow Sea and east coast of Korea Peninsula during the Ming Dynasty, *Agricultural History of China*, 2009 (02) 9-22; Li Yushang, The prosperity of Clupea Pallasi since 1600 and its ecological effects, *Agricultural History of China*, 2010 (02) 10-21; Li Yushang, The Fluctuations of Yellow Sea herring and abrupt climate change since 1816: The impact of Tambora volcano's eruption, *Academics in China*, 2009(5) 42-55.

	Annals of the Choson Dynasty-geography records			Augmented Survey of the Geography of Korea	
Jeolla	Jeonju Fu	Mankyung Buan	Jeolla	Jeonju Zhen	Mankyung Buan Heungdeok
Chungcheong	Gongju Mu	Yeompo Biin	Chungcheong	Gongju Zhen	Imcheon
	Hongju Mu	Hamdeok Taean Seosan Boryeong		Hongju Zhen	Hongju Seocheon Biin Nampo Taean Seosan Boryeong Gyeolseong
	Pungcheon	Pungcheon			
Gyeongsang	Gyeongju Fu	Dongnae Yeongil	Gyeongsang	Gyeongju Fu	
				Gyeongju Zhen	Ulsan Dongnae Cheongha Yeongil Janggi Gijang
				Yeonghae Duhufu	Heunghae
				An-dong Zhen	Yeongdeok
				Jinju Zhen	Namhae
				Gimhae Zhen	Gimhae Geoje Goseong Jinhae Chirwon Ungcheon
Hamgil	Gyeongwon Fu		Hamgyong	Hamheung Fu	
				Yeongheung Fu	
				Chongpyong Fu	
				Anbyeon Fu	
				Deogwon Fu	
				Anbyeon Zhen	Muncheon

Annals of the Choson Dynasty-geography records	Augmented Survey of the Geography of Korea	
		Continued
	Bukcheong Fu	
	Hoeryeong	Isong
		Hongwon
	Jongseong Fu	
	Gyeongwon Fu	
	Gyeongwon Fu	
	Buryeong Fu	
Pyeongan	Guseong Zhen	Seoncheon

Compared with the former situation from 1417 to 1450, the distribution region of the Yellow Sea herring expanded to the eastern tip of Shandong Peninsula, the eastern parts of Liaodong Peninsula and the coast of Seoncheon Kun, Pyeongan-do from 1451 to 1504. However this kind of distribution region expansion could be caused for the deficiency of Chinese historical records from 1417 to 1450. That is to say, just like the situation in the western coast of Korean Peninsula, there may be no significant changes in the distribution regions of herrings along the Chinese coast during the two periods (See Figure 15-3 and Figure 15-4). It was very clear that the herring school located in the northeastern coast of Hamgyeong-do extended its distributional ranges to the south southern coast from 1451 to 1504. The distribution range of herring were not limited in the coast beyond N 42° but widely distributed in the coast of Hamgyeong-do. And the distribution region ever expanded in Gyeongsang-do too.

However, the distributional ranges of herring school changed again from 1505 to 1602 (See Figure 15-5). The most notable changes in this period lied in the disappearance of herring in the coast of Yellow Sea. The herring school disappeared both in the tip of Shandong Peninsula and the west coast of Korean Peninsula. These distributional ranges appeared in the beginning of 16th century and did not change greatly until one century later. Compared with Figure 15-4 and Figure 15-6, Figure 15-5 showed the distribution region of herrings living in the eastern coast of Korean Peninsula began to shrink from 1505 to 1602.

Some major changes of the distributional ranges of the herring school appeared in the first half of 17th century seen from Figure 15-6 and Figure 15-7. The disappearing herring school came back to the tip of Shandong Peninsula nearly a century had passed. At first, herrings appeared in the coast of Jeolla-do in 1603, and then Hwanghae-do in 1629. Compared with Figure 15-6, both the distribution regions of herrings along the coast of Gyeongsang-do and Hamgyong-do expanded and the yields increased at that time.

Few and fragmentary records of herrings could be found in the Korean historical resources after the establishment of Qing Dynasty in 1644. It is obvious that herring stocks distributed in many regions disappeared from both sides of Korean Peninsula. For few historical resources were available in this period, it was impossible to draw the distributional ranges in the map. According to the ample gazetteers compiled in the reign of Kangxi(1662-1722), Qianlong (1736-1795), Daoguang (1821-1850), Tongzhi (1862-1874) and Guangxu (1875-1908) in Qing Dynasty, even many gazetteers published in 1920s and 1930s, the exact distribution map of the Yellow Sea herring along the Chinese coast could be drawn (see Figure 15-8 to Figure 15-12)[1].

Many stocks of herring ever swim southward to the coast of Zhucheng and Rizhao (N 35°-36°) around 1673 (Figure 15-8) and it is notable that this situation did not occur again in the past 600 years. However, herrings disappeared or seldom of them could be found in the two places around the year of 1764 (Figure 15-9). And high yields of herrings appeared along the coast from Jiaozhou to Yantai and the eastern coast of Liaodong Peninsula during the two periods (1662-1722, 1736-1795).

During the reign of Daoguang Emperor in Qing dynasty (1821-1850), relatively higher fish density still existed around the coast of Shandong Peninsula. What's

① Beijing Astronomical Observatories, Chinese Academy of Science. The Union Catalogues of Chinese Gazetteers, Beijing: Zhonghua Book Company, 1985.

more, it was noteworthy that the distributional ranges of herrings ever extended to the coast of Bohai Sea, which is the innermost gulf of the Yellow Sea (See Figure 15-10). And this situation only occurred once in the past 600 years too.

Herrings still appeared along the coast from Jimo to Fushan in Shandong province from 1850 to 1883. But the yields of herrings at that time became far less than the period of Daoguang reign. As herring stocks became gradually less, the herring fishery at Linyu county and Leting county finally disappeared around 1870 (see Figure 15-11). Differ from other fishermen, the fishermen lived in Changdao island still kept their fishing old traditions to go fishing near the coast of Weihai and the western coast of Korean Peninsula. They still went to the fishing grounds located in the coast of Jeolla-do after the local herring disappeared around 1850 (see Figure 15-12). And this half century long herring fishing tradition had been called "Da Zuo" (They went fishing in Korea and sold herring catch to locals and when they returned home, carried back a cargo of local oak for making charcoal used for getting warm by the fire on ship the next year) by the local people. However the herrings also disappeared in Jeolla-do around 1900. At this period, the former most important herring fishery had been replaced by the little yellow croaker fishery in the Yellow Sea and Bohai Sea. That is to say the position of cold water fish had been replaced by the warm water fish.

About 400 square nautical mile narrow regions along the coast from Shidao to Weihai always belong to the main spawning ground of Yellow Sea herring since the 15th century. As too many matured herrings swim to the spawning ground, it is believed that some of them could be found beyond this narrow region. It is interesting that the extension and shrink of the spawning ground range always differ in different high yields periods. And what caused this phenomenon?

15.5 CLIMATE CHANGE AND SPATIAL DISTRIBUTION OF HERRINGS DURING THE PAST CENTURIES

It was obvious that the herring fishery had ever experienced several times of fluctuations in Europe during the past centuries. Based on the studies of Bohuslän herring fishery, Norwegian spring herring fishery, south-western England herring and sardine fishery, French herring fishery in the English Channel and the Bay of Biscay herring fishery, the analysis of historical records and meteorologic resources indicated that these places had undergone large fluctuations during the last centuries. Moreover it is conclude that climate variation governed the alternating herring and sardine periods[1]. A long term study of herring fishery in the English Channel had revealed that periods of warmer weather favored the sardine fisheries, while colder climate was more beneficial to the herring fisheries[2].

Compared with the situation in the period of 1417 through 1450, there were no obvious changes in the distribution range of the Yellow Sea herring from 1451 to 1504. However, the situation in the eastern coast of Korean Peninsula was completely different. The red tide phenomenon which was regarded as the caution of the holly heaven in ancient Korea had been recorded in the Annals of the Choson Dynasty. There were ten times of red tide in Gyeongsang-do from 1399 to 1450, but only one red tide phenomenon was recorded in 1520 after that period. It is possible that the Tsushima Warm Current might be weaker after 1451 and then lead to the extension of distribution range along the eastern coast of the Korean Peninsula. However, the distribution ranges of herring did not change in Hwanghae-do and Chungcheong-do at the same time.

The herrings disappeared along the coast of Yellow Sea and the distribution range of them also shrank along the eastern coast of the Korean Peninsula from 1505 to 1602. At least, compared with the situation in 1950s, the weather in the middle of

---

① Jurgen Alheit, Eberhard Hagen, Long-term climate forcing of European herring and sardine populations. *Fisheries Oceanography*, 6 (2):130-139.

② A. J. Southward et al., Fluctuations in the herring and pilchard fisheries of devon and cornwall linked to change in climate since the 16th century, *Journal of the Marine Biological Association of the United Kingdom*, 68 (3) 423-445.

Jiangxi province was extremely warm-wet from 1593 *to* 1597[1]. The changes on distribution ranges of the two local herring populations might be related to the climate warming.

During the Little Ice Age of the late 17th century, cold-water marine fish were of major importance in the Baltic Sea fisheries and the fishing season for the major pelagic fish was substantially later in the year compared to the present, much warmer conditions[2]. And the distributional ranges of herring never changed sharply around the Yellow Sea in the same period.

Moreover great climate change also occurred in the early 17th century and 19th century in China[3]. The studies on ice core records[4], lake sediments[5], tree ring[6]

① Che Qun and Li Yushang, Abrupt climate change around 1600 reflected in *NongzhengQunshu*, *Agricultural History of China*, 2011 (01) 120-127.

② Gaumiga et al., Gulf of Riga (Baltic Sea) fisheries in the late 17th century. *Fisheries Research*, 87 (2007) 120-125.

③ Chu Ko-Chen, A Preliminary Study on the Climatic Fluctuations During the Last 5000 Years in China, *Scientia Sinica* 16(2) 226-256; Zhang De-er, The Little Ice Age in China and its correlations with global change, *Quaternary Science*, 3(2) 104-112; Zongtai Wang, The little ice age of the northwest region, China, Chinese Geographical Science, 2(2) 215-225; Wang Shao-Wu, Wang Ri-Sheng, Little ice age in China, *Chinese Science Bulletin*, 36(3) 217-220; Weihong Qian, Yafen Zhu, Little ice age climate near Beijing, China, inferred from historical and stalagmite records, *Quaternary Research*, 57(1) 109-119.

④ Yao Tandong, et al., Climatic variations since the Little Ice Age recorded in the Guliya ice core, *Science in China (Series D)*, 39(6) 557-596; Yao Tandong, Xie Zi-Chu, Wu Xiao-Ling, L. G. Thompson, Climatic change since little ice age recorded by Dun-de Ice Cap, *Science in China (Series B)*, 34(6) 760-767.

⑤ Jin Zhangdong, Wang Su-min, Shen Ji, Wang Yinxi, Carbonate verse silicate Sr isotope in lake sediments and its response to Little Ice Age, *Chinese Science Bulletin*, 48(1) 95-100, Ma Long, et al., The medieval warm period and the little ice age from a sediment record of lake Ebinur, northwest China, *Boreas*, 40 (3) 518-524.

⑥ Liu Yu, Cai Qiufang, et al., Amplitudes, rates, periodicities and causes of temperature variations in the past 2485 years and future trends over the central-eastern Tibetan Plateau, *Chinese Science Bulletin*, 56(28-29) 2986-2994; Guo Xiaohua, Deng Yang, et al., Tree ring based streamflow reconstruction for the upper Yellow River over the past 1234 years, *Chinese Science Bulletin*, 55(36) 4179-4186; Cai Qiufang, Liu Yu, et al., Tree-ring-based May-July mean temperature hiatory for LvLiang Mountains, China, since 1836, *Chinese Science Bulletin*, 55(26) 3008-3014; Duan Jianping, Wang Lily, Li Lun, Chen Kelong, Temperature variability since A. D. 1837 inferred from tree-ring maximum density of *Abies fabri* on Gongga Mountain, China, *Chinese Science Bulletin*, 55(26) 3015-3022.

and stalagmite records[1] indicated that large regions of China had ever experienced major varieties of climate in the past five centuries. What's more the climate fluctuation not only appeared in the Mainland China but also impacted the sea surface temperature (SST) in South China Sea. The study on the $D^{18}O$ in the Lagoon sediment of Nansha Island, China indicated that the SST was much cooler in the early 17th century and the first half of 19th century[2].

It is believed that the extremely cold weather pushed the herrings swim southward and lived along the coast of Zhucheng and Rizhao around 1673. And the herrings did not disappear until 1764 in the two places. The high yields of herrings along the coast from Jiaozhou to Yantai and the eastern coast of Liaodong peninsula indicated that the air temperature was always cold in general from 1662 to 1722 and 1736 to 1795. Compared with the situations from 1505 to 1602, the herrings distributed along the coast of Gyeongsang-do and Hamgyong-do expanded their distribution ranges during the following decades and the yields of herrings also increased. Synchronous changes on the distribution ranges of herring occurred along the coast of Yellow Sea and the eastern coast of Korean peninsula. It is believed that this change was related to the cliamte cooling.

The global abrupt climate changes occurred in 1230, 1600 and 1815, have been confirmed by plenty of studies[3]. And that of 1600 and 1815 may be caused by the

---

[1] Ming Tan, Tungsheng Liu, et al., Cyclic rapid warming on centennial-scale revealed by a 2650-year stalagimte record of warm season temperature, *Geophysical Research Letters*, 30 (12) 191-194; Dorte Eide Paulsen, Hong-Chun Li, The-Lung Ku, Climate variability in central China over the last 1270 years revealed by high-resolution stalagmite records. *Quaternary Science Reviews*, 22(5-7) 691-701.

[2] Zhao Huanting, Wen Xiaosheng, et al., The temperature changes recorded as $D^{18}O$ in the Lagoon sediment of the Nansha Island in the past 1670 years, *Tropical Geography*, 24(2) 103-108.

[3] Reid A. Bryson and Thomas J. Murray, Climate of Hunger: Mankind and the World's Changing Weather, University of Wisconsin Press, 1977; Kathleen R. Laird, Sherilyn C. Fritz, Kirk A. Maasch & Brian F. Cumming, Greater deought intensity and frequency before AD 1200 in the Northern Great Plains, USA. *Nature*, 1996 (382) 552-554; Zheng Jingyun, Ge Quansheng, Zhang Piyuan, Abrupt Climatic Change: Evidence and Implication, *Advance in Earth Science*, 1999, 14 (2) 177-182; R. B. Alley, J. Marotzke, et al. Abrupt Climate Change, *Science*, 299 (5615) 2005-2010.

volcanic eruptions of Huaynaputina[1] and Tambora[2] respectively. Actually, the volcano Huaynaputina erupted in year 1600, and three years later (1603) Yellow Sea herring began to boom in Jeolla-do, so did Gyeongsang-do and Hamgyeong-do. As a result of the insufficiency of parent fish amount, herring flourishing on hwanghae-do of Korea occurred in 1629, which is 29 years after the volcanic eruption.

In Baltic Sea, the herring fisheries were poor during the last decades of the 18th century, while herring occurred in great numbers in the Limfjord during the 1810s and 1820s. But the fishery of this stock collapsed and herring was caught at a level of less than 1000 tons until the second decade of the 20th century[3]. Moreover catches of herring and other coastal fish near Estonia in the mid and late 19th century varied probably due to climatic fluctuations, when fishing effort and methods were stable[4]. The herring catches in Scotland and Ireland also fluctuated sharply in the 19th century

---

① Fidel Costa, Bruno Scaillet. Massive atmospheric sulfur loading of the AD 1600 Huaynaputina eruption and implications for petrologic sulfur estimates, *Geophysical Research Letters*, 30(2) 40-44; Jie Fei and Jie Zhou, The possible climatic impact in north China of the 1600 Huaynaputina eruption, Peru. *International Journal of Climatology*, 29(6) 927-933; C. U. Hammer, H. B. Clausen & W. Dansgaard, Greenland ice sheet evidence of post-glacial volcanism and its climatic impact, *Nature*, 288 (5788) 230-235; David M. Pyle. Volcanoes: How did the summer go, *Nature* 393 (6684), 415-417; Alexandra Witze, The volcano that changed the world, *Nature News*, 2008.4.11; LaMarche, V. C. & Hirschboeck, K. K. Frost rings in trees as records of major volcanic eruptions, *Nature* 307 (1984) 121-126; K. R. Briffa, P. D. Jones, F. H. Schweingruber and T. J. Osborn, Influence of volcanic eruptions on Northern Hemisphere summer temperature over the past 600 years, *Nature*, 393: 450-454; Shanaka L. de Silva & Gregory A. Zielinski. Global influence of the AD 1600 eruption of Huaynaputina, Peru. *Nature*, 393: 455-458; Zhang De'er, The Little Ice Age in China and Its correlations with Global Change, *Quaternary Sciences*, 11 (2) 104-111.

② C. Edward Skeen, The year without a summer: A historical view, *Journal of the Early Republic*, 1 (1) 51-67; Richard B. Stothers. The great Eruption in 1815 and Its Aftermath, *Science*, 224 (4654) 1191-1198; Yang Yu-da, Man Zhi-min, Zheng Jingyun, A Serious Famine in Yunnan (1815-1817) and the Eruption of Tambola Volcano, *Fudan Journal* (*Social Science*), 2005 (1) 79-85; Wang Zheng, Zhou Qingbo, Zhang Piyuan et al. *Progress in Natural Science*, 5 (3) 323-329; R. K. R. Vupputuri, The tambora eruption in 1815 provides a test on possible global climatic and chemical perturbation in the past, *Nature Hazards*, 5 (1): 1-16.

③ Bo Poulsen, Poul Holm, Brian R. MacKenzie, A long-term (1667-1860) perspective on impacts of fishing and environmental variability on fisheries for herring, eel, and whitefish in the Limfjord, Denmark, *Fisheries Research* 87(2-3) 181-195.

④ Julia Lajus, Henn Ojaveer, Erik Tammiksaar, Fisheries at the Estonian Baltic Sea coast in the first half of the 19th century: What can be learned from the archives of Karl Ernst Baer? *Fisheries Research* 87(2-3) 126-136.

and it may be related to the impact of lunar cycles and sun spots[1].

However, the situations differed in Yellow Sea and Bohai Sea. Herring fishery became flourishing in the mid of 1810s and it did not collapse until 1850s. In fact, after the eruption of Tambora volcano in 1815, profitable herring fisheries ever appeared along the coast of Bohai Sea in the following years. If the sea surface temperature is the key environment factor that may impact the herring abundance, could we say that the eruption of Tambora volcano lead to different climate conditions in the Baltic Sea and Yellow Sea, Bohai Sea? And then lead to the difference in the variation of herring abundance. For the same reason, could we say the differences in the distribution ranges of Yellow Sea herring in two periods, 1662 to 1722 and 1821 to 1850, may indicate the impact to the sea surface temperature of the Yellow Sea caused by the eruptions of Huaynaputina volcano and Tambora volcano was different?

Both the European and Chinese fishermen had experienced the depression of herring fishery after 1850 when the climate became warmer than before. The profitable Yellow Sea herring fishery occurred again in 1960s and 1970s when the weather was cooler than before. However this fishery declined sharply in 1980s when the weather began to get warmer. According to the observation of fishermen, more and more warm water fishes such as blue fin leather jacket appeared in the Yellow Sea at that time.

15.6 RALATION OF DISTRIBUTION RANGES AND SEA SURFACE TEMPERATURE

It is notable that the prosperous periods of Yellow Sea herring fishery coincided with the cool periods both appeared in China and Korean Peninsula roughly. But we are still not sure whether there is any obvious changes in the distribution ranges of herrings caused by the variations of air temperature in the past several high yields periods. And the studies on the sea surface temperature (SST) and Catch Per Unit

---

① T. Wyatt et al., Deterministic signals in Scottish and Irish Herring (Clupea harenggus) catches, *Scientia Marina*, 59(3-4) 507-513.

Effort (CPUE) would be helpful to understand the changes in distribution of Yellow Sea herring due to different temperature value.

To examine the relationship between temperature and fish population, datum is available as follows: the modern statistical data include monthly SST from a set of five ocean monitoring stations (See Table 15-2), monthly Yellow Sea herring catches from the coast along Yan Tai and Weihai, motortrawler's fishing records of marine fisheries enterprises in the period of 1966-1982 (See Table 15-3) around Shidao fishing ground where is the most important spawning habitat for Yellow Sea herring, and the fishing intensity there was steady as well.

Table 15-2 March SST and Temperature from ocean monitoring stations (℃)

Year	Shidao		Qinhuangdao		Shijiusuo (Rizhao)		Xiaomaidao (Zhucheng)		Xiaochangshan (Changshan Islands)	
	T	SST	T	SST	T	SST	T	SST	T	SST
1966	3.8	3.5	1.7	1.7	5.3	6.6	5	5	1.4	1.8
1967	4.1	3.5	3.3	2.9	5.2	5.4	4.9	4.2	2.5	1.9
1968	3.5	2.4	3.8	3.6	5.3	5.2	4.7	3.3	2.8	1.8
1969	1.6	1.5	-0.7	-0.6	2.7	3.2	2.3	2.6	-0.3	0.2
1970	1.4	2.4	-0.5	1.3	3.5	4.7	2.8	3.7	-1.1	0.9
1971	1.7	2.3	0.6	1	3.4	4.2	3	3.3	-0.5	0.8
1972	3.4	3	3.1	3.1	4.4	4.8	4.2	3.8	2.5	2.6
1973	–	4.4	3.8	3.9	6.1	6.5	5.9	5.7	3.7	3.5
1974	3	2	2.1	2.1	4.4	4.4	3.9	3.9	1.6	1.3
1975	4.5	3	4	3.5	6	6.2	5.4	5.4	3.3	2.9
1976	3.7	4.2	2.3	3.1	5.3	5.9	4.6	5	2.2	3.1
1977	—	—	—	—	—	—	—	—	—	—
1978	3.5	3.4	2.8	2.9	5.1	5.5	4.4	4.7	1.8	2.6
1979	3.9	3.7	2.8	2.5	5.6	6.2	5.2	5	2.7	2.9
1980	3.2	3	3	3.8	4.5	5.1	4.3	4.5	2.2	2.2
1981	5.1	2.9	3.1	2.5	6	5.6	5.5	4.9	2.3	1.7
1982	4.3	4.3	3.5	3.4	5.5	6.6	5.3	5.3	2.9	2.9

Resources: State Oceanic Administration People's Republic of China. *Observed Materials of Oceanic observing station (1966-1972)*.

Table 15-3 Herring catches of Yanwei, Shidao fisheries from motortrawler's fishing records

Year	Catch of Total Fishing Effort (Box)	CPUE of February — May (Box/Net)	CPUE Annual Growth Rate
1966	0	0	—
1967	56 468	3.89	—
1968	24 360	3.44	−0.12
1969	32 149	15.51	3.51
1970	12 686	2.43	−0.84
1971	424 930	25.41	9.45
1972	1 943 373	49.06	0.93
1973	1 162 441	37.16	−0.24
1974	671 457	22.41	−0.4
1975	1 709 254	48.74	1.17
1976	1 144 435	51.11	0.05
1977	257 076	18.38	−0.64
1978	425 176	40.62	1.21
1979	910 617	60.99	0.5
1980	843 313	62.03	0.02
1981	717 986	46.73	−0.25
1982	73 078	23.06	−0.51

Resources: Yellow Sea fishery research institute and East China Sea fishery research institute, Chinese Academy of Fishery Sciences. *The compilation of trawl fishery catching data in the Bohai Sea, Yellow Sea and the East China Sea*, Qingdao and Shanghai, 1983.

For data processing, some variables are calculated for the model of temperature-herring relationship. Firstly, we took CPUE as the alternative parameter of herring population. Secondly, according to the equations as followed:

$$GR = BR\text{-}FMR\text{-}NMR \tag{1}$$

$$FMR = TFC/P \tag{2}$$

$$FMC = TFC/CPUE \tag{3}$$

Where GR is population growth rate, BR is population birth rate, FMR is fishing mortality rate, NMR is natural mortality rate, TFC is total fishing catches, P is population, FMC is fishing mortality coefficient, we took FMC as the alternative parameter of fishing mortality rate. Thirdly, we defined the theoretical value of CPUE annual growth rate to remove the influence of the fishing mortality by assuming CPUE annual growth rate appearing to be a linear negative correlation with TFC of previous year in the uniform natural environment. And Linear interpolation analysis was conducted to establish the theoretical value of CPUE annual growth rate by using CPUE annual growth rate as dependent variable, and TFC of previous year as independent variables. Fourthly, CPUE annual natural growth rate was obtained by CPUE annual growth rate minus the theoretical value, by which we obtained CPUE natural birth rate departures, then plus 2.508, the CPUE annual natural growth rate in the uniform natural environment. All the parameters for temperature-herring model had been established (See Table 15-4).

Table 15-4   Parameters for temperature- herring model

Year	Catch of Total Fishing Effort of the Previous Year (Box)	CPUE of Previous Year February-May (Box/Net)	CPUE of February -May (Box/Net)	CPUE Annual Growth Rate	Theoretical Value of CPUE Annual Growth Rate	CPUE Natural Birth Rate departures	CPUE Annual Natural Growth Rate
1967	0	0	3.89	—	—	—	—
1968	56 468	3.89	3.44	−0.12	1.24	−1.36	1.15
1969	24 360	3.44	15.51	3.51	1.89	1.62	4.13
1970	32 149	15.51	2.43	−0.84	2.33	−3.17	−0.66
1971	12 686	2.43	26.41	9.45	2.05	7.39	9.91
1972	424 930	25.41	49.06	0.93	1.05	−0.12	2.39
1973	1 943 373	49.06	37.16	−0.24	−0.95	0.71	3.22
1974	1 162 441	37.16	22.41	−0.4	−0.22	−0.17	2.33
1975	671 457	22.41	48.74	1.17	−0.11	1.28	3.79
1976	1 709 254	48.74	51.11	0.05	−0.55	0.6	3.11
1977	1 144 435	51.11	18.38	−0.64	0.55	−1.19	1.32

Year	Catch of Total Fishing Effort of the Previous Year (Box)	CPUE of Previous Year February-May (Box/Net)	CPUE of February -May (Box/Net)	CPUE Annual Growth Rate	Theoretical Value of CPUE Annual Growth Rate	CPUE Natural Birth Rate departures	CPUE Annual Natural Growth Rate
1978	257 076	18.38	40.62	1.21	1.29	−0.08	2.43
1979	425 176	40.62	60.99	0.5	1.59	−1.09	1.41
1980	910 617	60.99	62.03	0.02	1.2	−1.19	1.32
1981	843 313	62.03	46.73	−0.25	1.32	−1.57	0.94
1982	717 986	46.73	23.06	−0.51	1.17	−1.67	0.83

Then, the temperature-herring model was set up by curvilinear regression using CPUE annual natural growth rate as dependence, SST of Shidao ocean monitoring station. It was discovered that March SST appearing to be significantly related to CPUE annual natural growth rate, and the equation is as followed:

$$y = 2.561x^3 - 23.567x^2 + 67.907x - 57.997 \ (R = 0.68, \ P = 0.093) \qquad (4)$$

Where y is CPUE annual natural growth rate, x is March SST of Shidao ocean monitoring station.

According to the analysis, March SST appearing to be significantly related to CPUE annual natural growth rate. The effect of SST on herring population is supposed to be the impact of SST on the survival rate of eggs, as March is the key month of eggs' hatching. From this research, March SST is the main environmental factors on the generations' population.

The equation is established to describe the relations between SST and herring resources, by which it is possible to calculate the relations between the SST and the spread and shrinkage of the herrings' distributional ranges in history.

According to the equation, $y = 2.561x^3 - 23.567x^2 + 67.907x - 57.997$, of which two effective roots are 1.54 and 3.83. That is, it would be suitable for herring population growth when March SST of Shidao is in this range. And, it would be optimum when SST is around 2-3 ℃.

Based on the above conclusion, further analysis of the relationship between SST and the distribution could be conducted. The correlation coefficients of Shidao SST with Qinhuangdao, Shijiusuo, Xiaomaidao, Xiaochangshan SST, $r = 0.653$, 0.873, 0.850, 0.871 ($p < 0.01$) respectively, are significantly correlated, and linear regression equations are as followed:

$$\text{Shidao SST } (x), \text{ Qinhuangdao SST } (y): y = 0.937x - 0.355 \tag{5}$$
$$\text{Shidao SST } (x), \text{ Shijiusuo SST } (y): y = 1.002x + 2.282 \tag{6}$$
$$\text{Shidao SST } (x), \text{ Xiaomaidao SST } (y): y = 0.895x + 1.625 \tag{7}$$
$$\text{Shidao SST } (x), \text{ Xiaochangshan SST } (y): y = 0.97x - 0.934 \tag{8}$$

From equation (4), 1.54, 2.4, 3.83 are the three critical values of temperature-herring model. By equations (5), (6), (7), (8), relationship of SST structure was set up when various ocean monitoring stations equal to the critical values (See Table 15-5).

Table 15-5 Relationship of SST structure of ocean monitoring stations

Station	Xiaochangshan			Qinhuangdao			Shidao			Xiaomaidao			Shijiusuo		
	1.54	2.40	3.83	1.54	2.40	3.83	1.54	2.40	3.83	1.54	2.40	3.83	1.54	2.40	3.83
Xiaochangshan	—	—	—	1.01	1.90	3.38	0.56	1.39	2.78	-1.03	-0.09	1.46	-1.65	-0.82	0.56
Qinhuangdao	2.05	2.89	4.27	—	—	—	1.11	1.91	3.25	-0.42	0.48	1.97	-1.03	-0.22	1.11
Shidao	2.55	3.44	4.91	2.00	2.92	4.45	—	—	—	-0.09	0.87	2.46	-0.74	0.12	1.54
Xiaomaidao	3.91	4.70	6.02	3.42	4.24	5.60	3.00	3.77	5.05	—	—	—	0.96	1.73	3.01
Shijiusuo	4.84	5.73	7.20	4.29	5.21	6.74	3.83	4.69	6.12	2.19	3.15	4.75	—	—	—

Shidao SST would be in the region of 2.00 to 4.54 if Qinhuangdao March SST is in the suitable region of 1.5 to 3.83. The region of 2 to 2.83 is obtained by getting intersection elements. That is, it would be suitable for herring increasing around both Shidao and Qinhuangdao sea area when Shidao March SST in the region of 2 to 2.83. To this analogizes, it would be suitable for herring reproducing around Shidao, Yaitai, Qinhuangdao sea area when Shidao March SST in the region of 2 to 3.83, and spawning habitats would expand northern to sea area around Xiaochangshan. And also, the spawning habitats would expand southern to sea area around Rizhao, Zhucheng, when Shidao March SST in the region of -0. 09 to 1. 54, while it would be unsuitable for sea area around Shidao to be the spawning habitats.

The results above denied the possibility of sea area around the counties Rizhao, Jimo being the central spawning habitat of Yellow Sea herring when it flourishes all sea area around Shandong Peninsula. As the suitable temperature for herring spawning season is in the range of 0-8℃, whose optimum temperature is 2-6℃, and SST in the range of 6-20℃ is suitable for the current juvenile[1], sea area around Zhucheng and Jimo, Shandong province, provides survival space for parent fish school, although it does little to population recruitment. Therefore, the parent fish school would move to secondary spawning habitat when the population density of central spawning habitat reaches a certain level, and the distribution area would have been extended to its biological limits in case that population is large enough.

In the period of Little Ice Age, especially from 1550s-1730s, when herring flourished constantly, the Yellow Sea herring reached its maximum density and the most extensive distribution areas in the past 600 years, widely distributed on both sides of the Yellow Sea, which means Shidao March temperature was optimum for herring reproducing, that is, 2-3℃. When Shidao March temperature was 2. 4℃, that of Xiaochangshan, Qinhuangdao, Xiaomaidao, Shijiusuo was 1. 39℃, 1. 91℃, 3. 77℃, 4. 69℃ respectively, which are all in the optimum range of herring spawning. Therefore, we inferred that Shidao March SST was around 2. 4℃ in this period.

Subsequently, during the time of Daoguang in Qing Dynasty (1820s-1850s), relatively high fish density existed in Sea area around Shandong Peninsula, whereas the herring distribution expanded southern to Jiaozhou, north-western to Qinhuangdao, which is the most noteworthy, while the amount of fish schools around Xiaochangshan sea area declined apparently over the previous period (See Figure 15-9). The herring's flourishing around Qinhuangdao means the optimum SST there for

---

[1] Tang Qisheng, A preliminary study on the cause of generation fluctuation of the Yellow Sea herring, *Transactions of Oceanology and Limnology*, 2(37-45), 1981.

herring reproducing, that is, around 2.4℃, while that of Shidao was 2.9℃, which is 0.5℃ lower than that of small glacier epoch.

As March temperature of Shidao appearing to be significant related to Shidao March SST (See Table 15-5), linear regression was conducted and the equation is as followed:

$$\text{SST } (x), \text{ T } (y): y = 0.884x + 0.723 \ (r = 0.649, \ p < 0.01) \tag{8}$$

Based on the analysis above, the temperature of 1550s-1730s and 1820s-1850s were 1.9, 2.46℃ respectively, and that of 1966-1982 was 3.08℃ (See Table 15-5). In summary, the temperature trend line in Shidao March temperature of 600 years was plot as followed (See Figure 15-13):

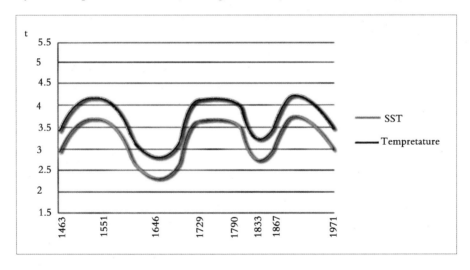

Figure 15-13　The trend line of average temperature on March in Shidao since 1463

15.7　DISCUSSION

The key natural factors which could impact the abundance of herrings differ in different sea areas. For the impacts of Tsushima Strait are different, the variations of yields and distribution ranges of the herring which distributed in Yellow Sea and the eastern coast of Korean peninsula may be inconsistent. Synchronous increases and declines of herring catches do not exist along the coast of Hokkaido and Karafuto[1].

It is notable that this issue is complex in Europe. One study on the overview of historical European herring fisheries indicated that long term variations of temperature could affect the abundance and spatial distribution of herring in Northern Europe[2]. Nevertheless one case study from Russia indicated that there is no relationship between herring catches and temperature in the White Sea according to the long term analysis[3]. Although the North Sea breach of Agger Tange in 1825 had profound impacts on the depression of whitefish and eel fishery, new study on the collapse of the herring fishery in Limjord from 1829 onwards revealed that the crisis of this fishery was mainly related the impact of fishing on adults, juveniles, larvae and eggs[4].

However, as a special local population which distributed in the southernmost sea area in the Northern Hemisphere, the abundance and distribution ranges of the Yellow Sea herring were mainly impacted by the variation of climate.

Based on the historical herring resources, the trend line of the sea surface temperature on March since the 15th century was almost coincident with the basic knowledge of the climate change during the past 600 years. During the profitable periods of the Yellow Sea herring, there were two main periods when the distribution ranges fluctuated sharply. These two variations of distribution ranges occurred after the eruption of Huaynaputina and Tambora respectively. The huge eruption of

---

① Kazuya Nagasawa, "Long-term variations in abundance of Pacific herring(*Clupea pallasi*) in Hokkaido and Sakhalin related to changes in environmental conditions", *Progress in Oceanography*, 49(2001), pp. 551-564.

② Jurgen Alheit and Eberhard Hagen, Long-term climate forcing of European herring and sardine populations, *Fisheries Oceanography*, 6(2) 130-139; James E. Overland, Juergen Alheit et al., Climate controls on marine ecosystems and fish populations, *Journal of Marine Systems*, 79(3-4) 305-315.

③ Dmitry L. Lajus, Yaroslava I. Alekseeva, Julia A. Lajus, Herring fisheries in the White Sea in the 18th — beginning of the 20th centuries: Spatial and temporal patterns and factors affecting the catch fluctuations, *Fisheries Research* 87(2-3) 255-259.

④ Bo Poulsen, Poul Holm, Brian R. MacKenzie, A long-term (1667-1860) perspective on impacts of fishing and environmental variability on fisheries for herring, eel, and whitefish in the Limfjord, Denmark, *Fisheries Research* 87(2-3) 181-195.

Krakatoa in 1883 slowed sea-level rise and ocean warming well into the following century[1]. However this beneficial period for the cold water fishes did not stop the great depression of the Yellow Sea herring in China. Moreover the eruption of Huaynaputina and Tambora just impacted the climate in several years[2], but the profitable periods of Yellow Sea herring lasted for quite a long time. And it is impossible to reveal the relations in the volcano eruption, abrupt change of climate and the abundance of Yellow Sea herring clearly in this paper.

(Li Yushang, Department of History, Shanghai Jiao Tong University, Shanghai, China;

Che Qun, Center for Historical Geography, Fudan University, Shanghai, China

Chen Liang, Department for History of Science and Philosophy of Science, Shanghai Jiao Tong University, Shanghai, China)

---

① Simon Winchester, *Krakatoa: the Day the World Exploded 27 August 1883*, the Penguin Group, 2003; P. J. Gleckler, et al., Volcanoes and climate: Krakatoa's signature persists in the ocean, *Nature*, 439 (7077) 675; Michael R. Rampino, Historic eruptions of Tambora (1815), Krakatau (1883), and Agung (1963), their stratosperic aerosols, and climatic impact, *Quaternary Research*, 18(2) 127-143.

② David M. Pyle. Volcanoes: How did the summer go, *Nature*, 393 (6684), 415-417; Richard B. Stothers, The Great Tambora Eruption in 1815 and its Aftermath, *Science*, 224 (4654) 1191-1198; Global influence of the AD 1600 eruption of Huaynaputina, Peru, Nature, 393(6684) 455-458. Fidel Costa and Bruno Scaillet, Massive atmospheric sulfur loading of the AD 1600 Huaynaputina eruption and implications for petrologic sulfur estimates, *Geophysical Research Letters*, 30(2) 40-44; K. R. Briffa, P. D. Jones, et al., Influence of volcanic eruptions on Northern Hemisphere summer temperature over the past 600 years, Nature, 393(6684).

图书在版编目（CIP）数据

亚洲的智慧：区域一体化和可持续发展的探索 = Asia's Wisdom：Exploration on Regional Integration and Economic Growth：英文/袁堂军、张怡主编. —上海：复旦大学出版社,2014.5
ISBN 978-7-309-10562-9

Ⅰ. 亚…　Ⅱ. ①袁…②张　Ⅲ. 区域经济发展-亚洲-文集-英文　Ⅳ. F130.4-53

中国版本图书馆 CIP 数据核字（2014）第 072804 号

亚洲的智慧：区域一体化和可持续发展的探索
袁堂军　张　怡　主编
责任编辑/林骧华　马晓俊

复旦大学出版社有限公司出版发行
上海市国权路 579 号　邮编：200433
网址：fupnet@ fudanpress.com　http://www.fudanpress.com
门市零售：86-21-65642857　团体订购：86-21-65118853
外埠邮购：86-21-65109143
常熟市华顺印刷有限公司

开本 787×960　1/16　印张 20.25　字数 323 千
2014 年 5 月第 1 版第 1 次印刷

ISBN 978-7-309-10562-9/F·2036
定价：40.00 元